CHILDREN IN CUSTODY

Children in Custody

Gill Stewart
Norman Tutt

Avebury
Aldershot · Brookfield USA · Hong Kong · Singapore · Sydney

© Gill Stewart and Norman Tutt, 1987

Published by

Avebury
Gower Publishing Company Limited
Gower House
Croft Road
Aldershot
Hants GU11 3HR
England

Gower Publishing Company
Old Post Road
Brookfield
Vermont 05036
USA

British Library Cataloguing in Publication Data

Stewart, Gill
    Children in custody.
    1. Juvenile corrections — Great Britain
    I. Title II, Tutt, Norman
    365'.42   HV9145.A5

Library of Congress Cataloguing-in-Publication Data

Stewart, Gill.
    Children in custody.

    Bibliography: p.
    Includes index.
    1. Juvenile corrections — Great Britain.
    2. Juvenile deliquency — Great Britain. 3. Juvenile
justice, Administration of — Great Britain.
    I. Tutt, Norman, II. Title.
    HV9145.A5S72   1987   365'.42'0941   87–8483

    ISBN 0 566 05075 7

Typeset in Great Britain by
Guildford Graphics Limited, Petworth, West Sussex.
Printed in Great Britain at the University Press, Cambridge

Contents

Tables

1 Introduction

The issue of locking up children and young people is not new. In 1838, as the result of a recommendation from a House of Lords committee, Parkhurst Prison for Boys was established. The Lords' committee, in an argument redolent of current proposals for reducing overcrowding in prisons in the 1980s, had asked:

> Whether the means might not be found in some unoccupied barrack or fort connected with, or in the neighbourhood of, the places of embarkation, of providing for the accomplishment of an object so important as the due custody, the effective punishment and the timely reformation of that large class of juvenile offenders whom the ingenuity of more mature and experienced delinquents renders the instruments of so much and such increasing criminality. (Carlebach, 1970).

Thus the 'Parkhurst Experiment' began with the recognizable intentions of protecting the young and 'less corrupted' juvenile offenders from the influence of their older peers, and offering more constructive and reformative methods of dealing with juveniles than adult prison or transportation.

The prison was duly divided into units, some based on arbitrary age divisions which are still in use today. The units comprised:

(1) The General Ward for boys 14 years and over.
(2) The Junior Ward for boys below 14 years.
(3) The Probationary Ward for boys for the first four months after admission.
(4) The Refractory Ward for punishment.
(5) The Infirmary Ward for boys who need in-patient treatment.

It is salutary to reflect, given the massive changes in society over the past 150 years, that in the 1980s juvenile offenders are still (in England and Wales) divided around the age of 14 years, that is, those over 14 are eligible for detention centre orders, and sentences are divided around the period of four months (in England and Wales), sentences of less than four months being served in detention centres and, if greater than four months, in youth custody centres.

It is interesting that the founders of Parkhurst Prison for Boys were well-intentioned but lacked any empirical basis for their

Table 1.1   *Previous convictions of boys admitted to Parkhurst Prison
in 1850 (report of the Directors of Convict Prisons 1851)*

No. of boys	Previous convictions
14	None
27	1
23	2
24	3
15	4
12	5
10	6
7	7
2	8
1	+9
11	10+
8	Not known

(Carlebach 1970)

arbitrary policy decisions and that today after more than a century
of 'scientific' thinking, the same mixture of motivation and ignorance
prevails in our policy of juvenile justice.

The staff of Parkhurst Prison were however determined to implement a scientific approach within their regime, and Chaplain Smith
proved to be an unlikely but effective social science researcher
meticulously recording a range of empirical data about all admissions.
For example, in 1851 Chaplain Smith recorded that there were 154
admissions in that year: of these 62 had both parents, 30 were orphans
and 62 had only one parent. He found that between 85 per cent
and 90 per cent had attended schools for from six months to seven
years but with very negative results. Chaplain Smith went on to
note that 'we seldom get a prisoner from a rural and scattered
population', and, with an accuracy which is hopefully echoed in
this study, he dutifully recorded the number of previous convictions
of each new admission (see Table 1.1).

His table read today is a remarkable indicator of how in some
respects little has changed.

In fact it is tempting to suggest, since Chaplain Smith was only
required to record 5 per cent of his cases as 'not known', that the
standard of record keeping more than a century ago shows greater
precision than today.

It is not the purpose of this chapter to carry out a definitive historical analysis but merely to point to the fact that there is a long tradition of state and voluntary provision of secure and custodial facilities for a minority of juvenile offenders. The size and definition of that minority will vary over time, just as the support or opposition to the expansion of secure facilities will vary with changes in social attitude and opinion. This study concerns itself with the four jurisdictions of England and Wales, Scotland, Northern Ireland and the Republic of Ireland.

It is a curiosity of historical development that a cluster of islands so small geographically that it could fit many times into the single state of America, should have developed four entirely separate and distinct systems of processing and treating juvenile offenders. This accident of development provides the ideal opportunity for analysts of social policy, since in effect it provides an opportunity for comparison between the outputs of different systems which are in general operating within the same cultural and social context. Yet, as will be seen later, the differences in social context may still be quite substantial. Moreover this study attempts to redress some of the imbalance which has occurred within juvenile justice whereby policy and practice in England and Wales or the Republic of Ireland is more influenced by what is happening in North America some 3,500 miles away than by what is happening in Scotland or Northern Ireland a mere 50 miles away. There is a certain irony in the fact that the Supreme Court of the United States of America decision in Re: Gault should have profoundly influenced arguments for justice in the Republic of Ireland and England and Wales, whereas the deliberations of 'The Task Force' or the 'Black Committee' are virtually unknown beyond the Republic or Northern Ireland.

There were two more immediate and pressing reasons for this study beyond the interesting historical development. The first of these was that despite the four very different jurisdictions there was a concern in each that the numbers of children entering custody by various means was somehow increasing. As this study will show it is very difficult to produce a totally accurate picture of how many children are locked up, where they are detained, how they were placed in custody and for what reasons. Consequently there is very little accurate or reliable trend data. In these circumstances the perceptions and beliefs of those working in the juvenile justice and welfare systems become paramount even if unreliable. Over the past decade each of the four jurisdictions have experienced pressure from policy makers and practitioners, often supported by their academic advisers, to provide both more and a wider range of secure facilities for young people. These pressures arose from diverse sources; for example the 'treaters' argued that it was impossible to treat certain adolescent behaviour such as self-injury or substance abuse unless the young person could be confined to avoid absconding. In these circumstances, it was argued, secure facilities were required to protect the child. Others however argued that juvenile crime was qualitatively increasing in severity, with more offences of serious violence or public disorder, and that in these circumstances the public needed to be protected from the depredations of a small but increasing minority. Indeed in England and Wales the Home Secretary pronounced that whilst a short detention centre order may be appropriate in some cases, longer youth custody sentences were appropriate for those who revealed their 'addiction to violence' (Brittan, 1985). In the Republic of Ireland, Cuin Mhuire, a new remand and assessment centre for females aged 12 to 16 years, was opened in 1984, and within a short time the experience of running this centre was indicating to the Department of Justice that long-term custodial facilities for females may be required. Also in the Republic of Ireland, but not within our terms of reference, a decision reminiscent of the Lords Committee of 1838 (see p. oo) was taken to reopen a barracks on a small island in Galway Bay as a secure facility for young people over the age of 17 years who stole and drove away motor vehicles.

Thus in each jurisdiction, regardless of the differences in age limits, legislation or ethos, there was pressure to develop more custodial or secure facilities for juveniles. This was not solely a feature of the British Isles and the Irish Republic, since in 1984 ministers of the Council of Europe became concerned with the same phenomenon and established a select committee of experts to examine:

(a) the recent evolution of trends in the reaction to juvenile delinquency in Council of Europe member states (influence of neo-classical ideas, increased use of imprisonment etc.);

(b) in particular, the reactions of authorities and the attitude of the public towards certain groups of juveniles, in particular second-generation immigrants.

The second pressing feature was that each jurisdiction was either in the process of implementing new proposals for dealing with juvenile offenders or undertaking radical and major reviews of its current system. In Northern Ireland the Black Committee had reported in 1979. The committee, more properly known as the Children and Young Persons Review Group, had received evidence from Scotland, England and Wales, and the Republic of Ireland, as well as North America, and had set out the policy proposals for government for the next few decades; one of its proposals was for a single secure unit of some 120 beds where previously some 80 or 90 such beds had existed. The Northern Ireland administration was, and still is, in the process of implementing the report's findings. In the Republic of Ireland a task force to review child-care legislation and services had been established in 1974 and reported in 1980. The task force, drawing on many similar sources to the Black Committee, put forward proposals for reform of the legislation, much of which was still technically unchanged since the 1908 Children Act passed more than a decade before independence and the later establishment of a written constitution. In England and Wales a Conservative government had been elected in 1979 with a specific reference in its election manifesto to increasing the powers of juvenile court magistrates by providing 'a secure and residential care order' to assist in combatting juvenile crime. The manifesto promise was embodied in varying forms in the Criminal Justice Act 1982 which was implemented in May 1983 and proceeded to have a profound impact on the numbers of young people receiving custodial sentences. In Scotland, at the same time, the children's hearing system established under the Social Work (Scotland) Act 1968 was subject to a major review which considered, but eventually rejected, extending the powers of the children's panels. The powers which were sought would have increased the 'judicial' nature of the hearing by giving the panel powers to levy fines and conditional discharges.

In the light of all of these developments it seemed timely to establish a study with the general remit to examine the use of custody for children in the four jurisdictions.

However this general remit required a great deal of refinement and was (eventually);

(1) To examine the current secure and custodial facilities for children and young people under the age 17 years within statutory, voluntary and social work, penal and health services.

(2) To examine and compare the processes by which children and young people enter such facilities.

(3) To learn from currently available information more about the background and circumstances of children and young people admitted to secure or custodial facilities.

(4) To examine the purpose of varying forms of custody and the methods employed within secure and custodial facilities.

(5) To analyze the results and findings from the above and make recommendations where appropriate.

The study began on 1 January 1984 and was generously funded by a grant from the Carnegie United Kingdom Trust and the Joseph

Rowntree Memorial Trust. A further small grant was received from the Francis C. Scott Trust.

The first issue for the study group was to define its terms. The three major questions to be answered were:

What is a *child?*
What is meant by *in?*
What is *custody?*

What is a *child*?

Concepts and definitions of childhood have varied widely across the boundaries of time, place and social position. Central to this concept is the perception of childhood as retaining innocence, as expressed in dependency upon adults, compliance to adult wishes and controls, and respect and imitation.

Each jurisdiction has a different arbitrary age at which a child is legally assumed to understand right from wrong and therefore be capable of prosecution for a criminal offence. Each jurisdiction however qualifies this minimum age by placing the onus on the prosecution (or its equivalent in Scotland) to prove the child actually knew what he or she was doing was criminal. Each of the four jurisdictions has legislation which embodies the concept of *doli incapax*, the rebuttal assumption of incapacity; in all cases this prevails until the fourteenth birthday, with the exception of Scotland which, as will be seen in the next chapter, bases its whole system on different premises.

It was decided for the purpose of this study to take as the lower age limit the age at which national legislation allowed an individual to be charged with a criminal offence, regardless of any qualifications concerning understanding on the part of that individual. Adopting this approach illustrated the first difference between the four jurisdictions, since in the Republic of Ireland a child can be charged with an offence from the age of 7 years. In Northern Ireland the age of criminal prosecution had been raised in 1968 to 10 years of age. In England and Wales, it is also 10 years. In Scotland, despite the reforming legislation of the late 1960s, the age of criminal prosecution remains at 8 years of age.

It was decided to investigate all those children over the age of 7 years who entered custody. However, the problem of defining a child is not solely concerned with the age at which the individual is held legally responsible for his or her actions, but is also concerned with the age at which the law indicates the young person will be treated as a fully responsible adult and not afforded any special protection or isolation from adult offenders. In the Republic of

Ireland and Northern Ireland the upper age limit was clearly 16 years of age. On the 17th birthday the young person could be placed before an adult court and receive a prison sentence. Even so, the young person over 17 years was likely to be placed into a prison department establishment dealing only with young adult offenders, thereby giving protection for a further period of time from exposure to the possible corrupting influence of fully mature and experienced adult offenders.

In Scotland the age was the 16th birthday; beyond that age the young person would normally not be dealt with by the childrens' hearing but instead by the sheriffs' court as with adult offenders. Again a custodial sentence would usually be served in an institution separate from the general adult prison population. In England and Wales the failure to fully implement the Children and Young Persons Act 1969 (which would have abolished all sentences in prison department establishments for those under 17 years of age) and the subsequent overlaying of this unimplemented Act by the Criminal Justice Act 1982 had led to a state of some considerable confusion with no clear dividing line at 17 years. The present position is that both juvenile magistrates and crown courts may sentence a young male between 14 and 17 years to junior detention centre for periods up to 4 months. No such centres currently exist for females. Similarly the same courts can sentence both females and males between 15 and 17 years to youth custody for periods up to twelve months. The crown court moreover can sentence this age group for longer periods. The same courts are able to remand young people to prison on unruly certificates in special circumstances but *only* males of 15–16 years. Nothing could more clearly illustrate the current state of confusion in the legislation surrounding custody for young people than this irrational outcome of pragmatic incrementalism.

The four jurisdictions in the study are out of step with their nearest partners in Europe. Table 1.2 shows the minimum age of criminal prosecution in law, and the age of transfer into the adult court system in a selection of European states.

It is difficult to draw any conclusion from this table other than that the four jurisdictions of this study, and consequently the values underpinning the legislation, view children and their rights differently to other European states.

How the four nations view children and protect their rights is discussed more fully in Chapter 3. What should be noted here is that this study has used the definition of child and young person as currently reflected in the four sets of legislation, namely an individual between the age of 7 years and 16 years. This does not mean that children younger than 7 years are never locked up nor

Table 1.2   *Ages at which children can be 'prosecuted for a criminal offence and are held fully responsible as adults in a selection of European states'*

State	Minimum Age	Adult
France	13	18
Federal Rep. of Germany	15	21
Netherlands	14	17
Portugal	12	16
Sweden	15	21
England & Wales	10	17
Scotland	8	16
Northern Ireland	10	17
Republic of Ireland	7	17

indeed that because the age of prosecution is 7 in the Republic, children of that age are automatically placed before courts. In fact the legal age limits can only ever be general guidelines and a means of limiting the scale of the study.

Certain aspects of 'custody' of young people were specifically rejected; for example, is a young baby placed in a cot harness by a concerned and conventional mother in custody? Is a hyperactive toddler or mentally handicapped child contained within a hospital ward by secure windows and door handles placed out of his reach in custody or merely subject to reasonable precautions? It was decided that using the legal age limits would restrict the study, rightly, to those children where specific state intervention precipitated by the child's personal behaviour or actions had led to placement in custody. This does not mean that other children are never, rightly or wrongly, legally or illegally, locked up by parents, guardians, teachers, nurses or residential social workers but that to uncover that informal practice is hardly feasible and if uncovered only identifies individual malpractice rather than state responsibility about which action can be taken in the form of legislative reform.

In order to limit the scope of the study to both practicable and relevant levels the term *child or young person will throughout the book refer to an individual between 7 and 16 years*. Childhood, it is assumed, ceases on the 17th birthday.

What is meant by *in*?
To anyone a child locked in a cell is obviously in custody. But

what should be made of a 'time-out room' attached to a classroom of a special school for the maladjusted? The 'time-out room' may to all intents and purposes physically resemble a cell. Does such a room constitute custody and is a misbehaving child who is placed for periods of never more than 15 minutes before return to the general classroom actually *in* custody for that short period? Alternatively, what of a large rambling Victorian house now used by a local authoirty as an observation and assessment centre? The centre, housed on the edge of a difficult inner-city area has a high wire net fence around the gardens and restricted opening windows and locked front door to the main living area of the children. The authority believes the provision of the fence and door locks is no more than many householders in the area would take as a precaution against burglary. The children in the home do not have door keys nor are they encouraged to open the front door unless accompanied by a member of staff because the centre is positioned on a busy and dangerous urban roadway. Are the children living in the centre *in* custody or are they only *in* custody if placed in the secure separation room housed within the main residence?

Does the word *in* carry with it connotations of time? For example should young persons resident in a secure unit during the week but going to their own homes at weekends, be recorded as *in* custody?

Whilst the study acknowledged all these real difficulties of defining when a person is *in* custody, an arbitrary decision was taken to carry out a census of a particular 24-hour period and to enumerate any child or young person who spent part or all of that 24-hour period in secure conditions. It seemed essential that the problems of definition should not hamper or even jeopardize the first serious attempt to discover how many young people are at any one time deprived of their liberty. It seems extraordinary that given the high value put on freedom by the four jurisdictions, the safeguards which existed to protect that freedom by habeas corpus and other means and, given the high financial cost of both placing and retaining anyone in custody we do not know, nor have any routine or simple way of discovering, how many young people are deprived of their liberty.

What is *custody?*
An individual's freedom of movement can be restricted by physical restraint, special clothing, purposely designed rooms or, ultimately, secure institutions.

Whilst it may be comfortable to believe that archaic forms of personal physical restraint are no longer used and do not feature in current methods of control of difficult behaviour, such a belief would be a delusion. It is still unfortunately true that hard-pressed staff, short of numbers and ideas, may still resort to extreme measures of physical restraint. During the period of the study a reliable report was received of a young 15-year-old mentally handicapped and apparently very difficult girl being bound by her ankles and wrists to a hospital bed to stop her self-injury and disruptive activity.

Whether or not children and young people restrained by such overt physical means are actually in custody is open to debate. However it was believed that such forms of restraint if they are in use should if possible, be identified, recorded and commented on. Accordingly the definition of custody used throughout the study included 'devices' which are used to restrain a young person's freedom of movement. There is of course a major methodological difficulty in that most of these devices are used informally, and if not actually illegal they are contradictory to the spirit of all current legislation and advice. This is obviously known, if not understood by the users of such devices, consequently they are unlikely if questioned about their means of restraint to openly and freely admit to using such devices. Therefore whilst the study has attempted to investigate this area of practice, any results, which are mainly negative, need to be viewed in the light of the above. Such practices although rare when compared with our historical past, have been observed directly by individuals involved in this study, and incidentally and importantly, reported to the relevant authorities. But it has proved impossible to establish how widespread is this form of custody which we chose to include in our definition.

Less dramatic than these overt physical means of restraint, but more common, are practices which place direct, but subtle, restrictions on the young person's movement. The most obvious method employed is to place a young person who is a (persistent) absconder into pyjamas or nightdress, and to remove all day clothes and shoes to a locked office. There may be no physical barrier, in the form of locks, to their further absconding, but such a child is obviously constrainted both by social embarrassment and/or by immediate identification. While this study has attempted to identify such practices, there is a fine balance between viewing such actions as 'custodial' as opposed to the actions of a 'reasonable parent'. In a recent appeal court decision, the court was considering an appeal by a local authority against a compensation order made by a lower court. The compensation order was to compensate an individual who had suffered serious financial loss due to the criminal action of a boy in the care of the local authority. The lower court had decided the local authority acting *in loco parentis* must pay for the damage committed by the absconding boy. The appeal court ruled that the local authority must be tested for neglience against the standard of 'what would a reasonable parent be expected to do'. It could be argued that confinement to a bedroom, and deprivation of clothing *for a limited period of time*, may well be the actions of a reasonable parent.

The other major form of 'personalized' custody which the study decided not to consider, since evidence was not available, was the use of drugs. It has been argued that various forms of major tranquillizers are used to control the behaviour of (difficult) adolescents. For example:

> It is unlikely that surgery is used frequently, if at all, in order to achieve security with youngsters. Medication is commonly [sic] used in psychiatric and general practice in order to help a youngster and those around him to cope better with his problem behaviour. A youngster who is put to sleep, is heavily 'tranquillised' or has difficulty in dragging himself from one place to another, does not present much of a risk to other people. With certain rare exceptions, the use of medication to control problem behaviour hardly ever arouses public concern. It is cheap and, as a means of control, is assumed to be administered in therapeutic settings which are centrally concerned with the welfare of the individual and the healing process. Without it the revolution in recent psychiatric practice would not have been achieved and a great many people would have remained or been put in locked wards than there are at present. (Hoghughi, 1978)

It should also be borne in mind that drugs need to be directly administered to be effective as a control device. Tutt (1971) points out that in some regimes it is the threat of the painful administration of 'the needle' which can itself be used as a form of punishment or control.

Whilst those connected with the current study were only too aware of the use of drugs with adolescents it was decided that the examination of such practice was beyond the scope of the study. The methods to be used to collect and analyze data on young people in custody were not sensitive enough to comment authoritatively on the use of drugs. Whilst all those involved recognize the seriousness and inherent dangers involved in the prescription of drugs to control and contain young people it must remain subject to investigation by means other than this study. Therefore the definition of custody employed specifically did not refer to the use of drugs of any type.

The continuum identified by the study is as follows:

Time-out room: This is normally a single room with little, if any, furnishings, restricted outward visibility, protected electric light fittings and possibly strengthened doors. No substantive security features are built in.

Single separation room: This facility differs from a time-out room in that it has been designed to withstand deliberate damage and attempts to escape and has viewing facilities for staff.

Police cell: Police cells do not require a full description but are obviously designed to hold prisoners. Some police stations have similar but separate facilities to keep juveniles away from adult prisoners.

Small short-term secure unit: A number of local authorities with observation and assessment centres have developed short-term secure facilities to hold difficult young people on remand or awaiting a court appearance. These units have separate single secure bedrooms adjoining some form of day/recreational/dining area. All is deemed secure and inspected and approved by officials acting on behalf of the relevant Secretary of State. Children may spend up to 28 days or beyond in these facilities. The details of one such facility is described later.

Secure unit linked to open unit: In the 1970s both in England and Wales and Scotland a number of open community homes with education, or List D Schools, were encouraged to build units of 6–8 beds into which particularly difficult young people could be admitted prior to passage into the open unit or if proving too disruptive in the open unit could be contained in security.

Closed psychiatric wards: Whilst the study identified only one designated regional secure unit for adolescents within the psychiatric services (Prestwich), it became obvious that a number of large psychiatric and mental handicap hospitals retained locked wards. A number of difficult adolescents were admitted to and held on such wards. Their legal position, as shall be illustrated in the next chapter, is particularly obscure.

Detention centres: Detention centres are obviously custodial facilities being run by the appropriate prison department. They take offenders on orders from the court. There young people are often accommodated in buildings converted from previous use, e.g. army billets. These are large, housing 100+ inmates, who are in association throughout the day and night, being accommodated in dormitories and occupied by classrooms or work parties. Security is by conventional high perimeter security fencing. Sentences are less than four months.

Youth custody centres; Young offenders' centres: Again these are obviously custodial facilities, usually accommodating those serving longer sentences. Accommodation may be dormitory or cellular. The degree of security will vary from an 'open centre', usually situated in an isolated rural area, to closed units which have very high degrees of security, with both perimeter fencing and electronic surveillance, internal cellular accommodation and (locked) barred doors on corridors. However, outside working parties and community service activities may still be part of the regime.

Large long-term secure units: A number of large independent units have been established by both local and central government outside of both the penal and health services. These units range between 24–60 young people. Nearly all admit both sexes, normally for relatively longer periods of care or sentence: 6 months–5 years. They have been developed on a basis reminiscent of the Parkhurst Prison for Boys to take very serious juvenile offenders who would otherwise be retained in prisons. The development of these units is described in Chapter 4, but much of the initiative for them came from the case of Mary Bell — a young girl found guilty of murder at the age of 10 years who precipitated a crisis in thinking on the issue of secure facilities and without whom no analysis of the development of secure facilities is possible (Millham, *et. al.*, 1978, Cawson and Martell, 1979).

The definition of *What is* custody? attempted to embody this diverse range of individual restraints and buildings. The study group was also conscious that a number of units which could be conceived as custodial would fall outside this definition.

Thus the definition which would guide the study and the remainder of the discussion in this book was agreed as:

> *A Child in Custody: means any individual between the ages of seven and sixteen years, i.e. to the seventeenth birthday, who is placed into any situation or device, for whatever purpose and by whatever means, which is intended, for whatever reason, and for however short a period of time, to remove or significantly restrict a young person's freedom of choice to leave.*

2 Law and policies

To conduct any comparison between legislation and policy in the four jurisdictions is difficult, since legislation is a dynamic process. Consequently it is never possible to identify four static and stable pictures of current legislation and juxtapose them to make comparison. The legislation in each of the jurisdictions is being tested continually and modified in the light of specific test-case decisions. It is constantly under review as practitioners and legislators identify loopholes, failings, unintended consequences or changes in public attitude. Also it is constantly being amended or overruled intentionally or unknowingly by newly enacted legislation.

This chapter will initially deal with the generality of children and young people who may be placed in custody, namely those charged with and admitting, or found guilty of, an offence and then placed in a secure facility by the decision of a court or tribunal. This is not by any means all the children who experience custody. The chapter will therefore continue by examining the specific and exclusive groups who do not fall into the general group because of their extreme behaviour or because of 'quirks' in the legislation. Finally, it will examine the small but significant group who may not be dealt with by either child-care or criminal proceedings but under the general mental health legislation.

Legislation

It is impossible to identify all the legislation which may be, depending on circumstances, relevant to the group of children under examination. Therefore only the major legislation governing the processing of these cases has been identified for each jurisdiction (see Table 2.1). Exceptions to these major Acts are discussed later. It is useful to re-echo the words of the House of Commons Social Services Committee for England and Wales (1984):

> The general situation was well summed up by a group of lawyers and social workers who told the Committee: 'The present state of children's legislation can only be described as complex, confusing and unsatisfactory... The effect and implication of this on children is diverse with far-reaching consequences for their welfare'.
> The time has arrived — indeed it arrived some time ago — for a thorough-going review of the body of statute law, regulations and

Table 2.1   *The major legislation in the four jurisdictions*

Jurisdiction	Legislation
Republic of Ireland	The Children Act 1908 as amended by Children Act 1941
Northern Ireland	Children and Young Persons Act (1968)
Scotland	Social Work (Scotland) Act (1968)
England and Wales	Children and Young Persons Act (1933) Children and Young Persons Act (1969) as amended by Criminal Justice Act (1982)

Table 2.2   *Ages of 'child and young person' as defined in appropriate legislation*

Jurisdiction	Ages	
	Child	Young Person
Republic of Ireland	7–14 years	15–17 years
Northern Ireland	10–13 years	14–17 years
England and Wales	10–13 years	14–17 years
Scotland	8–16 years (in exceptional circumstances 17.5 years)	Not applicable

judicial decisions relating to children, with a view to the production of a simplified and coherent body of law comprehensible not only to those operating it, but also to those affected by its operation. It is not just to make life easier for practitioners that the law must be sorted out; it is for the sake of justice that the legal frameworks of the child care system must be rationalised.

This committee has precipitated a major review of child-care legislation in England and Wales which may ultimately lead to a more concise consolidation Act, but even so legislation governing children who offend is excluded from this review's consideration and will therefore remain in a state of confusion for some considerable time.

These major pieces of legislation contain the definitions of child and young person which it should be remembered vary slightly within the four jurisdictions (see Table 2.2). The lower limit of 'child' in this study is defined by the age at which an individual can be charged with an offence.

The legislative framework

The Republic of Ireland

Children and young persons are defined by the Children Act 1908, as amended by the Children Act 1941, in which a child is defined as a person under the age of 15 years, and a young person as a person 15 years or upwards and under 17.

In the Republic the courts at the lowest level, the courts of summary jurisdiction, are called district courts. They are presided over by full-time salaried judges called district justices who sit on their own without assessors or a jury. They have both criminal and civil jurisdiction within certain limits.

The age of criminal responsibility is 7, but *doli incapax* (the rebuttable presumption of incapacity) applies up to the age of 14. Children and young persons are prosecuted in the district courts. When hearing charges against persons under 17 these courts are referred to as juvenile courts and must sit at a different time and in a different place from the ordinary sittings. To add to the confusion under the Courts of Justice Act 1924, the courts in the four county boroughs (Dublin, Cork, Limerick and Waterford) are designated 'children's courts'. The Dublin Metropolitan Children's Court is the only permanent full-time children's court with a district justice who deals exclusively with children and young persons. Charges against children and young persons are prosecuted by the police. The court is not open to the general public and though the press may attend there is a ban on the publication of the names of the accused.

A child or young person may be tried in a juvenile court (or special sitting of the district court) for any offence except homicide but he, or his parent, may in the case of an indictable offence demand to be tried by jury, which is a constitutional right.

The rebuttal of *doli incapax* is usually only a formality. Free legal aid is readily available from a limited panel of solicitors. There is no provision for assessment or a social report before conviction but after conviction the court will often remand the offender to the detention centre/remand home in Dublin for assessment or, more usually, for a report by the court welfare officer while he is at home.

The custodial sentences available to the court are discussed below. Other options open to the court are as follows:

dismissal under the Probation Act;
discharge on condition of recognizance;
probation order: supervision by probation officer;
committal to care of a relative or other 'fit person' (rarely used);
whipping (under the Summary Jurisdiction over Children (Ireland) Act 1884, Section 4(1), unrepealed but never used);
fining of offender;
fining of parent or guardian;
order to parent or guardian to give security for good behaviour of offender.

Constitutional considerations — In contrast to all the other jurisdictions participating in this joint study the Republic of Ireland alone has a written constitution. The use of habeas corpus proceedings to challenge prison policy has been developing over the past decade and has successfully focussed attention on prison conditions. Where serious doubts exist about the legitimacy of penal policy procedures, it is possible to mount a constitutional challenge through the courts to test such policies or procedures against the fundamental rights accorded to all citizens by virtue of Articles 40 to 44 of the constitution and other constitutional provisions. The full impact of this facility has yet to be felt. Its potential scope is extremely wide.

Northern Ireland

The 1968 Children and Young Persons Act (Northern Ireland) provides the current legislative framework for dealing with juvenile offenders and children deemed to be in need of care, protection or control. This piece of legislation is very similar to that which pertained in the rest of the United Kingdom prior to the enactment of the 1968 Social Work (Scotland) Act and the 1969 Children and Young Persons Act (England and Wales).

The juvenile court remains the judicial forum in which any statutory intervention into the lives of children and young persons takes place. The court is presided over by a magistrate who has at least six years experience as a practising lawyer, assisted by two members of a lay panel. In comparison with the 'welfare' orientated approaches of the Scottish and English Acts, the Northern Irish Act retains important decision-making powers in the control of the court.

Disposals available to the juvenile court under the 1968 Children and Young Persons Act are:

committal to a training school
committal to the care of a fit person order
supervision order (for children only)

attendance centre order
committal to a remand home

— under other legislation the court can order:

a period of probation
a period in the young offenders centre.

Options also include fines, and conditional discharges.

Juveniles can also be detained under the Emergency Provision Act, although the numbers currently being detained under this legislation are very low. There is, in fact, some suggestion that juveniles charged under this Act are more likely to be given low tariff disposals than otherwise. In 1976 a committee under the chairmanship of Sir Harold Black was established to review legislation and services relating to the care and treatment of children and young persons under the Children and Young Persons Act, and to make recommendations as to changes in legislation and organization in those services in Northern Ireland. The report was published at the end of 1979 and contains several radical proposals for the reform of the juvenile justice system. Heavily influenced by the 'Justice for Children' lobby the report suggests the total separation of juvenile justice and child welfare systems. Within the juvenile justice system it is suggested that disposal should be determined by the offence and not be affected by welfare considerations, and that a custodial disposal be reserved for the serious and persistent offender. Sentences should be determinate and they should be served in a single secure unit replacing the existing training school system, and to be run by training school staff. Whilst the Black Report has been accepted by two successive administrations 'in principle', the target date for implementation has been repeatedly postponed. Moreover it now appears that in its implementation a number of the specific proposals will be amended or dropped completely. At the time of writing, Black's proposals for determinate sentencing and a ceiling on the number of beds in custody look as though they will not be implemented. Moreover the 'Justice' model proposed by Black will be further diluted by introducing an assessment process as a precursor to the imposition of a custodial sentence.

England and Wales
These countries define 'child' and 'young person' at the same ages as Northern Ireland but beyond that there is very little similarity, since England and Wales introduced two major pieces of legislation since 1968, the date of the last legislation in Northern Ireland.

Up to May 1983 when the Criminal Justice Act 1982 was implemented the major legislation covering the prosecution, disposal and treatment of juvenile offenders in England and Wales was the Children and Young Persons Act (1969). The 1969 Act had two major objectives: the first to shift the emphasis in dealing with juvenile offenders away from a system based on the magistrates court's power to determine what disposal a child should receive. Instead an increase in formal cautioning by the police would, it was hoped, divert children from the courts. Those children found guilty by the court would be committed to the care of the local authority and specific decisions about the child's placement and treatment would be made by professional social workers. The second objective was to replace the traditional institution-based programmes of approved (training) schools with more community-based programmes which would lead to a greater integration of the child, his family and the community.

The sections of the 1969 Act which were agreed by parliament for implementation finally came into effect in January 1971. The judicial model, which had prevailed until that date, was replaced in 1971 by a more overt treatment model under which, after a finding of guilt, the only course of action available if the juvenile bench wished to sanction the removal of the child from home, short of sending him to detention centre or recommending his committal to borstal training (now youth custody) was to place the child into the care of the local authority. The actual placement of the child was to be determined by officers of the local authority, normally social workers. The placement under their discretion could be in any one of a range of residential facilities including secure units, or in a foster home, or in exceptional circumstances back in the child's own home.

It is important to remember that major sections of the 1969 Act were never implemented, if they had been the operation of all local authority child-care facilities would have been very different. Particularly influential provisions which remain unimplemented are Sections 4 and 7. Section 4 would have raised the age of ciminal prosecution from 10 years to 12 years and finally to 14 years. Thereby all under 14 years would be dealt with as civil child-care cases. Section 7(i) would have abolished borstal training and detention centres for all those under 17 years of age. Thus local authorities would have been required to cope with all juvenile offenders under 17 years of age.

Almost immediately after the partial implementation of the 1969 Act there were claims that it was not working. The House of Commons Expenditure Committee established a sub-committee chaired by Mrs Renee Short (Labour MP for Wolverhampton) in

December 1973, to begin an enquiry into the workings of the Act. The expenditure committee reported in 1975 and made over forty recommendations, two of which are relevant to this analysis:

(1)   The practice of remanding young persons to adult prisons should cease forthwith (p.xlix).

(2)   That when a juvenile already the subject of a care order appears before a court charged with an offence, the court shall have the power to make, if it thinks fit, a 'secure care order' requiring the local authority to place the juvenile in secure accommodation for a period of not less than that specified in the order (p.xlix). (Expenditure Committee)

The Labour administration in government at that time responded to this pressure for increased secure accommodation in two ways: firstly by taking powers under the Children Act 1975 to provide capital grants to local authorities to build secure accommodation, which became necessary since the very high capital costs of such provision was proving a block to expanding local authority secure provision. Secondly, the government responded with a White Paper (Home Office, *et al.*, 1976) which, whilst rejecting the idea of a secure care order, accepted the phasing out of remands to prison. Accordingly, following consultations with local authority associations, an Order was laid before Parliament under Section 34(7) of the 1969 Act which came into force on 31 March 1977 ending such remands of 14-year-old girls. A similar order ending such remands for 15- and 16-year-old girls was laid on 24 November 1978 and came into force on 1 March 1979. A further order under Section 69 of the Children Act (1975) restricting the circumstances under which certificates of unruliness could be issued came into force on 1 August 1977. In the twelve-month period after the order came into effect the number of certificates issued dropped by 28 per cent compared with the corresponding period before 1 August 1977 (DHSS, 1981a). These deliberate moves to phase out the use of remands to prison department establishments led local authorities to develop their own alternative secure facilities.

By the 1980s policy had changed substantially, partly as a result of the incoming Conservative government with its commitment to 'Law and Order' but also as a result of growing concern about the 'unintended negative consequences' of the 1969 Act. In October 1980 the government issued a White Paper — *Young Offenders* (Home Office, 1980). This formed the basis of the Criminal Justice Act 1982 which received the Royal assent on 28 October 1982 and came into operation on 24 May 1983. The Criminal Justice Act 1982 signified a return of power to the juvenile court by the:

retention of the detention centre, but with shorter maximum (4 months) and minimum (21 days) periods of detention;

powers for the magistrates court to impose on offenders aged 15–16 years medium sentences of youth custody (i.e. between 4 and 12 months);

powers for the court to impose conditions in supervision orders including supervised community activities and night restriction;

powers for the court to make a charge and control order, thereby limiting the discretion of the local authority to place the child.

The overall effect of the Criminal Justice Act 1982 on secure facilities is discussed later. In addition magistrates had options of discharge, fine, bind-over, supervision and care order all of which existed under the Children and Young Persons Act 1969.

Scotland

The position in Scotland is very different to that prevailing in the other three jurisdictions; indeed the reforms undertaken in Scotland in the late 1960s make its system for dealing with children and young people under the age of 16 unique internationally. The uniqueness of the system makes description difficult since it is avowedly not a justice system, deliberately choosing not to discriminate between children who admit guilt of an offence and those with various other social needs arising from neglect or incompetence on the part of parents.

Part III of the Social Work (Scotland) Act 1968 introduced the children's hearing system on 15 April 1971. From that date juvenile courts were abolished and children who were deemed to be in need of compulsory measures of care were referred to a lay hearing as opposed to a court. The reasons why a child might be deemed to be in need of compulsory measures of care included allegations that a child had committed an offence and various other categories such as that a child was beyond the control of his parents, that he failed to attend school regularly without reasonable excuse, or that lack of parental care was likely to cause the child unnecessary suffering or seriously impair his health or development or that he himself had been offended against. No distinction was made between those children who were referred on an allegation that an offence had been committed by the child, and the other grounds. Whatever the grounds, the welfare principle of whatever was in the best interests of an individual child was to be the sole criterion for decision-making.

For a child to be referred to a hearing on the basis of an allegation that he had committed an offence, the age of criminal responsibility is 8. A child is a young person under 16 years of age at the time of referral to a hearing. By statute if a young person is, at the age of 16, the subject of a supervision requirement, in theory at least he can continue to be treated as a child until he has attained the age of seventeen and a half, provided he remains the subject of a supervision requirement during the whole of that period. Hearings have the power to make supervision requirements incorporating a condition of residence for children who are referred, and that place of residence may be one which is 'secure'. The responsibility for naming the place of residence rests with the children's hearing, and that place of residence cannot be changed without a review hearing taking place, and the review hearing altering the place of residence.

Although the vast majority of 'children' who commit offences are referred directly by the police to the reporter to the children's panel, certain categories of offence must be reported by the police to the procurator fiscal for that official to decide whether or not the child should be prosecuted in court. Where the procurator fiscal so decides, it is possible that a child may be detained in a penal establishment. The principal law officers have recently issued instructions that unless there are exceptional circumstances those children who are so categorized by being the subject of a supervision requirement and over 16 years of age, should in the first instance be prosecuted in court. Prior to disposal of the case, the court must seek the advice of a children's hearing as to the most appropriate disposal, but are not required to accept such advice.

There are three main routes in which young people under the age of 16 can be detained in a penal establishment:

(1)   On an Unruly Certificate issued by a sheriff under Section 24 or 297 of the Criminal Procedure (Scotland) Act 1975 as an alternative to the child being detained in a place of safety by a local authority pending his appearance in court for disposal of his case.

(2)   In consequence of a committal under Section 206 of the Criminal Procedure (Scotland) Act 1975 where a child can either be placed temporarily for assessment in Longriggend Remand Centre or on placement in Polmont or Glenochil Young Offenders Institution; the placement decision in this case is taken by the Scottish Home and Health Department Prisons Group, since this committal is in connection with serious offenders and solemn procedure and placement in a penal institution is a possibility.

(3)   In consequence of a committal of a child for up to two years residential training under Section 413 of the Criminal

Procedure (Scotland) Act 1975; again the placement can either be in Longriggend for assessment or in Polmont or Glenochil; placement decisions in such cases are taken by Social Work Services Group on behalf of the Secretary of State, and a penal placement is a possibility. The Secretary of State may approve placement within the child-care system.

Children detained in secure accommodation outside the penal system — On 30 January 1984 new regulations relating to the use of secure accommodation were introduced to Scotland by the Health and Social Services and Social Security Adjudications Act 1983.

These regulations followed the earlier legislation introduced in England and Wales and set out the same conditions to be satisfied before a child (in Scotland, a young person under the age of 16 or under supervision and not yet 18) can be detained in secure accommodation.

These regulations specify the necessary conditions as:

(1)   that the child has a history of absconding, and
     (a)   he is likely to abscond unless he is kept in secure accommodation,

AND

     (b)   if he absconds it is likely that his physical, mental or moral welfare will be at risk,

OR

(2)   he is likely to injure himself or other persons unless he is kept in secure accommodation,

AND

in the cases of either (1) or (2) that it is in the child's best interests that he be placed in secure accommodation.

The authority to make decisions to detain a child in secure accommodation is vested in children's hearings. Decisions by hearings may be short-term when they issue a warrant for 21 days, or long-term when they make a supervision requirement. Such orders as are issued are not mandatory and only authorize the use of accommodation. The final decision as to whether or for how long the secure facility will be used rests with the Director of Social Work in conjunction with the head of the residential establishment in which the child is liable to be detained. All secure accommodation must be inspected and authorized by the Secretary of State as appropriate for such use.

The uniqueness and complexity of the hearing system in Scotland is perhaps best illustrated by the flowchart supplied by the Scottish

Education Department which shows the categories of children dealt with by the system and the outcomes of the hearings.

The decision makers

Embedded within these brief descriptions of the four legislative frameworks is an element of diversity which may be crucial: namely who makes the decisions about children and young people.

In the Republic of Ireland, Northern Ireland, and England and Wales, it is the police who initiate and take the prosecution. Since 1986 this has not been true in England and Wales where a separate 'crown prosecutor' has been established under the Prosecution of Offenders Act 1985. The crown prosecutor is responsible for taking all criminal prosecutions in both the juvenile and adult court. In Scotland the adult court has for a long time been served by the procurator fiscal, who brings the prosecution. For children, the reporter serves a similar role for the children's hearing. As can be seen in the flowchart of the system in Scotland (see Fig 2.1), the police can issue warnings, as is true of the other three systems. Police cautioning is particularly well developed in England and Wales where more than 60 per cent of all referrals of juveniles are dealt with by this means rather than by formal prosecution.

More importantly in Scotland, the discretion of the reporter should be noted since in a substantial number of cases (12,700 — see figure) the reporter chose to take no formal action and to divert the case from formal consideration by the children's panel.

The nature of the decision-maker in court or the hearing is also very different. In Scotland Lord Kilbrandon, the architect of the children's hearing system, was eager to involve the 'community' as much as possible in the problems of the children from that community. This eagerness has been translated and retained in the method of recruitment of panel members. Recruitment is by open advertising in local media, and members are lay members of the community who once appointed undertake a training programme. Martin et al. (1981) have pointed to the influence of this form of recruitment:

> It has been estimated that in the city of Glasgow, approximately 50 of every 100 newly-recruited panel members withdraw within the space of three years, and that the greater part of this loss is associated with a change in domicile. New recruitment is therefore essential. In Scotland as a whole about 400 members of the public are drawn each year into a form of voluntary service that carries little if any publicly recognised status and of course attracts no tangible rewards.

Martin et al.'s analysis of the personal characteristics and

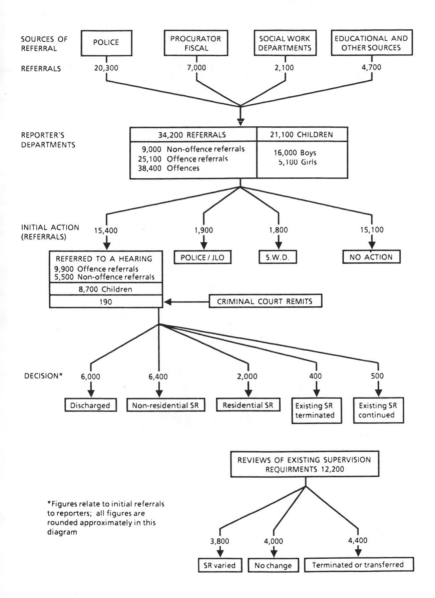

Figure 2.1 Representation of childrens hearings statistics, 1985

Table 2.3   *Panel members by sex and occupational class (Martin et al, 1981)*

Registrar-General's class	Males %	Females %
I	19 (22)	5 (11)
II	40 (45)	29 (56)
III Non Manual	11 (13)	12 (25)
IV Manual	11 (13)	1 (1)
IV & V	7 (8)	4 (6)
Not classified		
Housewives	–	43
Retired	2	–
Unemployed	1	–
Unclassifiable	9	6
(N = 100%)	449	457

backgrounds of panel members suggests they are a relatively hetero-genous group:

> The median age . . . was a little over 40. Exactly one-third fell in the age group 35–44, with one quarter younger than 35 and just over two-fifths aged 45 or above.

In England and Wales whilst the juvenile court magistrates are lay-people who receive no renumeration, they are drawn from the general 'pool' of magistrates because of their 'interest or knowledge of young people'. They are recruited in a much less open way than the panel members in Scotland. For example open advertising is still a new and relatively rare approach. Magistrates are appointed by the Lord Chancellor either formally after nomination from a recognized organization or through informal recommendation. Much of the recruitment and selection of magistrates is still surrounded by polite obscurity and, it is alleged, this gives rise to a narrowly drawn group, predominantly professional middle-class and of a narrow age band. Magistrates are required to retire from the juvenile bench at the age of 65 years and from the bench completely at 70 years. The court is of course advised by a legally trained clerk.

Northern Ireland has a mixture of legally trained and lay bench. The juvenile court is presided over by a magistrate who has at least six years experience as a practising lawyer, assisted by two members of a lay panel.

In the Republic of Ireland children and young people are dealt with by the court of summary jurisdiction, the district courts which are presided over by full-time salaried judges who sit on their own without assessors or jury. There is one exception to this general provision, in Dublin where there is a permanent metropolitan children's court presided over by an appointed judge. Indeed the written constitution of the Republic of Ireland specifically limits and discourages the involvement of a lay bench in criminal proceedings since it regards such practice as reducing the rights of the individual to a full judicial hearing. On this point the position has been summed up as follows: 'the Constitution militates against the participation of lay persons in the administration of justice (save in the case of jury service), both in criminal and in civil cases.' (Duncan, 1984) There are two cases in which a person who is not a judge may decide a civic matter:

(1) when the decision does not involve the administration of justice, and
(2) where the decision, though constituting an administration of justice, involves the exercise of limited judicial powers or functions.

It seems likely that the formal legal training undertaken by judges in the Republic and the magistrates in Northern Ireland would affect their attitudes and beliefs and possibly decisions when compared with the very much less formal and indeed marginal training in England and Wales. Whereas in Scotland the more diverse nature of the panel members and their more systematic but limited training may influence their final decisions.

Secure residential and custodial facilities

In Chapter 1 the difficulties in defining these terms were discussed. Even with these difficulties it was possible to identify the national provision which catered for the majority of children and young people within the four nations.

Types of secure accommodation

In the Republic of Ireland the main types of establishment in which children and young persons (in the relevant age range) could find themselves in custody are as follows:

(1) reformatories
(2) industrial schools
(3) places of detention/remand homes
(4) prisons
(5) St Patrick's Institution (borstal institution)

Children could also find themselves in custody in certain other types of establishment, for example:

(1)   the cells of police stations
(2)   psychiatric hospitals
(3)   establishments for the mentally handicapped.

These will be discussed later in the chapter.

Reformatories — There are at present three certified reformatories in the Republic: One, St Anne's, Kilmacud which takes 10–15 girls, and is run by an order of nuns with the assistance of lay staff. Scoil Ard Mhuire, Lusk takes 40–50 boys, was opened in 1970, and although run by the Oblate order the staff are mainly lay people; there is a management committee consisting of civil servants and interested outsiders nominated by the minister. The third, Trinity House, on the same site as Scoil Ard Mhuire, is so called because it consists of three units each designed for 10 residents, and was opened in 1983.

Unlike Scoil Ard Mhuire, Trinity House is run directly by the Department of Education. The main implication of that arrangement is intended to be that it will take all comers. Trinity House is self-contained though it shares some facilities with Scoil Ard Mhuire. There is an absolutely secure perimeter and the most modern provisions for internal security. The regime is said to be based on behavioural modification.

A court can commit to a reformatory only a person aged 12 years upwards but under 17. In practice a young person of 16 years or more is never sent there. The period of committal must be not less than two years and not more than four although there is a provision whereby the minister may extend the period to the time when the offender is at a maximum of 21 years. Again this extension is never made in practice.

Industrial schools — Children can be committed to industrial schools in a number of ways. They can be committed by the courts on care grounds. Under the law of the Republic there is no such thing as 'care proceedings'. However in Part IV of the Children Act 1908, which deals with reformatory and industrial schools, there are extensive provisions for the committal of children to industrial schools (Section 58) and, in a narrower range of cases, to the care of a relative or fit person (Section 59). It is under these sections that children in need of care or protection because of injury or neglect by their parents or guardians are brought to court. Only children (that is, up to the age of 15) can be brought and the grounds for bringing them as set out in the Act are expressed in out-of-date terms, and have been criticized as being inadequate in modern conditions. The Act provides, for instance, that a child may be brought to court:

(1) if he is 'found begging or receiving alms';
(2) if he is 'found having a parent or guardian who does not exercise proper guardianship';
(3) if he 'frequents the company of any reputed thief, or of any common or reputed prostitute.';

The grounds at (2) above are the most commonly resorted to.

Children can be committed by the courts following a conviction for school non-attendance. Under the School Attendance Act 1926 there is compulsory school attendance in the Republic between the ages of 6 and 15. In the past this provision was used extensively to take children into care because of the inadequacy of the other provisions.

Most establishments which are certified by the Minister of Education as industrial schools are also approved by the Minister of Health as children's homes. Under this latter heading, therefore, children can be placed by the health boards (acting as child-care authorities).

Two of the industrial schools (St Joseph's, Clonmel and St Laurence's, Finglas) are, together with the reformatories, classified as special schools. Those two establishments take most if not all of the children committed for offences.

On 30 June 1982, the last date for which published statistics are available, there were 28 certified industrial schools (a number have closed since then). Of the 945 children in them over two-thirds had been placed by the health boards; only 290 had been committed by the courts and only 77 of them, all boys, were in the two special schools.

The two special schools offer some measure of security but they are by no means closed custodial establishments. The rest of the industrial schools are various models of children's homes. Even today the Minister of Education may order a child over the age of 12 years detained in an industrial school 'who is found to be exercising an evil influence over the other children in the school' to be transferred to a reformatory (Children Act 1908, Sec. 69(2)(c)). In other words a child over 12 could be transferred from a non-custodial establishment to, say, Trinity House without reference back to a court.

The court determines the period for which a child is committed to an industrial school, but it cannot extend beyond the child's 16th birthday. He may be detained for one further year, until he is 17 if the minister so orders and his parent or guardian consents.

Places of detention — A child or young person convicted of an offence punishable with penal servitude or imprisonment may instead be sentenced to a 'place of detention' for a period not exceeding one month where the court considers that none of the other methods of dealing with him are suitable (Children Act 1908, Sec. 106). A recent supreme court decision states that this provision does not put a limit of one month upon the sentence of detention or imprisonment imposed upon a child where the court decides that imprisonment is a suitable option. So that a court which sentenced a young person aged 15 years and 7 months to two years' imprisonment in Mountjoy Prison was deemed correct by the supreme court. They asserted that the Section 106 provisions only operated where no other suitable method of dealing with the case could be found. There are two places of detention in Ireland in the form of which that term is used in Section 106. One is St Michael's, at Finglas in Dublin. In fact it is not used as a detention centre, but as a residential assessment centre to which the court can remand male offenders for a period of about three weeks for assessment before sentence/committal. Again, though not a secure closed institution, it offers a measure of custodial security. Cuin Mhuire is a similar facility for girls aged 12 to 16 years, opened in 1984.

Prisons — A child (i.e. 7–14 years of age) cannot under any circumstances be sentenced to imprisonment. A young person (i.e. under 17) who is tried summarily for an indictable offence may be sentenced to imprisonment if he is 'unruly and depraved' but for no more than three months. On indictment, there is no such limit but again he must be unruly and depraved. The courts have decided that there must be in existence a suitable establishment for young persons in relation to which a particular individual must be too unruly and depraved to be held there before he can be committed to prison.

The number of young people committed to prison has been low in recent years, approximately 10 per annum; however many of these have been girls for whom there is no alternative long-term secure facility.

St Patrick's Institution — St Patrick's Institution is housed in a wing of Mountjoy Prison in Dublin. It was opened in 1957 to replace a borstal institution. St Patrick's, which is termed a 'place of detention', is a secure institution which deals with male offenders between 17 and 21. But there is a provision under the statute which defines the status of St Patrick's (the Criminal Justice Act 1960) whereby an offender aged under 17 but over 16 may be sentenced to St Patrick's if he is convicted of an offence which would otherwise render him liable to imprisonment or penal servitude, and the other methods of dealing with the case which are available to the court are not deemed suitable. The period for which he may be detained is a period not exceeding the term for which he might, if he were over 17, be sentenced to penal servitude or imprisonment. St Patrick's is to all intents and purposes a prison establishment, run by prison officers. Associated with it is an open establishment, Shanganagh Castle, in the south-eastern suburbs of Dublin, to which the more amenable offenders in St Patrick's can be sent. A court can only sentence direct to St Patrick's; transfer to the open establishment is by ministerial order.

Statistical summary
The number of establishments which take children and young persons in each of the above categories is given in Table 2.4, which also shows the age range dealt with and the numbers of children and young persons in custody/care at any one time. It is not suggested that the total numbers shown refer to children in custody as defined in this study.

Northern Ireland

Residential provision — the training-school system
The training school system currently consists of four establishments, including one secure unit and one which provides some limited secure provision. Juveniles are allocated to establishments on the basis of sex and religion. There is no separate residential assessment facility. The schools carry out their own assessment with the assistance of a peripatetic team of psychologists.

Training schools can take young people on remand, or for a one-month order from a juvenile court, or on a long-term training school order. A training school order is a semi-determinate sentence of one to three years. It is imposed by the court and is used not just for young people convicted of offences but for non-school attenders and others deemed to be in need of 'care, protection or control'. The authority to release young people is, however, vested in the schools' management boards. The management boards are accountable to central government, specifically the Northern Ireland Office. The training school system in Northern Ireland is therefore separate from other child-care provision. However, following the publication of the Black Report the two larger open training schools have been

Table 2.4   Type and number of custodial establishments and the age range and numbers of occupants in the Republic of Ireland

Type of establishment	Number of establishments	Age range	No. in custody/ care (on a given date)
Prison	1 (Mountjoy Prison)	15+	(a)
Borstal	1 (St Patrick's)	16+	(b)
Reformatory	3	12–16	80(c) (30.6.82)
Industrial school	26 (approx.)	7–16	945(d) (30.6.82)
Place of detention/			(e)
remand home	1 (St Michael's)	7–16	19 (30.6.82)

Notes:

(a) Not available; 10 persons aged under 17 were committed to prison during 1981.

(b) Not available; 134 persons aged under 17 were committed during 1981.

(c) Including an estimated 27 in Loughan House, run by the Department of Justice and since 1983 replaced by Trinity House.

(d) This establishment is also a certified industrial school, but not used as such; there is no double counting.

(e) Including 141 in the industrial schools which are called special schools.

divided into care sectors and youth treatment centres. The former takes 'status' offenders, for example non-school attenders, and the latter only offenders. This innovation was made to facilitate Black's recommendation on the separation of 'justice' and 'welfare' systems.

The secure unit has a high level of physical security as it is housed in a purpose-built structure originally intended to be a closed borstal. Accommodation is available for 20 remands and 20 committed boys. The placement of committed boys in the secure unit normally takes place as a result of transfer from one of the open establishments. Although such a transfer requires the approval of the Northern Ireland Office it is essentially determined by negotiation between training school staff, in practice the directors of the establishments concerned. It is now theoretically possible to transfer females to the secure unit but up until the present this event has never occurred. Indeed the apparent inability of this unit to admit girls has meant that the only option for those who cannot be contained within the training schools is current the Young Offenders' Centre, a wing of Armagh Women's Prison. Although the numbers of such place-ments has only ever been small, it is barely satisfactory since the establishment is not designed or staffed to cope with juveniles, for example there is no educational facility. Once transfer to the secure unit has been effected, only in the most exceptional circumstances would an individual be moved again to an open establishment.

Although numbers of committals to training schools have declined since 1980, transfer rates from the open schools to the secure school have shown a slight increase. It has been several years since a juvenile has been confined in an adult prison in Northern Ireland.

There have been until recently several routes whereby a person under 17 can be committed to the young offenders' centre. A young person aged 14-17 years could have been held in remand at the centre providing the court has deemed him to be so unruly that he cannot be detained elsewhere. It is still legally possible and occa-sionally occurs in practice that a young person aged 16 but under 17 convicted of an imprisonable offence, may be sentenced to the young offenders' centre. A juvenile can also be sentenced to the young offenders' centre under Section 73 of the Children and Young Persons Act 1968 (equivalent to Section 53 of the Children and Young Persons Act [England and Wales]). Under Section 140 of the Children and Young Persons Act 1968, a young person having attained the age of 16 can be sentenced to the young offenders' centre for a period of up to two years for persistent absconding from a training school. A young person aged over 14 and subject to a training-school order may be transferred to the young offenders' centre for a period of five weeks, on the complaint of the training-school manager, having secured the signature of one justice of the peace. Current practice is for five-week warrants from the open training schools to be transferred to the secure training school, but it is still possible for the secure training school to use the same non-judicial process to transfer juveniles to the young offenders' centre.

The number of non-offenders are in general only a small pro-portion of those boys transferred to custody. The highest category of transfer consists of those individuals who have committed further offences. These may be related to absconding. Concern has been expressed that non-offenders can be transferred to security because developing legislation will bar such transfer. As a result pressure is being exerted by the DHSS and the social services boards for the extension of intensive-care units for non-offenders.

Northern Ireland has no detention centre order. Some juveniles actively prefer, many even seek, the short determinate young offenders' centre sentence which cancels the indeterminate training school order; however this is unlikely to be a significant factor with regard to trends overall.

Use of custodial provision for juveniles has been at very high levels in the past. In 1975 and 1977 the proportion of the juvenile population detained under Section 73 of the Children and Young Persons Act 1968 was respectively 22.6 times and 19 times the equivalent for England and Wales. However this situation had reversed by 1980. The special circumstances of Northern Ireland's political situation does occasionally give rise to uncharacteristic fluctuations in trends, such as the high numbers of Section 73 detainees in the early 1970s, but more usually the child-care and juvenile justice system are affected by intra-systemic factors. For example the absence of any psychiatric provision for adolescents is currently the source of considerable concern to residential child-care staff and is, according to some sources, the occasional justification for poor practice such as the inappropriate use of secure provision.

England and Wales

The growth of secure facilities and custody
Throughout the 1970s central government action appeared to demand that local authorities should expand the secure provision under their control. This demand was assisted by continual pressure from the Magistrates' Association. The association's campaign came to fruition in 1979 when the report of a joint working party of the Magistrates' Association, the Association of Metropolitan Authorities and the Association of County Councils was published. This report prepared under the chairmanship of the DHSS showed that whilst the constituent members were divided on a number of issues, there were large areas of agreement. One of these areas was secure accommodation. This is somewhat surprising since it is an issue which is both emotive and inflammatory for social service policy-makers and practitioners and yet the report clearly stated 'The provision of more secure places is both urgent and essential and more progress should be made by both the government and local authorities towards extra provision.'

To be fair to the working party it did qualify this emphatic statement with a further conclusion which states 'We consider that much more should be done to contain difficult young offenders within the existing community home system by means of close supervision rather than by physically secure accommodation.'

Given this apparently widespread agreement that more secure provision is needed it is not surprising that such provision grew rapidly throughout the 1970s. However, it is worth recording this growth since it has not only had a profound impact on local-authority expenditure patterns but as importantly has created difficulties in making it possible to staff such units with appropriate numbers of appropriately trained staff.

In 1971, when the 1969 Act was implemented, there were approximately 7,500 young people, boys and girls, in open community homes with education. However at that time there were less than 100 long-term secure places for young people. Some 60 of these places were accounted for by the three large secure units (approximately 22 each) at Red Bank School (Lancashire), Red Hill School (London Borough of Wandsworth), and Kingswood School (Avon). Some small units existed in girls' community homes with education and in general the only security available to observation and assessment centres were single separation rooms. By 1980 the picture looked quite different. There were by then less than 5,000 young people in community homes with education. This drop reflects a consistent downward trend since 1971 and is continuing, if not accelerating, and has led to the closure of a number of community homes with education.

At the same time as demand for open places was dropping the number of long-term secure places has increased rapidly and in proportional terms dramatically; by 1980 some 300 long-term places in security were provided. But the most rapid growth has been in observation and assessment centres, from virtually zero to over 200 places in the decade. This growth is particularly significant since it is in an area of previously untried and untested provision. Very little experience or knowledge exists on security in short-term establishments with a high turnover, provided in small, that is, three- or four-roomed units. There are some signs that a number of local authorities, normally under a Labour council, are deciding that secure facilities are excluded from their policy options, and accordingly some purpose-built units are not being brought into operation or are actually being closed.

The growth of secure provision would be sufficient to be a cause for concern; however, the figures given above exclude the growing number of young people in security in prison department establishments. These shifts in disposal patterns are even more significant than the figures suggest, since they occurred at a time when the official policy was in fact the reverse. Borstal and detention centres were, under the 1969 Act, initially to be phased out and yet over the decade showed a massive increase in use of over 200 per cent. For detention centres figures rose from 2,061 in 1971, to 5,412 in 1981; for borstal (both boys and girls) the numbers rose from 1,116 in 1971 to 2,382 in 1981. Thus these ten years saw a major growth in the use of security and custody of all types for young people. The implementation of the Criminal Justice Act 1982 has had a mixed effect on this growth. Early indications are that the use of detention centres for under 17 years is dropping (-15 per cent), whereas youth custody is increasing ($+69$ per cent), more particularly for girls.

Table 2.5   Places in approved secure units by region (June 1984)

Region	Observation and Assessment Units			Community Homes with Education				Total
	Boys	Girls	Mixed	Boys	Girls	Mixed		
Northern			22			36	(58)	58
Yorks. & Humberside	9		7	18			(48)	34
North-western	22	4	6	34	13	8	(110)	87
West Midlands	7		10		4		(26)	21
East Midlands	2	2	12	3		8	(38)	27
East Anglia	6	6					(12)	12
Thames Valley	3		15		3		(40)	21
London	54	12	2		3		(120)	71
Southern			11				(13)	11
Wessex	10	3					(19)	13
South-west			12	26			(38)	38
Totals	113	27	97	81	23	52	(522)	393

Notes:
Figures shown in brackets are those proposed by DHSS on 1 July 1982.

The current provision of secure facilities
The tables presented in this section are culled from various sources and attempt to illustrate trends in the use of local authority secure provision and prison department custody.

Detention centre orders — The number of males aged 14 to 16 sentenced to detention centre nearly doubled between 1973 and 1982. The proportionate use of detention centre orders rose during this period from just under 6 per cent of male juveniles sentenced, to just under 10 per cent of those sentenced. Figures on sentencing in the year following the introduction of the 1982 Criminal Justice Act in May 1983, show the proportion increasing. However, figures on *receptions* of juveniles into prison establishments show that the number of detention centre receptions of males aged 14 to 16 was 16 per cent lower during the period July 1983 to June 1984 (4,670) than in 1982 (5,570). The average length of detention centre orders

Table 2.6   Secure units — patterns of use

Type of unit	No. of units	No. of places	Average length of admission (in days)	Occupancy
Observation and Assessment Units 6 or more places	9	88	48	66%
Community Homes with Education 6 or 9 places	6	40	31	64%
Community Homes with Education 10 or more places	6	134	413	95%

Notes:
Units with fewer than six places are not included in this table. Tables 2.5 and 2.6 are taken from figures provided by the DHSS (London).

Table 2.7   Persons aged under 17 held in adult prisons in England and Wales (in March 1985: by type of prisoner)

	Number[*] Untried and convicted unsentenced	Sentenced
Adult prisons with remand units/wings for prisoners aged under 21[†]	1	20
Remand centres taking remand prisoners of all ages[§]	35	15
Other adult prisons	6	22

Notes:
[*] The figures are those recorded centrally.
[†] Cardiff, Dorchester, Exeter, Liverpool, Manchester, Norwich, Swansea and Winchester.
[§] Ashford, Low Newton, Manchester, Pucklechurch and Risley.

in the year ending June 1984 was 10 weeks (with remission, 6 to 7 weeks).

Borstal training/youth custody orders — Between 1973 and 1982 the number of males aged 15 to 16 sentenced to borstal training fluctuated; the proportional use of the borstal training order remained fairly constant at 3 per cent, dropping to 2 per cent in 1982. In the first year of the Criminal Justice Act's operation, the number of male juveniles received into youth custody (1,850) was 41 per cent higher than the number of borstal receptions in 1982 (1,310). The number of females aged 15 to 16 sentenced to borstal training also fluctuated during the period 1973 to 1982; the proportional use of the order was around 1 per cent of those sentenced. In the first year of the Act's operation the number of female receptions into youth custody (95) was more than double the number received into borstal in 1982 (45).

In the year ending June 1984 the average length of youth custody for males aged 15 to 16 was under 8 months (with remission, just over 5 months), and for females aged 15 to 16, 5.5 months (with remission, about 3.5 months).

Scotland
Under the children's hearing system the only secure units attached to List D schools are those at Rossie, Montrose (The Macdonald Wing), capacity 25 boys; Kenmure St Mary's, Bishopbriggs, Glasgow (The Ogilvie Wing), capacity 24 boys and girls; and the new unit attached to Kerelaw School, Stevenson, Ayrshire, opened in December 1983, capacity 18 boys and girls. These three schools also have open wings and there are at present 17 other List D schools in Scotland which are open establishments. (It should perhaps be noted that this figure has already been considerably reduced from 28 in 1971 and the Secretary of State is again considering reduction of such schools that he would license, having recently withdrawn the licences from four other List D schools.) Some of these schools do employ or have employed 'custody' rooms or cells where disruptive children may be held for 'cooling off' periods. Further, hearings may detain children in assessment centres, and some of these establishments, notably Howdenhall in Edinburgh and Larchgrove in Glasgow, were secure until 1984. All now have secure facilities within their premises. Children may either be held in such establishments for a set number of days on a requirement pending a further decision by a hearing, or indeed may be detained there as the subject of a supervision requirement incorporating a condition of residence in that secure establishment. At present it would be possible for

a social work director to detain a child in such an establishment without reference to a hearing if parental rights were vested in the local authority or even, in exceptional cases, if a child were in the voluntary care of the social work department.

Children found guilty of serious crimes
So far this chapter has been concerned with the majority of children who may be placed into secure provision. However most jurisdictions also allow for exceptional cases. Some already referred to are those children sentenced under Section 53 of the Children and Young Persons Act 1933 in England and Wales, or Section 73 of the Children and Young Persons Act 1968 (Northern Ireland). These are normally children who are dealt with as exceptional due to the nature of their crimes, typically homicide, rape or arson. Whilst in each of the four jurisdictions there are only a very small number of cases they pose specific problems for both legislation and provision and neatly crystalize the dilemma of balancing the welfare of a young person against protection of the community.

In England and Wales Section 53(1) of the Children and Young Persons Act 1933 provides that a person found guilty of murder committed when under the age of 18 must be sentenced to be detained during Her Majesty's pleasure in such place and under such conditions as the Secretary of State (the Home Secretary) may direct. Moreover Section 53(2) provides that where a person under the age of 17 is convicted on indictment of an offence for which an adult may be sentenced to imprisonment for 14 years or more, the court may, if it considers that no other method of dealing with him is suitable, order him to be detained in such place and under such conditions as the Home Secretary may direct. This period of detention (which may be for life) must be specified in the sentence and it must not exceed the maximum term of imprisonment with which the offence is punishable in the case of an adult.

Except where the charge is homicide, or there is a joint charge with an adult, children under the age of 14 may not be tried by the crown court. It follows that these are the only circumstances when somebody under the age of 14 may be detained under Section 53(2).

The effect of an order for detention under Section 53 is that decisions on placement, transfer, home leave and parole are matters for the Home Secretary. Most of the young people detained in this way are held initially in prison establishments, but where children might be considered suitable for admission to a community home the Home Secretary consults the DHSS about placement. When an appropriate placement has been arranged, the Home Office issues a removal order to the establishment having charge of the child, authorizing his removal to the place where he is to be accommodated. If transfer to another establishment, whether closed or open, is subsequently necessary the same procedure is followed. In both cases the holding establishment remains responsible for the child's detention until the Home Secretary formally directs his removal elsewhere.

Obviously these young people, most of whom have been found guilty of very serious crimes, are likely to spend considerable periods in custody with massive restrictions placed on their movement and liberty. For a number of these young people life in the secure unit of a child-care establishment is a precursor of a longer period of detention in a prison department establishment to which they are transferred on reaching adulthood.

As has been suggested the number of young people is in fact small. In 1984 in England and Wales 74 young people were sentenced under Section 53 of the Children and Young Persons Act 1933. Of these 17 were indeterminate sentences, either at Her Majesty's Pleasure, Section 53(1), or life sentences under Section 53(2). In 1984 51 cases were referred for placement to the DHSS from the Home Office. Of these, 41 were placed into youth treatment centres or local authority child-care establishments, predominantly secure accommodation. This group placed in 1984 added to those young people previously sentenced meant that by 31 December 1984 71 such cases were accommodated in youth treatment centres or child-care establishments. This number included 13 life sentences. Of the 71 cases, 25 were in youth treatment centres.

The number of young people being sentenced under this provision has increased dramatically over the past 15 years, from less than 10 per year to over 70. However it should be noted that these trends in sentencing are not immutable or irreversible. As stated earlier, in Northern Ireland the use of Section 73 of the Children and Young Persons Act 1968 was widespread in the mid-1970s; 22.6 times the rate of Section 53's in England and Wales. By the mid-1980s this situation had reversed. It should be noted that nearly all of those so detained in Northern Ireland have been detained in penal settings, commonly adult prisons. This is the outcome for those Section 53 in England and Wales not placed by the DHSS, but retained by the Home Office. In the Republic of Ireland there is now no equivalent of Section 53. The courts have held that under the constitution the power to determine the length of any sentence is vested exclusively in the courts [The State v O'Brien, 1973, Irish Report, p. 50].

The legislation described so far covers the vast majority of admissions to secure or custodial facilities. In the main the reason precipitating the admission is the acceptance or finding of guilt of the child. However, there is another group of children who can and at times do end up in custodial provision. This is the group which is admitted into 'care' for reasons of neglect or abuse or temporary inability of the parents to care for children who, once in the care of the statutory authorities, demonstrate such difficult behaviour or challenge to the staff of residential institutions that they are transferred to secure accommodation.

As has already been illustrated, in the Republic of Ireland a child over 12 years, admitted for non-criminal reasons to an industrial school, *may* be transferred to a 'reformatory school' including Trinity House, a totally secure custodial establishment, by administrative action as opposed to a court decision. The action is based on a judgement by the Minister for Education or her officers that the child 'is found to be exercising an evil influence over the other children in the school.' (Children's Act 1908 Sec. 69 (2)(c)). 'In the two years ending March 1985, eight boys were transferred from open Industrial Schools to Trinity House' (Reply to Parliamentary Question, 27 March 1985).

In Northern Ireland a young person committed to a training school as in 'need of care and protection', or as an offender if found to be too unruly, can be transferred to the secure unit at Lisnevin on the approval of the Northern Ireland Office. Such a transfer is normally conducted through negotiations between the directors of the two institutions involved, namely the open training school and the secure unit. It is not a judicial decision and is not dependent upon a further finding of guilt or hearing of further evidence.

In Scotland the two areas of civil and criminal matters merge totally. As has been shown the hearing system deals with the full range of childhood problems whether civil or criminal (indeed such a distinction is of itself meaningless within the Scottish hearing system). Consequently if at a hearing or at a review the panel are convinced the child's best interests are served by placement in a secure unit, for example because of persistent solvent abuse, the panel has the power to authorize the admission of a child to a named secure establishment, and given the agreement of the Director of Social Work and the head of the named unit, the child will then be admitted. In England and Wales until recently the same lack of clear boundaries prevailed. Indeed the DHSS (1981a) stated:

> We have sought advice about the powers of local authorities to place in secure accommodation other legal categories of children in care. [*Author's note*: other than those placed in care as a result of a criminal offence.] The absence of case law makes a definitive statement difficult but we understand the position may be summarised as follows: The

regulations (with respect to the conduct of community homes including the admission to secure accommodation) apply to all children in care, and this covers children received into care under the 1948 Act or matrimonial legislation, and the placement may be for an indefinite period. It will be readily seen that the powers vested in the executive are very extensive and wider than we originally envisaged.

Thus it emerged that children admitted to care for a range of non-criminal reasons could be admitted to secure accommodation by administrative decision without any finding of guilt or judicial hearing. This situation appeared to be in contravention of the European Convention on Human Rights, and legislation was drafted and eventually passed to rectify the position, if only partially. The detail of this more recent legislation is discussed later in this chapter.

In three of the four jurisdictions it is legally possible for young people to be deprived of their liberty without a judicial hearing. Recognizing this problem, each has adopted different means to rectify the situation. The Republic of Ireland would claim that protection of the individual's rights are guaranteed by the written constitution. Scotland has attempted to guarantee the individual's rights by means of a code of practice against which professional behaviour can be judged and, in the extreme, approval by the Secretary of State can be withdrawn. In England and Wales legislation has been used to determine criteria for admission to security and judicial review of professional judgements, and to produce new regulations. Rights of appeal to a higher court exist.

In each of the jurisdictions a great deal of attention has been paid to the means by which individual rights may be breached. However it should be noted, and this is confirmed by the census later in the chapter, that relatively few children in custody are placed in 'child-care' secure accommodation; the vast majority of young people who experience custody do so by sentence of the court to a prison department establishment.

Young people subject to the authority of the mental health systems may be placed in secure conditions, without explicit reference to their rights and without a judicial hearing or access to appeal.

Mental health legislation in the four jursidictions: anomalies and implications for legal minors

The term 'legal minor' is used here to describe any person under the age of 18 years in the four jurisdictions. Since mental health legislation uses different definitions to the child-care law so far discussed, the new definitions are stated in this paragraph. The terms 'child', 'adolescent' or 'young person' are not used in the mental health legislation. The term 'patient' is used throughout without distinction of age except in two specified instances to be discussed later. However, legal minors are variously described in other legislation and, as discussed previously, with little overall consistency. In Scotland a 'child' is any person under 18 years of age. 'Pupils' are boys under 14 years of age or girls under 12 years of age. Boys and girls above these respective ages are then described as 'minors' until they are 18 years old. Therefore it is important to check carefully, in any specific piece of legislation, the precise definition of the terms used.

This discussion refers to newly enacted and prospective mental health legislation in the four jurisdictions. References are to the Mental Health Act 1983 (England and Wales only), which is now in force, unless otherwise specified.

The Health (Mental Services) Act 1981 (Republic of Ireland) awaits implementation at a date to be announced. With regard to criminal offenders in the Republic, an inter-department committee on mentally ill and maladjusted persons (chairman, the Hon. Justice Henchy, Judge of the Supreme Court) published a third interim report in November 1978. Further debate is awaited.

In Northern Ireland a review committee on the mental health legislation reported in 1981 but re-drafted law has not yet reached the statute book, a similar position to the legislation on juvenile offenders. Currently it is intimately linked with child-care law which differs from that in the other jurisdictions. These links are much more extensive than were those between child-care law and the Mental Health Act 1959 (England and Wales) or the Mental Health Act (Scotland) 1960.

In the Republic legislation for mentally abnormal offenders is without lower age limit and dates from the Lunacy (Ireland) Act 1821 to the Criminal Lunatics Act 1884 with four intermediate acts still on the statute book. These current statutes have been the subject of intensive and continuing debate within the relevant jurisdiction, as indicated above, and will disappear as new legislation is implemented.

The common law (that is, the law which does not come from legislation) in England and Wales, the Republic and Northern Ireland is generally the same. However Scotland, which has its own legal system, possesses rules of common law some of which are similar and some different to those applicable in the rest of the United Kingdom. An attempt will be made to link the issue of common-law rights regarding consent to medical treatment with issues specifically connected with mental health legislation. The re-drafting and partial enacting of mental health legislation in the four jurisdictions is taking place at a time of complementary social and legal change which influence both the wording of the legislation and the uses to which it may be put. These are as follows:

(1)   Legislators, acting on behalf of society, are less likely than when drafting the Mental Health Act 1959 to regard doctors as necessarily benevolent or as the appropriate sole or major guardians of their patients' rights.

(2)   An increasingly complex debate continues about the civil and legal rights of the individual vis-à-vis the state. In this debate it is relevant to consider potential or actual conflict between the rights and needs of children and those of parents.

(3)   There is a continuing debate also about the rightful boundaries of psychiatry with particular reference to behaviour unacceptable to society. Confusion is peculiarly intense when badly-behaved children break the law or disrupt their schools and families. They may be regarded as mad, bad or 'in need of specialised help'.

(4)   The new terms 'mental impairment' and 'severe mental impairment' are used in the Act for those cases of mental handicap which are associated with 'abnormally aggressive or seriously irresponsible conduct'. They replace the previous terms 'sub-normality' and 'severe sub-normality' in the 1959 Act (in England and Wales). This terminology was introduced to avoid including the term 'mental handicap' in mental health legislation. An unfortunate side-effect may prove to be that in practice there will be an unclear and worrying boundary between these concepts and those of psychopathic disorder or severe conduct disorder in mentally handicapped children and adolescents.

(5)   The Criminal Justice Act 1982 has strictly limited and regulated the use of secure accommodation for children subject to care orders in England and Wales. It may be hypothesized that parents or guardians of badly-behaved children, faced with this dilemma, may turn to psychiatric services and request use of the mental health legislation.

It is proposed to discuss implementation of the legislation under three headings:

(1)   Informal admissions.

(2)   Civil legislation in respect of mental illness and mental impairment.

(3)   Legislation regarding mentally abnormal offenders.

Each of these headings should be considered:

(a) in respect of all legal minors under the age of 18 years. The redrafted statutory law regarding compulsory admissions to a psychiatric centre, for assessment or treatment, or regarding consent to treatment, applies to young people over 16 years of age if they had reached their full majority.

(b) The legislation should also be considered in respect of those legal minors who additionally are in care of parents or guardians able to give or withhold consent to medical treatment.

Therefore young people under heading (b) are included with those under heading (a) but there are, or may be, additional constraints on professionals offering psychiatric treatment to group (b) whatever the legal status of these people within the mental health legislation.

Informal admissions
It is consistently stated within the new legislation that informal admission to a psychiatric unit or nursing home does not differ, or will not differ (the Republic and Northern Ireland) under normal circumstances in any way from any other form of hospital admission.

For example, the Mental Health Act 1983 Part X, Section 131(1) states:

> Nothing in this Act should be construed as preventing a patient who requires treatment for mental disorder from being admitted to any hospital or mental nursing home in pursuance or arrangements made in that behalf and without any application, order or direction, rendering him liable to be detained under this Act or from remaining in any hospital or mental nursing home in pursuance of such arrangements after he has ceased to be liable to be so detained.
>
> (2) In the case of a minor who has attained the age of 16 years and is capable of expressing his own wishes, any such arrangements as are made in sub-section 1 (above) will be made, carried out and determined notwithstanding any right of custody or control vested in law by his parent or guardian.

Section 17(2) Mental Health (Scotland) Act 1984 is analogous to Section 131(1) above. There is *no equivalent* to (2) in the Scottish Act. The Health (Mental Services) Act 1981, Eire (Part 3) (Admissions and Discharges Procedures) states:

> Nothing in this part shall be read as preventing or discouraging a person from being admitted voluntarily for care and treatment to a psychiatric centre.

The consent of young people aged 16 or over is valid in this context. Section 8 of the Family Law Reform Act 1969, which is valid in England and Wales, therefore applies to informal admissions of young people over 16 to psychiatric centres. It states that consent of a minor who has attained the age of 16 to medical or dental treatment, which in the absence of consent could constitute a trespass to the person, is as effective as if the minor were of full age. This is congruent with the mental health legislation within the same jurisdiction, and with that in Eire.

However, sub-section 3 of the 1969 Act confuses the issues, using wording designed to sustain the common-law rights of legal minors by stating:

> Nothing in this section should be construed as making ineffective any consent which would have been effective if this Section had not been enacted.

Legal opinion is that this means that parents cannot override a consent or refusal to consent of the young person aged 16 or over, though parental consent may be relied on when a young person in this age group is incapable of expressing his views, for example when in need of life-saving procedures. In Scotland there is no statutory equivalent to the Family Law Reform Act 1969, and the Mental Health (Scotland) Act, as indicated above, does not legislate on the rights to informal psychiatric treatment of young people over 16 years of age. Lessels (1985) considers that it is a moot point in Scots law whether a person under 18 years could give or withhold consent to medical treatment. Lessels opines:

> If a child is capable, regardless of his age, of understanding the whys and wherefores of being admitted to hospital, and is capable of expressing his own wishes on the matter, then he should be entitled to object to a parental request for informal hospitalisation and he should also be allowed to veto parents from stopping him admitting himself voluntarily. Where the child's level of understanding does not come up to the suggested standard, parents would have full powers to give or withhold consent.

Applying this test it would seem possible for minor boy of 15 or a minor girl of 13 to give (or withhold) consent, assuming of course that each had the necessary capacity to understand what was involved. Furthermore it is even possible that a pupil child of, say, 11 years, could give consent, but in such a case it might be difficult to establish that at such a young age the child could appreciate the implications of consenting to treatment.

The consent of parents (or guardians or legal custodians) to medical treatment for pupil children is, in practically all cases, mandatory as they have control of the child's person. In emergency situations, or where local authorities have assumed parental rights, parental consent is not required, but these are exceptions to the well-accepted rule that it is the parents who are entitled to consent. So far as minor children are concerned, then, unless the child has the necessary understanding to consent for him or herself, the parents again would have to give consent. In England and Wales the Gillick decision *as it currently stands* implies that there is now such a legal requirement. This requirement on the part of doctors has arisen as a result of practice supported by judicial statements and is based on the assumption that parents have the right to control their children, although doctors have been supported by the law when acting without parental consent in medical emergencies. A local authority acting *in loco parentis* to a legal minor in care, may be asked for and give consent to his admission to a psychiatric centre.

Hoggett (1984) points out that Mental Health Act compulsion has hardly ever been used for patients under the age of 16 (in England and Wales) who below this age have been regarded as subject to their parents' control, which may include the power to admit a child to hospital. Furthermore, if the child or his parent is opposed to care or treatment thought appropriate to his needs he may, if under 17 years old, be brought before a juvenile court in care proceedings under Section 1 of the Children and Young Persons Act 1969 or, if under the age of 18, may be made a ward of the high court.

The Children's Legal Centre, using figures from the DHSS says that, during 1980, there were 34 out of 2,674 compulsory admissions of children under 16 years old under the Mental Health Act (1959) (Childright, 1983).

With reference to the rights of parents to 'volunteer' their children for psychiatric treatment, Hoggett comments:

> These principles leave a great deal of discretion in the hand of parents and doctors. There is every reason to believe that parents of handicapped or mentally disturbed children will find it hard to put their children's interests first all the time.

In the four jurisdictions under discussion, test cases, some dramatic and well-publicized, have not so far related to psychiatric treatment. For example, in Re. D. (1976) FAM. 285, a high court judge ruled that the sterilization of an 11-year-old girl with Sotos-syndrome was not in the child's interests although the child's mother had consented to the operation. This child was a ward of court and her views were not made explicit.

In common law it is argued that a young person 'old enough to understand the nature of the treatment and its implications' may be free to give consent in preference to the parents. However, Gillick versus West Norfolk and Wisbech Health Authority and the DHSS 1983, a case referring to the freedom or otherwise of doctors to prescribe contraceptives to girls under the age of 16 years without their parents' consent, has wide implications. Currently the court of appeal has supported Mrs Gillick's right in this respect, and though Mr Gillick is not mentioned, nor are the Gillick sons, the implications are that the court of appeal denies the freedom of doctors to give contraceptive treatment to girls without their parents' consent and also to give any other form of medical treatment without parental consent. If parents have full control over their children until the age of 16 years it may be that this enables parents to give permission for 'detention' in a psychiatric centre irrespective of the wishes of the legal minor concerned.

As the law stands, test cases regarding informal admission of young people under 16 years of age at the request of their parents or guardians are likely to arise only in Scotland where the law allows a relevant framework for debate. In the USA test cases have already arisen (Krisberg and Schwartz, 1983; Schwartz *et al.*, 1984) with regard to the in-patient treatment, with parental consent, of young people under 16 years of age who in law may be 'old enough to understand the nature of the treatment and it implications'.

Civil legislation in respect of mental illness and mental impairment: legal minors under 18 years of age

With regard to compulsory admission, the legislation applies to 'patients' irrespective of their age. There is no lower age limit in current or prospective legislation throughout the four jurisdictions and there seems to be no discussion of this issue in commentaries upon the legislation.

In a provision unique in defining age limits, the Mental Health Act 1983 described guardianship (Sec. 7–13) (Sec. 36–52 Mental Health (Scotland) Act 1984). This allows a patient who has attained the age of 16 years to be placed under the supervision of a guardian approved by a department of social services. The application is made to the social services authority and must be based on medical recommendations from two doctors (one approved), each of whom has examined the patient, with no more than five days having elapsed between these examinations. An approved social worker must be involved in this procedure. The local authority in turn may become the guardian or may approve an individual, such as a relative of the patient. Discharge may be by the medical officer, the authority or the nearest relative and the patient may apply to a mental health review tribunal within each six-month period.

The powers of the guardian are: to require the patient to reside at a specified place; to require the patient to attend at specific places and times for medical treatment, occupation, education or training; to require access to the patient to be given at the patient's residence to any doctor, approved social worker or other specified person.

The guardian has no power to make the patient accept treatment and guardianship does not allow detention under secure conditions.

Legal minors under 16 years of age
With regard to this group of young people and bearing in mind the possibility of test cases under Scots law, it seems possible that both parental rights and the rights of the child may be overridden in the course of compulsory reception into a psychiatric centre since none of the legislation gives a parent or guardian indisputable rights ahead of other relatives, or even non-relatives, with whom the child has been living for over five years. The rights referred to are specifically those of applying for admission and discharge.

Section 26 of the 1983 Act defines 'nearest relative' in great detail (Section 53 Mental Health (Scotland) Act 1984). A father no longer automatically takes precedence over the mother but, other things being equal, the older of the two takes precedence. Relatives, usually living with or caring for the patient, take precedence as may a person of either sex who has resided with a patient for five years or more. He or she comes last on the list.

The Health (Mental Services) Act 1981 (Eire), Section 15, lists various people who may act as nearest relative in making a recommendation for a 'Section' without listing them in rank order. The terms 'parent' and 'guardian' are not further defined, but have an established legal meaning, that is, 'parent' is both parents of a legitimate child or the mother of an illegitimate child; guardian is the legal guardian.

The enacted legislations nowhere state that where two married parents, who have never been involved in civil litigation regarding that marriage, share custody of a legal minor, both must be consulted with regard to their child's admission to a psychiatric unit. This may create problems where a child is labelled as psychiatrically ill in the course of a battle between separated or divorcing parents.

Section 28 of the Mental Health Act 1983 (Section 54 Mental Health (Scotland) Act 1984) states that where legislation has resulted in a 'Court Order' regarding custody, the 'person or persons having the guardianship or custody of the child shall, to the exclusion of any other person, be deemed to be the nearest relative'. In this section a 'Court Order' includes a court in Scotland or Northern Ireland.

Where powers are vested with a local authority (Sec. 27), that authority is deemed to be the nearest relative in preference to any other (Sec. 54 Mental Health (Scotland) Act 1984).

A child who is compulsorily admitted may be treated without parental consent, subject to the power of the parent or nearest relative to seek discharge. Save where special safeguards apply to certain treatments, compulsory patients may be treated without their consent or that of the nearest relative. A second opinion for specified treatments will be required for children under 16 years of age as for other compulsorily detained patients.

Nothing in the legislation indicates whether or not the locking up of legal minors or indeed, for example, the locking up of severely mentally handicapped people over 16 years of age, is acceptable as an adjunct to or pre-condition of psychiatric treatment, if the admission was informal but with parental consent. Behaviour modification programmes or the prescription of psychotropic medication without the consent of the legal minor but with the consent of the appropriate guardian are likely to provide further sources of controversy (see for example Childright, 1983).

Mentally abnormal offenders — Mental Health Act 1983
This legislation has been fully implemented in England and Wales from 1 October 1984, but is not yet implemented in Scotland nor enacted in the remaining jurisdictions. The age boundary of 16 years is not necessarily relevant; it is important, where legal minors are involved in criminal offences, to cross-check with relevant criminal justice legislation within the jurisdiction.

Section 35: remand to hospital for report — This empowers either a magistrates court or crown court to remand an accused person, awaiting trial and accused of an imprisonable offence, or awaiting sentence, to a specified hospital for a report.

Section 36 — This empowers a crown court to remand an accused person to a specified hospital for treatment. It refers to an accused person who is in custody awaiting trial before a crown court for an offence punishable with imprisonment (other than an offence the sentence for which is fixed by law) or who at any time before sentence is in custody in the course of a trial before the courts for such an offence.

In respect of both sections the court must be satisfied on the written or oral evidence of the registered medical practitioner who would be in charge of the preparation of the report or of the treatment, or of some other person representing the manager of the hospital, that arrangements have been made for admission to that hospital and for the admission to be within a period of 7 days beginning with the date of the remand.

Section 37: hospital and guardianship orders — This section applies only to individuals found guilty of an imprisonable offence except murder. The same rules of acceptance apply.

These sections could apply to children and young people. For the purpose of criminal law in England and Wales, a 'child' is aged between 10 and 14 years, and a 'young person' is over 14 years but under 17 years of age.

In Scotland a 'mentally disordered' child may be brought before a children's hearing because he/she is in need of compulsory care. This could mean a child under the age of 16 or one who, although over the age of 16 and less than 18, is already subject to a supervision requirement of the Children's Hearing Social Work (Scotland) Act 1968, Section 30(1). In Scotland children under 16 who have committed criminal offences usually do not come before the criminal courts and indeed cannot be prosecuted except with the consent of the Lord Advocate. Instead such children are usually referred to children's hearings by the children's reporter as being in need of compulsory care.

The Criminal Procedure (Scotland) Act 1975 describes the powers of the criminal courts in dealing with mentally abnormal offenders including those over 16 years of age.

In English and Welsh law the term 'sentenced to prison' applies to young people subject to youth custody or detention orders. Thus Section 38: *interim hospital order*, and Section 47: *the transfer of sentenced prisoner to hospital* may apply to young people under 17 years of age or to young people under 14 tried and sentenced with an adult.

It should be noted that the legislation throughout refers to 'detention' and at no point is this defined. Though there is detailed legislation about the rights of detained patients to consent to or refuse treatment, there is no comparative discussion in the *mental health* legislation, in any of the four jurisdictions, about the physical environment and conditions of security under which patients may be detained.

Also it seems anomalous that, if a child is in care, so that the 'nearest relative' is a local authority, an employee of that authority's department of social services, an approved social worker, may act on its behalf in applying for the child's compulsory admission to a psychiatric centre. At this point the local authority acts *in loco parentis and* offers an 'independent' social worker to the prospective patient. Similarly, an approved social worker may apply for guardianship in respect of a patient, and his employing local authority may then become the guardian of that patient.

This seems inappropriate given the care taken currently, and in prospective legislation throughout the four jurisdictions, to specify that *doctors* must be unrelated to the person to be admitted and must receive no legal or financial advantage from the admission. They must be seen to be clinically independent and one doctor must not be under the 'direction' of the other.

In summary, despite a trend towards clearer definition of civil and legal rights in respect of the individual patient, who is never defined except in respect of informal treatment as a legal minor except in the specific, limited and so far rarely used provisions about guardianship, it seems that the mental health legislation is being, or has been, re-drafted with considerable reliance on the good will and good faith of the parents of psychiatrically disturbed or severely mentally impaired children and with an even more touching dependence on the good will and good faith of their psychiatrists. The said psychiatrists have been given remarkably few guidelines in respect of their work with legal minors and their parents or guardians, although they work in a young specialty whose boundaries are subject to debate.

Hoggett says:

> It may be necessary to invoke the Mental Health Act procedures a little more frequently than has previously been thought. From the child's point of view, this is by no means a bad thing, for he will then have access to the Mental Health Act Commission, to the Mental Health Review Tribunal, and to the greater safeguards applicable to the medical treatment of detained patients. There would indeed be something to be said for regarding all child patients as detained patients for these purposes. Their numbers are not large, for strenuous efforts have recently been made to get them out of hospitals and back into the community, but these in no way mitigate the situation for those who remain.

This no doubt is controversial given that it may be argued that legal minors have exactly the same rights as the rest of the population of informal admission to psychiatric centres, particularly since compulsory admission may still carry lasting penalties such as difficulties with employment or emigration.

Meanwhile, the above-mentioned right of access to the Mental Health Act Commission is analogous to that available in Scotland, since the enactment of the Mental Health (Scotland) Act 1960 created an important precedent for the protection of civil rights including theoretically those of legal minors, as this legislation was also drafted without lower age limits. The new legislation broadens the remit of the Mental Health Act Commission, allowing it to work actively rather than reactively. Precedence may be created for a critical evaluation of the rights of legal minors which will merit critical examination by legislators in all four jurisdictions.

In the meantime, Hoggett's emphatic statement highlights the need for urgent and continuing debate concerning the rights of legal minors when they, their guardians or the courts seek, on their behalf, psychiatric advice and treatment including informal or compulsory admission to a psychiatric centre.

Recent developments

Increasingly observers of the juvenile justice systems and child welfare systems, as well as the practitioners within the systems, have become concerned that developments in practice have outstripped legislation, or alternatively changes in general public attitudes are out of step with current professional practice. This has led to pressure to reassess practice, realign legislation, and re-establish some questioning of professional judgements. It is not so relevant or obvious in the Republic of Ireland since the written constitution should, in theory, adequately protect the rights of individuals and therefore realignments are conducted on the rulings, if necessary, by the supreme court. It is however clearly seen in the other jurisdictions, who are attempting to redress the balance by means other than a written constitution.

The acknowledgement of the need to rethink some fundamental views has been clearly expressed by central government departments. England and Wales provides a useful case study of these developments, the underlying concepts of which are discussed in chapter 4.

The DHSS published a report of an internal working party on *Legal and Professional Aspects of the Use of Secure Accommodation for Children in Care* in 1981. This report neatly summarized the problem:

> Two aspects of the legal provisions relating to secure accommodation have given cause for concern. Firstly, the expansion in the provision and use of secure accommodation has increased doubts and uncertainties about the powers of local authorities and voluntary organisations to place the different legal categories of children in care in secure accommodation. Secondly, whilst the 1969 Act sought to promote the flexible use of treatment facilities thereby increasing the importance of assessing and meeting a child's needs one unintentional consequence has perhaps been a devaluation of the importance attached to his rights as a citizen which as an adult would be taken for granted.
>
> [It is important to note] the 1969 Act when passed made no direct reference to 'secure accommodation'. It empowered local authorities to restrict the liberty of certain children in care. Moreover the Act contained no requirement that a child should be offered legal representation in criminal proceedings when he was made subject to a care order — unlike the provisions relating to sentence to detention centre

or borstal, even though a child in care may be detained for a longer period of time than under either of the two custodial sentences.

This report concluded:

> We believe that the law and departmental guidance on such an important subject as the restriction of liberty of children and the use of secure accommodation by local authorities and voluntary organisations should be clear, as simple as possible and provide adequate safeguards for children. As far as the law is concerned we have reached the conclusion that in many respects it satisfied none of those objectives. (DHSS, 1981a)

There could be no clearer statement that practice and legislation were out of step. The government of England and Wales chose to redress the balance by two means. Firstly, to make use of legislation in preparation of the Criminal Justice Bill to incorporate specific changes in legislation and also through that legislation to introduce new regulations governing the use of secure accommodation.

The government's policy over the past decade has reflected the contradiction felt by most authorities and individuals when faced by the prospect of locking up a young person in secure accommodation, namely that whilst acknowledging that in certain exceptional cases loss of liberty is justifiable there is concern that the numbers for whom such a loss is justified is kept to an irreducible minimum.

This dilemma has produced a number of contradictions in the stance of central government, the most recent and obvious being in the Criminal Justice Act 1982, which, in many respects, makes it easier for magistrates to sentence young people to custody, whilst at one and the same time constraining the powers of local authorities to place young people into secure accommodation.

The effect of these new provisions in operation since 24 May 1983 is to reduce the discretionary judgement of social workers as to whether or not a child should be in security, and via the court to make the local authority account for its decision-making and bring the conditions of loss of liberty for children in line with the European Convention of Human Rights which demand that nobody should be placed in custody without a court hearing. Another effect is no longer to enforce the statutory requirement to appoint an 'independent person' to act on the young person's behalf when the local authority reviews the appropriateness of the use of secure accommodation.

These new provisions may have little impact on practice. As yet firm figures are difficult to obtain, but not untypical is the London region where there was a reduction in the numbers of children in security in the run up to the implementation date (24 May). This seemed to be caused by care authorities withdrawing some young people already in security and also by a reduction in referrals. Thus there was a total of 20 children (5 girls and 15 boys) where the care authority intended to go to court for a secure accommodation order. These applications should be seen against the background of 55 secure places available in the London region. All 20 applications were successful. By 1 July the position had changed drastically, there being a total of 38 children (11 girls and 27 boys) in security, an increase of almost 100 per cent in one month (Richards, 1983). It appears from these figures that magistrates tend to grant the order if asked.

The new regulations issued by the DHSS in England and Wales proved comprehensive and for the first time began to define the concept of secure accommodation and to limit the discretion of professionals as to when and how they could deprive children and young people of their liberty.

In summary the regulations state that the children affected by the new regulations are those:

(a) received into care under Section 2 (Child Care Act 1980);
(b) subject to care orders;
(c) remanded to care under Section 23(1) of the Children and Young Persons Act 1969.

The regulations do not yet apply to any other category of child (e.g. those subject to place of safety orders, in the care of local authority following arrest or detention). The government is considering amendments to extend the safeguards to other categories of children who may be accommodated in community homes. In the meantime the present arrangements continue.

The liberty of children in care may be restricted in youth treatment centres provided by the Secretary of State under Section 80 of the Child Care Act 1980, or in secure accommodation approved for that purpose by the Secretary of State (under *new* Regulation 3).

The following forms of accommodation are features of secure accommodation only:

(a) the locking of a child or children in a single room at any time, when accompanied by a responsible adult or adults;
(b) the locking of internal doors to confine a child or children in a certain section of a home, when accompanied by a responsible adult or adults.

N.B. The use of secure separation rooms in approved secure accommodation was to be phased out by 31 December, 1983.

The following procedures are not be considered as constituting the restriction of liberty of children, though they may be adopted where they are acceptable to the fire prevention officer, are consistent with building regulations, and are conducive to a domestic atmosphere within the home:

(a)   the locking of external doors and gates at night, consistent with normal domestic security;
(b)   the locking of external doors and gates during the day time where the purpose is to prevent intruders from gaining access to the home, provided that children are not prevented from going out;
(c)   the securing of windows.

Control imposed or implied by staff or other responsible adults is not considered to constitute the restriction of liberty (though control should always be imposed or implied in a manner consistent with good child-care practice).

Procedures designed to ensure the safety of children which also have the effect of restricting their liberty may not be adopted unless they have been drawn to the attention of the Secretary of State, who will decide whether such procedures are acceptable.

Where a home is surrounded with walls or fencing continuously more than six feet high, this must be drawn to the attention of the Secretary of State so that he may decide whether such restriction of liberty is acceptable.

No children under *10* years of age may be placed in secure accommodation without the prior permission of the Secretary of State.

The criteria which must apply before a child in care may have his or her liberty restricted are that:
(a)   i   s/he has a history of absconding and is likely to abscond from any other description of accommodation;
       ii.   if s/he absconds it is likely that his or her physical, mental or moral welfare will be at risk; *or*
(b)   that if s/he is kept in any other description of accommodation s/he is likely to injure herself/himself or other persons.
N.B. For children remanded to care charged with or convicted of serious crimes (i.e. where charged with an offence imprisonable, in the case of a person 21 +, for 14 years or more, or where charged with an offence of violence, or where previously convicted of an offence of violence), these general criteria do not apply if it appears that accommodation other than that provided for the purpose of restricting liberty is inappropriate because that child is likely to abscond from such accommodation, or to injure himself/herself or other people if kept in ordinary accommodation.

In practice this means that the local authority may arrange for such a child to be placed in security for a period of not more than 72 hours. Placement beyond that period is subject to the general procedure outlined below.

If it appears that a child's placement in secure accommodation should exceed 72 hours, an application for this must be made to a juvenile court. The child's right to legal representation must be explained and facilitated, the local authority must ensure that the child's parent or guardian is notified as soon as possible of the decision to retain the child in secure accommodation and of the court hearing date. The local authority should also ensure that the child's independent visitor, if one has been appointed, is similarly informed.

Law and policies 57

The maximum period a juvenile court may authorise continued placement in accommodation for restricting liberty is three months in the first instance. Where the local authority believes a secure accommodation placement should continue beyond the period specified in the initial order, procedures regarding legal representation and the court hearing must be repeated, but the juvenile court may authorise a child in care to be kept in accommodation for restricting liberty for further periods of six months on each application to the court.

Where a child is placed in secure accommodation which is not managed by his or her care authority, the managing authority must notify the care authority within 24 hours of the placement.

The cases of children in secure accommodation must be reviewed at intervals not exceeding three months, by at least two people. The review should include consideration of the appropriateness of secure accommodation and should take into account the views of the child and the child's own local authority, parents and others who have had care of the child, and the independent visitor (if one has been appointed).

Detailed records of all placements, dates, court dates, reviews, etc., must be kept. Officers authorising placement/discharge etc. must be named.

There is provision for appeals to the crown court against decisions of a juvenile court. Where such an appeal is against an order authorising a child's placement in secure accommodation or a youth treatment centre, the placement may continue during consideration of the appeal. Where a juvenile court has refused to make an order and the care authority is appealing against that decision, the child must not be retained or placed in secure accommodation during consideration of the appeal. In either case an appeal must be made within 21 days of the decision of the juvenile court (the period of 21 days starts on the day after the day on which the court's decision is given).

Where a child is sentenced to detention under Section 53 of the Children and Young Persons Act 1933, and a local authority is directed under Section 30 of the Children and Young Persons Act 1969 to detain him in approved secure accommodation, the local authority must comply with the directions and with any guidance issued by Department of Health and Social Security in respect of the child concerned. The only requirements in the regulations that apply are those relating to the keeping of records.

In the event of a juvenile court adjourning its consideration of an application, it may make an interim order authorising the child's care authority to make arrangements for him to be placed in approved secure accommodation or in a youth treatment centre for the duration of the adjournment. An interim order will be made only where the court is not in a position to decide whether the criteria ... in respect of remanded children, have been met. If the court adjourns its consideration of an application and does not make an interim order, the child may not be placed in secure accommodation during the period of the adjournment unless circumstances subsequently change when the normal procedures will apply. (Gelsthorpe, 1983).

In Scotland at approximately the same time secure units were being developed within a very different 'welfare' system which was not readily amenable to legislative control in the way adopted by England and Wales and described above. Nevertheless, in 1985 the Social Work Services Group of the Scottish Education Department issued a code of practice 'The Use of Secure Accommodation for Children', in which it states unequivocally:

> The Secretary of State considers that the overall effect of the arrangements for the use of secure accommodation should be that:
> (a) the use of secure accommodation for children is seen as an exceptional measure.
> (b) only those children who genuinely need secure accommodation are placed and kept there.
> (c) where it proves necessary to use that type of accommodation, the length of time during which any child stays in it is restricted to the minimum necessary to meet the child's particular needs; and
> (d) the use of secure accommodation is seen in the context of an appropriate child care framework which is fully consistent with the 'welfare principle' contained in Sections 20 and 43(1) of the Social Work (Scotland) Act 1968.
> Managers and heads of establishments should seek to ensure that these objectives are achieved.

The code of practice continues to outline the type of secure accommodation to be granted approval by the Secretary of State, and arrangements for regimes, for example type of admission, education opportunities, access to relatives, reviews and recording, permissible forms of control and staff levels.

In Scotland two new pieces of legislation have been introduced which underpin these developments. Firstly, the Health and Social Services and Social Security Adjudications Act 1983: with effect from 1 January 1983 various amendments have been made to the Social Work (Scotland) Act 1968. The most important of these amendments relate to secure accommodation. As from that date a child may not be kept in secure accommodation unless that accommodation is approved for that purpose by the Secretary of State. The present indications are that the Secretary of State will be extremely sparing in his approval of secure accommodation.

Secondly, the Criminal Justice (Scotland) Act 1980: Section 45 of the Act introduced new arrangements for those from the ages of 16 to 21 who are sentenced to detention by the courts, namely that those sentenced to a period of detention serve that detention in a young offenders' institution unless the period is from 28 days to four months when it will be served in a detention centre which the Secretary of State indicated would have a 'tougher regime'. The semi-determinate sentence of borstal training and the fixed sentence of three months in a detention centre are no longer available to the courts.

In Northern Ireland the thrust of recent developments is perhaps less clear, since whilst the Black Committee report addressed the problems of justice within a welfare system the progress of implementation is patchy. It now appears certain that many of the report's proposals will not be implemented in their original form. The present training school secure unit was to become the custodial unit but it will now only form part of the residential training school system, and detention in secure accommodation will be reserved for only a minority of those made subject of residential orders. However, it is expected that secure provision within the child-care system will be sufficient to permit the attainment of one of Black's objectives: that no juveniles need be detained in penal establishments.

The open training schools are committed to the operation of separate provision in accordance with the justice/welfare division. Determinate sentencing for offenders is expected to be introduced but will be available in an open setting.

At the time of writing it is not clear whether there will be access to the secure unit for juveniles who are not offenders although it is highly probable that pressure will be exerted from child-care staff to have some form of specialist provision for the particularly difficult non-offender.

3 Children, staff, regimes, and routines

This chapter examines the operation of secure facilities for children and young people in the four jurisdictions, not in terms of the detailed timetable and routines, but in terms of the philosophy and principles underlying the provision, how this is reflected in the training offered staff, and the types of regime which exist.

It can be argued that the current philosophies arise from two sources; firstly, the historical development and present view of 'childhood' within our society, and secondly, the penal philosophy and reformers of the last two centuries.

As has been argued elsewhere (Tutt, 1984) the boundaries of childhood are not absolute, indeed childhood is a social construct of relatively recent historical development and is capable of change and redefinition as social attitudes shift.

The locking up of children predates any discernible positive society policy towards children. Consequently, while the concept of children as a delineated social group has a recent history, policies toward them derive largely from those devised for adults.

In parallel with the emergence in post-feudal Europe of a concept of childhood a fundamental shift arose in social policy toward those charged with criminal offences or held to be culpably deviant. The enactment of punishment as a ritualized ceremony is described and discussed by Michel Foucault (1977).

For the most part, and until well into the nineteeth century children were dealt with as adults in miniature and were thus exposed to the conditions of adult prisons. In their origins, prisons had been places of containment until the completion of sentence and, the 'Bridewells' apart, could not be judged as representing an instrument of penal philosophy until the beginnings of the penitentiary movement in the latter half of the eighteenth century.

Sydney Smith, distinguished as writer and churchman, described the penitentiary regime as follows:

> Prisons are really meant to keep the multitude in order, and to be a terror to evildoers. . . . There must be a great deal of solitude; coarse food; a dress of shame; hard, incessant, irksome, eternal labour; a planned and regulated and unrelenting exclusion of happiness and comfort.

This view can still be seen as underpinning contemporary policy on law and order. For, in October 1979, the Home Secretary announced his plans to the Conservative Party Conference, for a 'new, tougher experimental regime' to be introduced as a 'short, sharp shock for young criminals'. He described the new rigorous regime as follows:

> ... life will be conducted at a brisk tempo. Much greater emphasis will be put on hard and constructive activities, on discipline and tidiness, on self-respect and respect for those in authority. We will introduce on a regular basis drill, parades, and inspections. Offenders will have to earn their limited privileges by good behaviour ... these will be no holiday camps, and I sincerely hope that those who attend them will not ever want to go back there. (Whitelaw, 1980)

The operation of secure provision for children is influenced by two strands of opinion. The first is represented by the current view that children should be dependent, responsive if not obedient to adults and, in the extreme, that they require protection from themselves and others. Or indeed the community may regard itself as needing protection from them. These views ensure that children have few if any rights of their own, and therefore can when necessary be deprived of their liberty by benevolent and well-intentioned adults. The second strand arises from our penal history and current penal philosophy. Specialist secure facilities for children have nearly always been developed as a reaction against the imprisonment of young people in adult prisons; however, this positive reaction has not created an alternative 'penal' philosophy for young people. Indeed most secure units for young people have always had to appear to be 'firm' with young people in order to gain credibility and therefore to be used by the judiciary. Only a minority have been able to develop credibility on the basis of their 'therapeutic' approach. The same attitudes which ensured that it took Mary Carpenter many years hard fighting to 'rescue' boys from Parkhurst prison in the 1850s (Carlebach, 1970) underlie the current arguments that 'unruly certificates' placing young people into the prison system can only be stopped when sufficient local authority secure units are available. In other words the child-care secure units are nearly always seen as lesser prisons but nevertheless as performing the same function, often with only minor modifications in philosophy, though the judiciary would claim that their sole concern was to ensure that during the period of remand the child was not 'free' to commit other offences and that following the period of remand he was available to be produced in court for trial or disposal. Millham, *et al.* (1978) point out that at least one of the secure units built in the 1960s quite unnecessarily adopted a design which ensured that 'slopping-out' was an essential part of the morning routine.

Previous studies of secure provision for juveniles suggest that the issues surrounding such provision have been a perennial feature of the child-care and juvenile justice field (Cawson and Martell, 1979; Millham *et al.* 1978). To quote from Cawson's study:

> The history of residential provision for young offenders in Britain shows that since its inception some closed facilities have always been regarded as necessary. (Cawson and Martell, 1979).

Imprisonment has been retained as a possibility for older children and for those convicted of serious crimes. Provision for the remand of 'unruly and depraved' young persons to prisons and later to remand centres has also been a constant feature of legislation to deal with young people across all four jurisdictions.

There has never been a time when all children subject to legislative orders were being contained, treated or cared for in open conditions. Demand for closed facilities has, however, fluctuated significantly. Thus, in the 15 years following the passing of the Children and Young Persons Act (1933), use of closed provision (in England) for juvenile offenders was at its lowest this Century (Cawson and Martell, 1979).

It is the trend beginning in the 1950s and accelerating throughout the 1970s up to the present, in which the demand for use of secure provision has increased, which would appear to require some analysis. The growth of secure provision is discernible throughout all four jurisdictions despite widely differing legislative and institutional frameworks. The nature and direction of the increased use of secure custodial facilities for juveniles is subject to local variations, but overall the trend is sufficiently general to suggest the influence of significant macro-political factors underpinned by, or reflecting, a substantive shift in attitudes towards young people and their misdemeanours. Indeed it has been suggested that the world-wide economic recession has exacerbated a pre-occupation with youth as a source of public disorder, thus effecting a shift in the emphasis of intervention from 'help' to control (Mungham and Pearson, 1976).

The arguments for the provision of secure institutions appear to transcend ideological and party-political distinctions insofar as there is an assumption that at least some juveniles will prove to be beyond the scope of current open establishments. Thus policy documents as wide apart as the Longford (1966) and the Black Committee (1979) reports identify a 'hard core', Longford referring to 'violent and disturbed adolescents' and Black to 'serious and persistent offenders', for whom secure provision is a necessity. The stated purpose of security does differ according to whether a 'welfare' or a 'justice' model is invoked. For a welfare-based system security is a means of providing 'intensive care' or at least having the child available for 'help'. Within a 'justice' perspective placement in secure conditions is the ultimate sanction available, a deterrent to offending. In both systems security is seen as an extreme measure to be used only for 'extreme' children. In practice the use of secure provision often seems to be related less to the behaviour of juveniles and more to the operation of the juvenile justice system, the perceptions of professional participants and the organizsational pressures presented by the agencies involved.

This is best illustrated by the frustration and helplessness often expressed by all agencies in the juvenile justice system: police, courts, social work agencies and residential staff. Representatives of all of these bodies periodically express their difficulties in trying to balance their responsibility to the child with their responsibilities to society while at the same time respecting the child's and family's rights. When faced by such conflicting demands secure accommodation appears to offer at least a form of solution. For example how do staff ensure that children with a previous history of absconding attend court on a required day, how do staff charged with the child's care stop him indulging in self-damaging behaviour? When faced by the need for rapid decision and response it is easier to reach for a solution with superficial validity than to explore more imaginative approaches.

There is currently provision within all four jurisdictions for secure accommodation for juveniles within (a) the child-care system, (b) the penal system, and (c) mental health provision. The last category, at first sight, would seem to be least important. Its functioning is governed by different legislation but, more importantly, issues surrounding the physical restraint of individuals are formally identified as medical or treatment problems rather than legal or moral problems, but the balance has shifted, as reflected in the recently enacted mental health legislation and the development of the Mental Health Commission. This results in some difficulty in making meaningful comparisons between the first two systems and the third. The statistics collected in the mental health system do not categorize juveniles separately; this, along with the numbers involved, makes it more difficult to comment with any certainty on the treatment of juveniles within it. The other two systems overlap to a considerable extent. The manner in which they are used for juveniles is affected by the same legislative and policy considerations.

The child-care system

Historically a major theme in services for juvenile offenders has been the provision of alternatives to the adult prison. The end result of a series of legislative and institutional developments was the creation of a system of residential establishments specifically concerned with the care and training of juvenile offenders; the approved schools in England and Wales and Scotland, training schools in Northern Ireland, and the industrial and reformatory schools in the Republic of Ireland.

The approved schools tended to base their regimes on a model of the client as recalcitrant and therefore primarily in need of 'training' (Millham *et al*., 1978), following the traditions set in the adult prisons by Howard and Bentham. However as Carlebach (1970) and others have noted, juvenile justice systems have always been subject to the influence of the competing interpretations offered by the 'welfare' model. The post-war years in particular marked the beginnings of a new emphasis on child care with the work of Melanie Klein and the post-Freudians, John Bowlby (1953) and the concomitant rise of the social work profession.

A new psychodynamic treatment-oriented technology was promoted by a group of influential and visible practitioners, Barbara Docker Drysdale, David Wills, and Richard Balbernie (1966). It cannot be said that their ideas changed the approved school system practice and philosophy drastically or rapidly, but the rhetoric if not the reality of a 'medical' model of delinquency gained currency through their influence. Ultimately this ideology was to become the official one with the enactment of the 1968 and 1969 legislation in Scotland, and in England and Wales. However the difficulties posed by the competing ideologies continued to bedevil policy in this field. For example, a DHSS working party set up to examine the observation and assessment of children (DHSS, 1980) clearly had difficulties in deciding which model it should adopt for the assessment of children and young people.

Concurrent with the changes at the conceptual level the approved school system was experiencing a number of other practical problems. In the immediate post-war years success rates were falling and absconding was rising (Millham *et al*., 1978). Practitioners sought to justify difficulties by explanations based on characteristics of the client group; generally these suggested that the young people were more difficult than they had been in the past, and particularly that there existed a minority 'hard core' of exceptionally delinquent adolescents who could not have been coped with in the normal regime. This gave rise to the 'rotten apple' theory, namely that the small minority corrupted the majority and therefore should be removed.

The 'rotten apple' explanation appears to have been extremely important in the genesis of secure provision. It has been presented as the reason for the Carlton 'riots' (Durand, 1960). The 'riots' at Carlton, an approved school in Bedfordshire, were little more than the breakdown of institutional control, when some insensitive mass punishment by staff led to wholesale absconding by the boys who 'terrorized' a nearby village and generally raised anxieties about such institutions; these riots are regarded as highly significant in the aetiology of recent secure unit provision. Although the Home Office had already set up a working party to look at the issue, the Carlton affair attracted considerable media and public attention. It was almost inevitable therefore that the working party should recommend the establishment of secure units within the approved school system (Millham *et al.*, 1978).

Three units attached to the classifying schools at Redbank, Redhill and Kingswood were developed by 1964. The closed units were designated to take persistent absconders, exceptionally unruly and uncooperative boys, exceptionally disturbed boys requiring psychiatric help, and children with serious medical conditions such as epilepsy and diabetes whose behaviour put them further at risk (other categories of children were added later). According to Millham *et al.* (1978), the Home Office intended the regime of the closed units to be 'brisk', (a term that re-emerged in the 1980s with the establishment of new regimes in detention centres). Scotland already had a secure unit, the McDonald Wing at Rossie Farm School. Ireland, North and South, did not at that time seem to experience the same problems with recalcitrant youth, or at least did not accept secure accommodation as the desired policy option.

It has been suggested that the functions of secure accommodation in the child-care system are: (a) to contain, (b) to control, (c) to care, (d) to treat, and (e) to rehabilitate (Wilkie, 1985). But in their implementation these objectives are difficult to combine, creating difficulties for practice which are reported to be particularly acute in long-stay secure provision (Millham *et al.*, 1978). In addition staff bring to their posts competing ideologies derived from education and social work, and a host of popular conceptions about security and the young people placed therein. These conflicts have to be tackled systematically during any induction training (see p. 79).

The 1969 Children and Young Persons Act and the 1968 Social Work (Scotland) Act embodied in their provision a welfare model, and in the case of England and Wales changed the administrative and financial framework of the approved school system. In England and Wales the schools were renamed community homes with education; the residential child-care system was expected to meet policy guidelines which were explicitly treatment-orientated, as outlined in the DHSS booklet *Care and Treatment in a Planned Environment* (DHSS, 1971). In Scotland the approved schools became List D schools because when invited by the central department to find a new name for the schools no one in the field could suggest one, so they were described as 'Schools on the Scottish Education Department List D' or for short, List D schools.

Following the enactment of the 1969 (England and Wales) and the 1968 (Scotland) legislation, demand for secure places increased in a manner that appears inconsistent with the 'welfare' principles which officially underpinned provision within the new child-care system. According to DHSS figures (England and Wales) there were about 150 secure places within the child-care system in 1969. By the end of 1981 the figure was estimated to be between 400–500 places (DHSS, 1981b).

The significance of this trend is best illustrated not by the growth in numbers but by the changes in ratio between secure and open provision. In England and Wales in 1969 there were approximately 150 secure beds and 6,000 beds in open institutions, a ratio of 1:40. By 1984 many open community homes with education had been shut down giving a residue of 3,500 beds whereas secure accommodation had expanded rapidly to some 300 in long-term establishments giving a ratio of 1:11.6. In Scotland the same growth can be seen. In the 1960s there were 25 secure beds and 1,700 open beds, a ratio of 1:68; by 1981 the List D schools had 49 secure places and 1,200 open (1:25); by 1984 there were 69 secure places to an overall population of 700 (1:10); and in addition a further small number, some five or six Scottish children, were being accommodated in English secure units. However it should be noted that in Scotland the numbers of children, as defined in law, placed in long-term penal establishments was, and is, negligible compared to England and Wales. Moreover the development of large regional social work departments and with it the expectation on the part of these departments to be self-sufficient in terms of facilities led to pressure to develop more smaller units for each individual region.

The massive increase in provision of secure accommodation in England and Wales following the 1969 Act is undoubtedly related to an escalation in the use of penal establishments for the detention of young people. In particular something of a national scandal erupted over the issue of 'unruly certificates'. The House of Commons Expenditure Committee found that by 1974 over 3,000 certificates of unruliness were issued annually. Its response contained the following statement:

> We condemn in the strongest possible terms the use of certificates of unruliness as a means of achieving secure accommodation. We recommend that the practice of remanding young persons to adult prison must cease forthwith. (Expenditure Committee, 1975).

This issue also attracted considerable media attention (for example, 'Children Behind Bars — The Scandal that must end', *Daily Mirror*, 10 May 1976). Government response to the problem was (a) to provide capital grant funding for the building of secure accommodation within the child-care system, and (b) to make it more difficult for local authorities to obtain unruly certificates.

The use of unruly certificates was reduced by one half between 1974 and 1981. This was achieved by the use of legislation and statutory instruments which both excluded some young people from the possibility of an unruly certificate (that is, girls under 17 years) and placed restrictions on their use (see Chapter 2). Nevertheless there remain considerable regional variations in England and Wales in the use of this provision, which are apparently unrelated to the availability of other forms of secure accommodation (DHSS, 1981b). The unruly certificate remains a problem in other jurisdictions, particularly perhaps in Northern Ireland, as a juvenile, subject to a training school order and aged over 14 years, may be transferred to the training school's secure unit. Transfer requires only the signature of a justice of the peace. Current practice is for these 5-week warrants from the opening training schools to be transferred to the secure training school, but it is still possible to use the same non-judicial process to transfer juveniles to the young offenders' centre. As females cannot be placed in the secure training school, they must therefore be placed in the young offenders' wing attached to an adult prison. There is considerable practitioner concern about this procedure.

In the Republic of Ireland only the courts, the juvenile courts, can certify a young person as unruly. In a number of cases taken to the higher courts on grounds of constitutional rights strict guidelines have been laid down about certificates of unruliness:

> It is the duty of the Courts to protect the rights of citizens and in particular the rights of 'young persons' within the meaning of the Children's Act, 1908, . . . very definite and specific evidence of the unruly nature of the general character of a convicted young person would be necessary before he was committed to prison rather than to a place of detention . . . the Court must conduct an enquiry as to the general character of the convicted young person and the convicted young person should have the right to challenge and rebut any evidence given. (State [Holland] v District Justice Kennedy and Another; quoted in Shatter [1977], p. 224)

The position in Scotland was surveyed by Elizabeth Denham (1984):

> A juvenile aged between 14 and 16 years may be remanded in custody pending an appearance in court if a Sheriff is satisfied that the child is of a character so unruly or depraved that he/she cannot be committed safely to the care of the local authority.

Senior police officers also have the power to certify unruly, under Section 296 of the Criminal Procedure (Scotland) Act, 1975. They may detain a juvenile on police premises, usually a detention room but sometimes a cell, until he/she can be brought before a Sheriff sitting summarily. This takes place normally within 24 hours when the appropriate police certificate must be produced.

The number of certificates has fallen from 264 in 1977, to 134 in 1981, 139 in 1982, and 141 in 1983, thus suggesting that a plateau has been reached. Denham found substantial agreement by police, sheriffs, procurators fiscal, reporters to the children's panel and social workers that some form of custodial provision is required. The route to this conclusion varied from the 'ultimate sanction' of the procurators fiscal, the police's need for containment of serious offenders, to the belief of social workers who recognized 'a group of children who need and benefit from treatment in secure accommodation'. Sheriffs in their turn require the production of the child in court and will understandably press for containment should a child seem likely to abscond from open accommodation. Despite the variations in the value systems represented there was agreement that there is need for improvement in remand conditions. This reflects a general concern that children should not be detained in prison establishments.

Denham found that of the children certified as unruly, 14 per cent later received non-custodial sentences; 30 per cent were remitted to the children's panel for disposal (this implies a substantial referral to List D schools), though in a number of cases the court would be aware that the proposed disposal by the hearing was in one of the secure units attached to schools, a facility not readily available at the time of the initial appearance in court); 41 per cent were placed under Section 413 or 206 orders which normally led to a direction by the Secretary of State for the child to be placed in a List D school, psychiatric provision or other residential facility. The remainder were returned to the care of the local authority for placement in children's homes. These figures confirm the view that a high proportion of children are certified as unruly on the basis of an immediate response rather than a long-term view of their needs.

Rushforth (1978) considered that boys entering the List D system by an 'unruly' or court route were likely to be 'stigmatised', while Pope (1978) viewed detention in prison remand conditions as reinforcing poor self-image or delinquent identity.

While such considerations apply equally across the borders of judicial systems it is noteworthy that Scotland certifies, on a per capita calculation, about one-third of the number of children so certified in England and Wales. Moreover Denham found regional variations within Scotland, each region being served by its own police force, procurators fiscal, reporters and children's panels, and social work departments, suggested that the use of unruly certificates varied more in accord with local factors and cultural traditions than individual factors of children. In the Republic of Ireland 21 children under 17 were committed to prison during 1983, having been certified as unruly.

The difficulty of examining the real need of provision is not only a problem with regard to unruly certificates; the whole issue of secure accommodation is influenced by extraneous factors. For example, it is difficult to assess how influential the media are in shaping policy on social welfare issues but certain policy decisions appear to have been precipitated by unusual levels of public interest. The case of Mary Bell is in retrospect regarded as an important factor in the setting up of youth treatment centres in England and Wales. The case highlighted a number of factors which were already under consideration. An inter-departmental working party was set up in 1968 by the Home Secretary to examine the need for facilities for the younger disturbed children who could not adequately be catered for in existing facilities.

At that time in England only secure places for boys were provided, consequently Mary Bell was placed in a secure unit accommodating only boys. Shortly after her admission there a girl was admitted to the McDonald Wing at Rossie Farm School in Scotland. Her distinction and isolation there as the only girl led the staff to encourage her to correspond with Mary Bell. Subsequently, with the opening of the new women's prison at Cornton Vale, provision was made for girls within the penal system and this situation remained until the opening of the girls' unit in the Ogilvie Wing then attached to Kenmure St Mary's List D school.

Two factors in particular are reputed to have been a major consideration in the Home Office working party's recommendations, both of which were highlighted to an extreme degree by the Mary Bell case: (1) the total absence of secure accommodation for disturbed girls, and (2) the problem of some Section 53 cases and other highly problematic children.

According to Cawson and Martell (1979) the creation of youth treatment centres was to provide a solution to the situation 'in which the Home Secretary is given the responsibility for placing severely disturbed children but has no resources for doing so under his own control'. The new centres were to provide long-term care in gradations of security for seriously disturbed children. The units were to attempt to arrest deterioration in the children's behaviour, to prevent further personality damage and to increase the understanding of severe disturbance in juveniles. They were given an explicit brief to test out and report on treatment strategies. The first youth treatment centre, St Charles, opened in 1971, the second, Glenthorne, in 1978.

A similar consideration in Scotland led to the conclusion, in 1975, that while there was evidence of need to explore alternative methodologies, this would be properly undertaken within the development of existing services rather than the creation of a new youth treatment centre or its equivalent. On the base date for this study four Scottish children were resident in English youth treatment centres. One of these children was transferred from the state institution at Carstairs, the equivalent of England's Broadmoor.

The development of the youth treatment centres serves to illustrate the ambiguous significance of custodial provision within a child-care context. Youth treatment centres are administered directly by the DHSS and are extremely well-resourced. The intention behind the development of these centres appears to have been the creation of a resource of 'last resort'. As stated by a psychologist working in Glenthorne, 'YTCs are intended to meet the needs of the minority of children for whom every other facility had proved inadequate' (Reid, 1982). As there are only two youth treatment centres with 70 beds between them, places are limited. Cawson and Martell noted that only 26 per cent of initial referrals to St Charles Youth Treatment Centre were accepted at the time of their study, that is in the mid-1970s (Cawson and Martell, 1979). Consequently, it was deemed necessary to screen referrals to youth treatment centres and apply strict criteria in the acceptance of referrals. These guidelines, as described by Reid (1982), established the intent that:

(1) Youth treatment centres admit children between the ages of 12 and 18;
(2) Children have been committed to the care of the local authority, or local authority has assumed parental rights, or the child has been sentenced by a court to a period of detention under Section 53 of the Children and Young Persons Act, 1933;
(3) Authorities are able to demonstrate that other resources have been tried first and have proven inadequate.

Recent research carried out in Glenthorne Youth Treatment Centre by the Dartington Social Research Unit (personal communication to director) indicates that these criteria are implemented in the selection of children for admission. Only 26 per cent of admissions are aged 13 or under, and 70 per cent have had three or more previous long-term placements. However, marked regional variations in both referrals and admissions are evident.

The processes underlying the changing criteria for admission of children into residential care following the implementation of the 1968 and 1969 Acts are described by one commentator as:

> A period of unending growth and opportunity ... the therapeutic function laid on residential institutions by the new legislation had a net widening effect as these establishments could claim to exist to help children in need rather than to train and control young offenders, consequently the inmate population became younger and less delinquent. (Thorpe *et al.*, 1980).

Thorpe's research indicated that as many as 90 per cent and generally at least 50 per cent of children in local authority provision had no need to be in residential care when assessed on objective criteria and could be dealt with in their own homes by community-based facilities (Thorpe *et al.*, 1980).

At the same time the perception became current among magistrates, police and others that some of the worst juvenile offenders were remaining at home because of a lack of suitable resources to deal with them, despite the imposition of care orders by the courts.

The expansion of secure provision was a concomitant of a generalized expansion of the residential child-care sector, but it is more difficult to understand the reasons for the continued expansion of secure provision (including the penal sector as part of this provision), in a period when the open residential system has been subject to a rapid and dramatic decline.

For example, in 1982 there were fifteen fewer community homes with education than there had been approved schools, and because many of the remainder have been reduced in size they provide in total only two-thirds of the places formerly available. In the Republic of Ireland the number of places in children's homes, including industrial schools, has declined very dramatically since the 1960s.

Although the decline of the residential child-care sector is commonly attributed to the financial and administrative structures under which it now operates, this, although a factor, is not in itself a sufficient explanation. The content of Northern Ireland's Black Committee Report (1979) suggests an underlying dynamic which may ultimately be more significant than financial considerations. This document recommended the closure of the 'open' training school system and its replacement by a single secure custodial unit reserved for serious and persistent offenders, with all other juvenile offenders being dealt with by community-based provision. In conjunction with this it advised that the child-care system be kept strictly separate from the juvenile justice system.

The Black Report makes quite clear the increasingly widespread perception by policy makers and practitioners that residential staff are losing their traditional skills of being able to provide care and control for delinquent juveniles while failing to develop those newer skills appropriate to their expanded 'therapeutic' function. As a senior practitioner engaged in devising programmes for Glenthorne Youth Treatment Centre has noted:

> Clearly many treatment programmes within the Child Care system fail to meet their stated therapeutic goals. Often failure reflects practical difficulties, e.g. staffing, finance, etc., but frequently it is a result of a deeper deficiency within the Child Care system itself. While the commitment of most care workers is beyond question, their therapeutic value may be suspect. Indeed, many workers in the field readily question their own efficacy as 'agents of change'. The fault is not theirs. In addition to the practical questions they face, at least two other factors play a part: 1) the translation of theoretical concepts behavioural or otherwise into practical, replicable therapeutic techniques is frequently inadequate, and 2) the training that many residential staff receive (if any) to equip them to become competent therapists is frequently directed towards nebulous or inappropriate goals, e.g. a disproportionate amount of time appears to be devoted to self analysis and the importance of relationships (often ill-defined) and significantly less attention to what could be done about problem behaviours and the means of doing so. (Reid, 1982).

The perceived purpose of custodial units within a child-care service is to contain and treat the most disturbed and difficult children referred into the system (Hoghughi, 1978). The evidence available to date does not support this perception entirely. Two previous major studies conducted in the 1970s on secure units, Millham *et al.* (1978), and Cawson and Martell (1979), both failed to find that the behaviour and personal characteristics of children referred to secure units differed to any significant extent from those of children in open units. Petrie (1980) in her study of 100 boys admitted to a secure wing in the List D system (Scotland) supports this finding.

A similar conclusion is drawn from all these studies. To quote Cawson:

> The unavoidable conclusion from the research is that save in a small number of extreme cases troublesome behaviour in an institutional setting is produced by the institution rather than being an attribute of the individual. (Cawson and Martell, 1979)

Millham found that the schools which were most prone to send their difficult boys elsewhere were also those with the poorest reconviction rates after discharge, although the removal of the most difficult boys ought to have given them an advantage. All three studies also report high recidivism rates for secure units. However it may well be that more recently, with the increased professional concern and costs connected with the use of security, children and young people admitted are more rigorously selected than previously.

Public anxiety and discussion about secure custody for children and young persons is a fairly recent phenomenon in the Republic of Ireland. In 1970, when the report on the *Reformatory and Industrial Schools Systems* [The Kennedy Report] was published, there was a large reformatory school for boys and two reformatory schools for girls. These establishments and, indeed, the registered industrial schools for the younger age group, were in most cases grim and institutional. The regime was harsh and in many cases the schools were in remote areas, but they were not secure in the sense in which we have used that term in this study. The Kennedy Report recommended the replacement of the reformatory schools by what is called special schools, junior special schools for the 12–15 age group, and senior special schools for the 16–17 age group, separate schools for boys and girls. They envisaged that only boys over 18 would be sent to St Patrick's Institution. The special schools 'should be run on "open" lines with a small closed wing for difficult cases.' Five years later the old catch-all boys' reformatory school had been replaced by a new 'special school'. The task force on child care services which had been established the previous year had to face the problem of:

> boys in the 12 to 16 age range for whom residential care is appropriate, but who will not be taken into any of the existing residential establishments because the particular form which their aggressiveness and disruptiveness takes is inconsistent with the programmes of care which these establishments see it as their function to provide,

that is, the new special school was being selective. The task force in its *Interim Report* in 1975 came to the conclusion 'that the question of providing secure accommodation should be approached with caution, and that we should guard against over-provision in this area.' It recommended that another special school should be established in the Dublin area for 25–30 boys in the 12 to 16 age group and that it should be 'organised on the basis of three units — secure, intermediate and open, respectively.' However, this minimalist approach was soon overtaken by events. A new government came into office in 1977 and a new hardline approach was adopted to the problem of the boys the existing special schools would not take. Loughan House, a prison establishment in a remote rural area which was being operated as an annexe to St Patrick's Institution for younger prisoners, was reserved for boys in the 12 to 16 age group. Although it continued to be run as part of the prison service, and was staffed by prison officers, it was certified as a reformatory school by the Minister for Education. The decision was controversial and there was a good deal of public discussion on it. It was justified as being a temporary expedient pending the provision of a new purpose-built facility. But now the plan was for a new totally secure 30-place establishment. By the time the task force presented its *Final Report* in 1980 a majority of its members accepted this plan. The task force dealt with the whole area of residential care in a wide-ranging and innovative way, but did not separately discuss the need for secure provision. The task force also dealt with court proceedings in relation to young offenders. In its report it opted to retain the main features of the existing system of juvenile justice, including the age of criminal responsibility of 7 and the other age limits. But as one of the modifications to the system the task force recommended that where a court was making an order following the admission or proof of an offence it should be required to adopt a course calculated to 'avoid sending the child to a custodial institution unless there is no acceptable alternative that will satisfy his needs or afford society a reasonable protection.' Two members, in a *Supplement to the Final Report*, adopted a radically different approach to juvenile justice based on decriminalizing offences by children under 15. They envisaged two types of proceedings under which compulsory orders could be made by a court in respect of a child: welfare proceedings and restraint proceedings. In the latter case before an order could be made there would have to be proof that voluntary measures had been exhausted, that welfare proceedings had been tried or would be inappropriate and that restraint for a certain period was necessary 'for the protection of the community.'

The discussion about the opening of Loughan House was the highpoint of public concern about custody. Loughan House operated as a reformatory for over four years and the last 14 boys there were transferred by ministerial order to Trinity House, a new totally secure 'special school', when that establishment opened in March 1983. Trinity House operates under the 1908 Act. In 1984 the government introduced a Bill to deal with the 'care and protection' of children. No proposals for the reform of the juvenile justice system have been announced and the introduction of legislation in this area has been postponed.

The penal system
While all four jurisdictions make provision for juvenile offenders to be detained within penal establishments, variations occur in the institutional frameworks and the circumstances in which the use

of such provision is deemed appropriate. Custodial sentences in England and Wales are of three kinds:

(1)   Detention centres (14–20-year-olds);
(2)   Youth custody (15–20-year-olds); and
(3)   Prison (17-year-olds upwards) with the exception of juveniles sentenced under Section 53 of the Children and Young Persons Act 1933.

In Scotland similar provision is made for young people aged 16 or over or, very exceptionally, for 15-year-olds. Northern Ireland has no detention centre or youth custody but has one penal establishment, the young offenders' centre, for young offenders primarily of 17-21 years. Sentences to the YOC are subject to a maximum limit of three years. If a sentence of more than 3 years is made it is then imprisonment. Juveniles can only be sentenced for periods longer than six months. The Republic of Ireland has St Patrick's Institution, a penal establishment which takes offenders in the age range 16-21, and a number of annexes. As we have seen, young persons (i.e. those aged 15 at least, but under 16 years) can be sent to prison if certified as unruly.

The objectives of penal provision in England and Wales have been stated as: (1) to punish; (2) to reform the offender; (3) to deter the offender and to deter others from similar acts; and (4) to remove the offender from society. In practice the reformist aspirations of the penal system have never been a significant factor in penal administration and have been increasingly de-emphasized in official policy (Cohen, 1974). The history of custodial sentencing for juveniles again reflects the ambiguity permeating perceptions of juveniles' offending, deterrence being presented as the reason for this form of disposal.

Detention centres were introduced in 1948 with the intention that the regime should be punitive and deterrent (the 'short, sharp shock'). It has been suggested that the punitive emphasis in detention centre regimes was a necessary trade-off for the abolition of corporal punishment and of middle-range prison sentences for under 17s (Crowe, 1979). However, development was slow, and in England and Wales it was not until the Criminal Justice Act 1961 that the expansion of detention centres occurred. By 1964 nearly 6,000 offenders experienced detention centres, a four-fold increase on 1960.

Under the 1969 Children and Young Persons Act, junior detention centres along with borstal training for under 17s were to be phased out. Despite this, in the years following the Act the number of juveniles committed to borstal rose from 818 in 1969 to 1,683 in 1979, and the numbers sent to detention centres increased from

2,228 in 1969, to 5,478 in 1979, an increase substantially greater than the rise in juvenile crime over the same period (Parliamentary All-Party Penal Affairs Group, 1981).

The 1969 Act gave the power to decide on the placement of children in care to local authority social services. The only form of direct sentencing open to the courts remained the penal option. The increasing reliance on these disposals for juveniles is attributed to a perception among magistrates and police that the 1969 Act had no teeth and that a small minority of 'tough, sophisticated juvenile offenders' had emerged who 'deride the powerlessness of the court to deal with them', and who 'are led to think they can break the law with impunity' (evidence to the Expenditure Committee, 1975). Reliance on custodial provision was said to have stemmed directly from the shortage of other forms of secure provision, that is, within the child-care system, although many questioned this assumption (Cawson and Martell, 1979).

The available evidence suggests that custodial sentencing is not reserved for the highly delinquent and sophisticated offender. For example, in 1979, 16 per cent of the juveniles received into detention centres had no previous convictions, and 43 per cent had either one or two previous convictions. In addition, for a substantial number of juveniles committed to penal institutions no previous attempt had been made to deal with their delinquent behaviour in the community. A Home Office study found that of juveniles entering borstal in 1977, more than a third had not previously been subject to a supervision order. The figure for detention centres appears even higher; of 130 junior detention centre trainees from the Prison Department, South West Region, and adjoining counties in November 1977, 78 per cent had not previously been under supervision (Parliamentary All-Party Penal Affairs Group, 1981). Yet DHSS figures suggest that a full half of those going to detention centres are, or have been, in care (DHSS, 1981b).

It is important to stress that with a five-fold increase in the number of juveniles in penal establishments in England and Wales since 1965, less than one-fifth can be related to increased offending, the remainder reflecting an increased tendency to give custodial sentences whatever the offence, a tendency on which the much higher provision of secure accommodation within the child-care system has had little impact. Similarly the reduction of juvenile remands in custody did not follow the increase in local authority places of security but followed from legislative restrictions on the courts' powers to make custodial remands.

The (English) Criminal Justice Act (1982) replaced borstal training in England and Wales with the determinate sentence of youth custody, and decreased the length of sentence permissible in detention centres. The result has been another sharp increase in the number of juvenile offenders given custodial sentences. Despite the objective of the Act to reduce custodial sentencing, in the first months of 1984 the number of juveniles sent to penal establishments was 21 per cent higher than in the second half of 1983 (NACRO, 1985).

England now has one of the highest rates of custodial sentencing for juveniles in Europe, yet in 1976 75 per cent of juveniles leaving detention centres, and 84 per cent of those leaving borstal, were convicted of further offences within two years (Parliamentary All-Party Penal Affairs Group, 1981). Dependency upon custodial sentencing reflects the evidence that the imposition of punitive custody fails to deter others from offending. Certainty of detection is probably a more significant influence on offending than the nature or severity of the punishment.

The apparently irrational reliance on punitive measures of control for juveniles cannot be attributed entirely or even primarily to a distorted and regressive instinct of the authoritarian bodies operating the juvenile justice system. Magistrates in dealing with juveniles more often than not accept the recommendation of the social worker (Thorpe *et al.*, 1980). Prison authorities have declared their objection to accepting juveniles, as is witnessed by the Governor's Branch of the Society of Civil and Public Servants which advocated the ending of detention centre training for juveniles.

Staff and their training
So far this chapter has shown that the general social attitudes, views and expectations of children and young people and how they should behave and be disciplined is continually changing and is the source of many dilemmas and arguments. Similarly the role, function and objectives of secure provision or penal institutions have a mixed history which produces either a lack of clarity of objectives or more likely a range of contradictory institutional objectives. This history has affected the recent development of secure provisions in which such disparate solutions for the same children as 'long-term intensive care' and 'short, sharp shocks' have been advocated.

In the middle of this maelstrom staff have to operate daily, attempting to maintain institutions demanded by a society which cannot determine their function. With few clear objectives it is difficult for staff to know what form of regime they should operate, more especially since many will be untrained (Millham *et al.*, 1980) in the requirements of a child-care service or will have been recruited to work in adult prisons and yet find themselves operating a daily regime for young offenders who are still school-children. To add to these problems, the perceived value of residential care and the subsequent demand for training have undergone major changes in the past decade as large institutions are closed and replaced by a diverse range of community facilities or by benign neglect. In these circumstances, not nearly enough recognition has been given to the task staff are expected to undertake if working with children in a secure setting. Both induction and in-service training and continuing supervision are necessary if staff are not to suffer unnecessarily from their experiences, and are actually to undertake constructive help and treatment with the children forced to remain in their care.

The view that closed facilities provide an 'intensive' care service for residential child care is not supported by the low priority given on training courses and the disapproval such work arouses in many child-care practitioners. In England and Wales qualifying training for residential work with children, for many years a specialism within child-care training, is now included as a small topic within the curriculum of courses for the Certificate of Qualification in Social Work (CQSW) and the Certificate in Social Services (CSS). In the majority of courses, with the exception of the Newcastle post-qualifying 'Advanced Course in Residential Care and Education', and the 'Diploma in Social Learning Theory and Practice in Applied Settings' at the University of Leicester, there is seldom reference to the uses of security, let alone the special skills, attitudes and knowledge needed by practitioners.

In 1982 the University of Leicester, following consultation with Glenthorne Youth Treatment Centre, introduced a 'Diploma in Social Learning Theory and Practice in Applied Settings' (1982). This collaboration between clinical psychology and behaviourist practice is a model of a relationship of academic to practitioner which is uncommon given the low-status tradition of residential work. An important innovation, in its own right and as a model, the course offers an appropriate level of sophisticated practice primarily for one establishment and does not claim to occupy the more general gap. Its objective is to provide a 'training course in behavioural principles and techniques' not specific, though relevant, to custodial care of children. As a part-time 'release' type course students are expected to apply their learning within their own agencies.

In the Republic of Ireland it is acknowledged that little or no attention has been paid to this specialized work, and that recently there has been reduction rather than increase in the already limited residential child-care training; there is now only a part-time course for a college certificate, and this does not include reference to work in security in its curriculum. In Trinity House, the secure unit, there has been a very high turnover of staff since it opened which may be attributed to the problems of inappropriately or untrained staff.

In Northern Ireland, while there is a strong residential element within one of the CQSW courses, there is no special focus on the needs of staff working with children in custody. There is a great need for the development of better assessment techniques to assist in decisions for the use of custody, and for more support for the staff undertaking the children's care. Secure accommodation in all four jurisdictions has, like 'Topsy', just grown, with no commensurate growth in training for those staffing secure units in penal and child-care systems. It may be that prison authorities disregard the particular vulnerabilities of the very young, and assume the relevance of their traditions of discipline and control. Certainly we have no evidence of specific training for prison staff who may be posted to junior detention centres or youth custody centres with a high number of young offenders resident therein. Less understandable perhaps has been the lack of interest shown by the universities and colleges responsible for social work training. This can only be rectified nationally by decisive action from the Central Council for Education and Training in Social Work. Meantime secure units within the child-care services have tended toward a development of internal, unit-based, staff development programmes.

Those sensitive to this specialized work acknowledge that it is not simply residential child care with the added element of locked doors, but has different and difficult characteristics and responsibilities and also some special opportunities. The difficulties arise from the emotional and physical factors related to turning a key on people, especially children, and the challenges this presents to staff and children. Responsibilities spring from the withdrawal of certain human rights from the children, and since there is a danger of doing more harm than good while a child is in custody there is need for extra special care.

Four factors influence staff functioning in any work setting: recruitment, induction training, further training, and leadership. Recruitment criteria and training are affected by the dilemma in which many employers find themselves; it seems against all good child-care principles to lock up children and yet it is necessary to provide and staff secure units. This dilemma prevents many committed child-care workers from applying for such work and may therefore lead to recruitment of inexperienced and untrained applicants. However this difficult dilemma is resolved it is essential that suitable people with appropriate experience are appointed, trained, and led if they and the young people in their care are to take full advantage of the experience; otherwise further harm will be done to children already damaged, and low staff morale will discourage the recruitment of good staff.

Secure units established as small adjuncts to open institutions present both training and organizational problems. For much of the year these units may be unoccupied. In some instances staffing structures have been agreed for the open institution, but no special provision made for those occasions when the unit is in use. As an alternative to the redistribution of staff already fully occupied in the open institution an alternative arrangement can exist whereby further help is introduced from a 'stand-by' group employed on a short-term basis to serve within the unit and to provide cover for full-time residential staff who might then be transferred for part of the day. Such a 'stand-by' group, if consistent in composition, would build up an experience of the work but without pretension to general or specific training. The established professional staff, despite their interest in and concern for children deemed to require security, would not give high priority to specialized training, their primary task lying elsewhere. Ideally, all staff in the open unit should be professionally qualified and have received induction training in the use of the closed facility.

The management and staff of closed facilities, whether attached to open units or isolated secure establishments, will require specialist training for their responsibilities which, at the present time, is not adequately provided on any qualifying or post-qualifying course. The areas of training required will include much common to generalist professional training for social work, teaching, child health and psychology, but should contain additional study and emphasis on a number of subjects crucial to working with young people in custody:

> Legislation, both in child care and mental health fields, is now extremely complex, due among other things to the incremental introduction of statutes, and the issue of the rights of children and parents.
>
> Codes of practice have developed which interpret legislation and inform practitioners of standards to be applied to selection and admission procedures.
>
> The aims, objectives and methods of custodial care, the quality of such care and the procedures to protect the rights of children and parents should be explicit, studied and discussed.
>
> Current developments and uses of custody have historical, social and developmental perspectives which should be known to those in the fields of social work, education, psychology and

medicine likely to have responsibilities relating to children held in security.

Design and the use of space is specially significant when living and working with others in confined conditions and is a related subject essential for study. Consultation between planners and practitioners is, in this instance, a fundamental mechanism for planning.

The use of consultancy, both internal and external, is vital to the practitioner working in stressful conditions and should be examined and experienced within specialised training.

Training of staff is the obvious way to ensure good practice in an institution which safeguards both the residents or inmates and staff. Another method of ensuring good practice is to have some form of external monitoring and evaluation. Such external monitoring may be provided by central government in the form of an inspectorate (for example in England and Wales the Social Services Inspectorate both inspect and sanction the use of secure accommodation on behalf of the Secretary of State). Alternatively the local authority may employ external consultants to work directly with the residents and staff by monitoring day-to-day practice. Finally research funded both locally and nationally may prove valuable in monitoring and evaluating the function of units, in terms of both their process and their outcome.

Consultancy remains an underdeveloped resource to practitioners and to their institutions. A major function of consultancy is to provide a consistent check on practice and management.

Consultancy is a specific task requiring specific skills, which may be available by contractual agreement from within some psychiatric and psychological services, some university departments, including social work departments, and from relevant institutions working in the field of human relations (as the Tavistock Institute in London, and the Scottish Institute of Human Relations in Edinburgh).

Consultancy to the institution provides for a reflective study and analysis of the procedures of management and working practices as these affect staff and residents and influence the relationships within and between these as distinct groups, and within and between the sub-groups inside the institution.

Where external consultancy has been established as integral to monitoring procedures, attention is given to the definition of institutional objectives, the provision and allocation of resources to attain these objectives, and the management of these resources. Resources in this context include the selection, training and support of staff, administrative personnel, the use of space and time and facilities whether recreational, educational or expressive. It is a function of management to monitor the relevance and feasibility of the institutional objectives. The complexity of the objective of secure units is seen in the range of consultants appropriate to different aspects of the unit's task. For example the list, while not exhaustive, is likely to include general physcians, to deal with public health issues in institutions, rather than advising on individual residents, lawyers, educationalists, architects, systems analysts and paediatricians. All of these have skills likely to be required by units on various occasions.

Consultancy is one way of attempting to open secure provision to public scrutiny. Such professional scrutiny should complement rather than replace other strategies aimed at making the institution more publicly accountable. One means of ensuring independent safeguards is by making a requirement (for all establishments with secure units attached) that objectives and criteria for the use of security are clearly stated and published and made available to those having an interest in the children for whom the facility might be invoked. Referring authorities and parents have an evident right to this information.

The circumstances which has led to a decision to confine a child, the identity and status of the decision-maker, the environment for confinement, the period in confinement, the content of staff action, and the outcome should be recorded and communicated without delay to the employing authority, as the mangement arm of service, and to the parents. Parents, or those standing in their place, should have access to a complaints procedure external to the agency and its management. The appointment of a 'befriender', who should not be an employee of the interested statutory agencies, should be made in the absence of responsible parental interest; the advocacy role of befriender should be acknowledged by the responsible authorities. Befriending schemes are of recent origin and have yet to extend their impact to the total residential scene, but in some instances are prescribed by statute.

The English law, (Children Act 1975, Sec. 59, and Child Care Act 1980 Sec. 18) requires that in reaching any decision relating to a child in their care the local authority shall give first consideration to the need to safeguard and promote the welfare of the child throughout his childhood, and so far as is practicable ascertain the wishes and feelings of the child regarding the decision and give due consideration to them, having regard to his age and understanding.

A child who has to be locked up may have been behaving in such a way that some would consider that he has forfeited the right to have his wishes and feelings given due consideration, but this is not so (Regulations 12:2 and 12:3 of the DHSS Secure Accommodation Regulations (1983b) are specific on this point), and it is especially important that he recognizes his rights. It is difficult for a child locked up because of persistently difficult or delinquent behaviour to trust that those taking decisions about his present and future care are giving first considerations to safeguarding and promoting his welfare, and giving his wishes and feelings due consideration.

The appointment of someone independent of those responsible for planning and caring for any child who has to be locked up to visit and offer opportunities for the child to express his wishes and views is one way to help the child in his peculiarly isolated and helpless situation. It also offers a safeguard for the child and those responsible for his care should there be any mismanagement giving cause for complaint. Where such a person is appointed it appears that the children value the opportunity offered and are responsible and trusting in what they communicate. It also appears that professional care staff as well as those with overall responsibility for standards of care generally welcome such an independent visitor, recognizing the safeguards relating to their functioning, and the value to the child.

The regimes
The penal history which has influenced the development of secure facilities along with the competing philosophies of education and child development can easily be discerned in the range of regimes currently existing within long-term custodial facilities for children and young people.

Three clear forms of regime have been observed and are described below, but, it should be noted that these 'pure' forms do not exist in reality, since to survive any institution is likely to respond pragmatically rather than ideologically. Consequently many regimes exhibit a mixture of theoretical approaches; some indeed see this as praiseworthy, claiming a greater effectiveness because of their 'eclectic' approach.

The vast bulk of young people experiencing short-, medium- and long-term custody are 15 to 16 years of age and contained within penal establishments — remand centres/institutions, detention centres, youth custody or young offenders' centres. These institutions are centrally established and controlled by the Scottish Office, Northern Ireland Office, Ministry of Justice or Home Office, and their staff are centrally recruited, trained and managed. Prison officers and governors will be rotated from adult prison to young offenders' institutions. Staff behaviour is governed by their experience and expectations of the wider prison system, and formally by the prison rules and regulations.

In these circumstances it is not surprising that the regime manifested by most of these institutions can be described basically as 'humane warehousing', the current *raison d'être* of the adult prison system. This is most clearly illustrated at the remand stage when even juveniles may spend up to twenty-three and a half hours a day in a cell.

The regime is preoccupied with custodial objectives, its major concern that offenders serve their time. This is encouraged by current legislation that allows determinate sentencing, remissions and little executive discretion on release date. Such establishments will provide the minimum requirements of the regulations, that is those of school age serving detention centre orders receive 15 hours classroom education per week by regulation. Those regimes may develop secondary functions of rehabilitation, for example literacy or vocational classes, or welfare and social skills training or group discussion. However these are secondary and are currently discouraged by official policy. An article by Tutt (1981) written soon after the introduction of the new experimental regimes in detention centres illustrates many of the directions and dilemmas of these regimes in the following extracts:

'New Hall — old way'

The trainees, as they are officially called, or the lads as viewed by the staff, all live in dormitories except during the two weeks induction when they are in cubicles for two containing bunk beds.

As far as education is concerned, only those who are 'clearly backward' receive remedial education during the day, all others have evening classes. Swimming, art, crafts and woodcraft have been stopped and wood and metal work substituted as evening activities.

An hour per day is set aside for formal drill instruction in which trainees are taught to march to command.

The officer in charge of weaving recognised working a loom as very hard work, much tougher in fact than drill, and wryly commented that since he was no longer allowed to hang and flog criminals they let him run the weaving shop.

The feeling I was left with after discussion with the staff was of men in confusion. A short time ago they were being encouraged to be 'social workers' concerning themselves with the welfare of trainees and teaching them constructive activities, now they are also expected to march young men back and forward on the basket-ball court. As one officer, formerly in the parachute regiment, explained: 'Drill in the Army has a purpose, to move a large number of men from A to B in the shortest possible time. What purpose is there in marching backwards and forwards for eight weeks?'

'We're not doing them much harm, but then we're not doing them much good either'.' (Tutt, 1981)

Tutt's scepticism was well-founded, as shown by the eventual report from the Home Office's own Young Offenders' Psychology Unit (1984); which concluded 'The introduction of the pilot project regimes had no discernible effect on the rate at which trainees were reconvicted' (para. 8.21), and 'Apparently the announcement of the policy did not affect crime rates generally; there was no interruption of trends in crime among young people generally, nor in the catchment areas of the two pilot project regimes especially' (para. 8.22), and 'It does not seem to have much improved trainees' conduct within the centre' (para. 5.46).

The two other forms of regime exist within both the child-care and the mental health systems and are prevalent within the special education sector catering for disturbed or maladjusted children. The two forms can be characterized by those based on the behaviourist or learning theories and those on the 'psychoanalytic' approaches to treatment.

Contemporary behavioural practice, at its best, requires a systematic application of a calculated and communicable set of responses to acts of behaviour. Reward replaces punishment as a fulcrum for change. The sequential nature of the system encourages sequential change reaching toward the achievement of a rich and rewarding personal environment and discharge (except for those held at Her Majesty's Pleasure under Section 53).

Basic staff on whom the system is finally dependent carry authority in their own right as professional practitioners, and consequently morale is high.

Behavioural systems so developed have achieved credibility and recognition as effective systems of institutional control. Final credibility of the behavioural system must however depend upon the validity of the supposition that patterns of behaviour adopted within the institution are substantially retained on discharge from the institution.

Beyond this an appraisal of behavioural methods must recognize current value systems as applied to human conduct. The emergence of a children's rights lobby illustrates such a value perspective, which has begun to criticize the assumptions of behavioural techniques with children (Childright, various). How far philosophical questions may properly intrude upon a scientific evaluation remains an issue not exclusive to behavioural scientists.

An alternative practice based in psychoanalytical theory, carried into social work and case-work practice by psychiatric social workers and supported by organizational initiatives such as those of the Tavistock Institute for Human Relations, in general, and by key practitioners — for example Barbara Docker Drysdale, Richard

Balbernie (1966) in particular — has had little impact upon the custodial scene. This may reflect an abhorrence to the practice of locking up children, but it may also reflect the denial of public sympathy with the concept that disruptive children should be understood rather than controlled.

Child-care practice is an expanding though inadequately defined field of knowledge which legitimately may draw on and contribute to research and practice in child development, psychoanalytic theory, behavioural and cognitive psychology and systems theory including family assessment and therapy and the study of institutions. Child-care practitioners and researchers should also be in continuing dialogue with their counterparts in the field of education.

Currently, practitioners, drawing on psychodynamic theories as applied to child-care practice in institutions, base their work on the supposition that children within those institutions who re-experience themselves in new forms of relationships with others will achieve autonomy as responsible individuals within a wider social setting. This position requires validation which has yet to be attempted.

Conclusion
It has been argued in this chapter that society's views of childhood are confused and ambivalent, accepting both that children are dependent and yet that they have to be taught independence and accountability. Sheriffs, judges and magistrates are only too ready to produce courtroom homilies to 16-year-old youths, about how they must learn 'to stand on their own two feet'. At the same time more privileged youth remain outside the labour market in full-time education until their early twenties, often living in state-provided and subsisized student accommodation away from too close a scrutiny of the police.

The confusion over the concept of childhood is exacerbated by the historical traditions of an education and penal policy which emphasized training, control, punishment and segregation. Much of this history is still influential on institutional practice even if the language has changed. John Howard, in the eighteenth century, encouraged segregation to avoid corruption. Today 'time-out' rooms are used as 'non-reinforcing' environments. This long tradition combines with a range of conflicting popular current social pressures which demand that offenders are made to suffer but which are equally vociferous in their offence if they suffer too much. This ambivalence is neatly illustrated in a recent report in a popular national newspaper which described the violence of a young man who had abused his child, and then in its leader column offered a comment on the imprisonment of the young man (which implicitly sanctioned violence):

> Of course he is guaranteed a rough time in prison, where convicts have their own rule of law. And if he does fall foul of this 'law of the jungle', few, if any, will shed many tears.

The management of secure facilities, whether in care, prison or mental health systems, is affected by this popular ambivalence and is unable to produce clear and non-contradictory objectives, which inevitably means that staff and their training needs remain confused and obscure.

In the latter part of this book it will be seen that the position is further compounded by the diverse range of children admitted to custody. In these circumstances it is unsurprising that many secure institutions are judged successful if they survive without collapse or political scandal, rather than by the success of their inmates in returning to the community without recourse to continuing offending.

4 Children's rights and child-care ideologies

This chapter will examine a number of issues relating to children's rights and compulsory state intervention in the context of the philosophies and practices employed in the four jurisdictions. It is not the intention here to describe in detail the 'rights' afforded to young people in the different systems. Rather, the purpose of the chapter is to look thematically at a range of issues relating to 'rights', 'due process', 'justice' and 'welfare' which seem common to our jurisdictions. These issues seem to create critical decision-points in systems of state intervention. In turn, these force policy makers and practitioners to confront the issues of the role of children in society and the nature of systems for their compulsory socialization. The decisions which are made on these issues are a litmus test of how the balance is struck (if at all) between respecting individual rights and regulating state intervention.

Concern with the rights of children under compulsory measures of state intervention is a relatively recent phenomenon, one on which there are very diverse views, some legal (Freeman, 1983) and others philosophical (Wring, 1981). Historically the social construction of 'childhood' and 'adolescence' had at its base a conception of the young as innocent, weak and powerless (Aries, 1962). The need of protection, discipline or control was vital if the child was to mature and be enabled to fit into adult society. 'Rights' in such circumstances were not merely unrecognized but rather an alien concept. The first bulwark of child protection and control was, of course, the family but its authority could always be supplemented or supplanted by the state — acting as *parens patriae*.

For those children in conflict with the law the role of the state became mediated through a range of 'disciplinary networks' (Foucault, 1977). Over the past two centuries these networks have developed away from the merely negative punitive aspects of legal control into a range of bureaucracies which seek to achieve regulation of the young by promoting their 'best interests'. Medicine, psychology, psychiatry, education, law enforcement and social work provide a network of regulation — what Donzelot (1979) calls 'the tutelary complex' — which blurs the boundaries of social control.

Acting under a broad remit to promote the 'best interests' of the child, such organizations have acquired a range of statutory and administrative powers and responsibilities which enable intervention to take place. The basis of that intervention is rarely precisely drawn. Apart from voluntary reference of troublesome children by their family, intervention is usually justified not only by reference to proven wrongs but also to a range of conduct or states which in adulthood would not constitute illegality. Indeed, inherent in the jurisdictional basis for intervention of these welfare bureaucracies are professional judgements. These judgements may need to be predicated on the demonstration of objective states of affairs, for example physical neglect, parental abandonment, or a criminal offence, but equally they may be founded on professional value judgements, for example being beyond control, or in moral danger.

Once the prerequisite conditions for intervention are satisfied, however (and any authorizing tribunal appraised of the case), then control over the professional discretion exercised by those seeking to promote the 'best interests' of the child is rare. Indeed the very nature of the professional expertise embodied in these organizations is frequently seen as inimical to external (lay or legal) review and control. The respect for professional autonomy is reinforced by legislative and administrative devices which expunge, transfer or suspend parental rights over children so that discretionary decision-making in the child's 'best interests' may proceed. What takes place within the sphere of legitimated professional discretion is, moreover, beyond the purview of those who may be directly affected by the decisions. For example, parents of children whose rights have been expunged, tranferred or suspended may frequently find that they have no *locus standi* to challenge professional practices which they find objectionable. Similarly, the children who are the subject of intervention may find their rights — such as to refuse treatment — not only unenforceable, but unrecognized either in the professional or the judicial domain.

Crime, control and child care

In the realm of controlling juvenile offenders all four jurisdictions historically demonstrate a move away from the merely crude form of punitive social control over young people. To a greater or lesser extent, all four jurisdictions have developed a range of welfare bureaucracies which currently provide a network of regulation operating under the 'best interests' doctrine. In none of the jurisdictions have these networks totally expunged the ability of the state to intervene directly in the life of a young person due to the nature of the offence they have committed. But all of the jurisdictions are able in appropriate cases to reduce the significance of the offending behaviour to one of symptomal value and elevate other aspects of personal and social functioning as potentially material. In so doing the professional diagnosis, assessment, judgement and decision-making powers of those operating welfare bureaucracies have become integral elements of the juvenile justice system.

In the Republic of Ireland the modifications of the criminal law system have been of an informal nature: The Children Act 1908 still operates without, for instance, the requirement introduced in England and Wales in 1933 that a court, even in a criminal case, has to have regard to the child's welfare. Some of the tendencies in the law and in social services practice observable in the United Kingdom would, in any case, be limited by provisions of the Irish constitution relating to family autonomy, procedural justice, and the exclusive role of the judiciary in certain areas of decision-making.

In recent years all four of the jurisdictions have begun to reappraise the philosophical and operational bases of delinquency control. The prerogative of welfare professionals to determine the child's 'best interests' has come under close scrutiny. This scrutiny is not limited to professional decision-making in the delinquency sphere. The issue of parental autonomy, resuscitated in the United States by the work of Goldstein, Freud and Solnit (1979), has informed reviews of child-care systems in the Republic and Northern Ireland, England and Wales. However the 'best interest' is most closely questioned where 'best interest' decisions are perceived to be inadequate in meeting other legitimate demands of a system of social control — such as the 'appropriate' restraint of liberty and public protection. In all four jurisdictions review of the adequacy of professional decision-making has led to a discussion of the extent to which professionals ought to be subject to external (lay or judicial) review, and with this the extent to which those subject to intervention may refer their case to some form of external arbitration. That this check on discretionary practice has usually (although not invariably) meant the resort to legal processes raises anew questions of legality and rights in existing systems of delinquency control.

Two main reasons or areas of debate seem to underpin the questioning of the existing basis of delinquency control.

(a) The welfare v justice debate
The philosophical and empirical bases which underpin the welfare ideology towards troublesome children have recently come under critical scrutiny. Starkly put, critics argue that welfare systems of delinquency control have been more concerned with who children

are rather than what children *do*, and as a conseqence have justified greater intervention into the lives of young people than would be merited on the basis of their conduct alone. Such intervention might be justified on the basis of it efficacy, but consistently the available evidence has contradicted this assumption, raising directly the issue of the justice of welfare-based systems. The competing assumptions of welfare and justice have been well rehearsed in all four jurisdictions (Morris *et al.*, 1980; Taylor *et al.*, 1980; Martin *et al.*, 1981; Black Committee, 1979; Taskforce, 1980; Morris and Giller, 1983). Briefly they may be illustrated here by extracts from the Black Committee Report.

The assumptions of the welfare model:
(a) delinquent, dependent and neglected children are all products of an adverse environment which at its worse is characterised by multiple deprivation. Social, economic and physical disadvantage, including poor parental care, are all relevant considerations;
(b) delinquency is a pathological condition; a presenting symptom of some deeper maladjustment out of the control of the individual concerned;
(c) since a person has no control over the multiplicity of causal factors dictating his delinquency he cannot be considered responsible for his actions or held accountable for them. Considerations of guilt or innocence are, therefore, irrelevant and punishment is not only inappropriate but is contrary to the rules of natural justice;
(d) all children in trouble (both offenders and non-offenders) are basically the same and can be effectively dealt with through a single unified system designed to identify and meet the needs of children;
(e) the needs or underlying disorders, of which delinquency is symptomatic, are capable of identification and hence treatment and control are possible;
(f) informality is necessary if the child's needs are to be accurately determined and his best interests served. Strict rules of procedure or standards of proof not only hinder the identification of need but are unnecessary in proceedings conducted in the child's best interests;
(g) inasmuch as need is highly individualised, flexibility of response is vital. Wide discretion is necessary in the determination and variation of treatment measures;
(h) voluntary treatment is possible and is not punishment. Treatment has no harmful side effects;
(i) the child and his welfare are paramount though considerations of public protection cannot be ignored. In any event, a system designed to meet the needs of the child will in turn protect the community and serve the best interests of society;
(j) prevention of neglect and alleviation of disadvantage will lead to prevention of delinquency.

The assumptions of the justice model:

(a) delinquency per se is a matter of opportunity and choice — other factors may combine to bring a child to the point of delinquency, but unless there is evidence to the contrary, the act as such is a manifestation of the rational decision to that effect;

(b) insofar as a person is responsible for his actions he should also be accountable. This is qualified in respect of children by the doctrine of criminal responsibility as originally evolved under common law and now endorsed by statute;

(c) proof of commission of an offence should be the sole justification for intervention and the sole basis of punishment;

(d) society has the right to re-assert the norms and standards of behaviour both as an expression of society's disapproval and as an individual and general deterrent to future similar behaviour;

(e) sanctions and controls are valid responses to deviant behaviour both as an expression of society's disapproval and as an individual and general deterrent to future similar behaviour;

(f) behaviour attracting legal intervention and associated sanctions available under the law should be specifically defined to avoid uncertainty;

(g) the power to interfere with a person's freedom and in particular that of a child should be subject to the most rigorous standard of proof which traditionally is found in a court of law. Individual rights are most effectively safeguarded under the judicial process;

(h) there should be equality before the law; like cases should be treated alike;

(i) there should be proportionality between the seriousness of the delinquent or criminal behaviour warranting intervention and the community's response; between the offence and the sentence given.

Both 'models' listed here are ideal types and, as such, cannot be said to be operating in any of the jurisdictions under review. Moreover, these 'models', as constructed by the Black Committee, are by no means exhaustive of the typologies commentators have constructed in analyzing the variety of approaches to juvenile delinquency control (see, for example, the supplementary report to the Taskforce 1980, pp. 350-54). While there are undoubtedly real (and often concealed) dangers associated with such 'modelling' exercises (Martin *et al.*, 1981) the intention here is not to endorse the Black Committee's analysis but rather to illustrate the nature and breadth of the debate surrounding the appropriate orientation of juvenile justice systems, and to highlight critical operational features.

For example, the welfare model is claimed to vastly over-simplify the nature of delinquent behaviour and ignore the selective operation of criminal justice agencies. Correlations between social disadvantage and recorded crime have been regarded inaccurately as causal relations (Rutter and Giller, 1983). The selectivity operated by the police, courts, social workers, and others in their processing of 'real problems' creates a self-fulfilling prophecy of the nature of delinquency and delinquents. The search for the 'real problem' in delinquent conduct means that individual rights and liberties may easily be overridden in the search for the child's 'best interests'. The belief in the efficacy of individualized treatment, again over-simplified the issue. As Tutt notes, 'there is no proven treatment of delinquent behaviour and the treaters tend to concentrate on behaviour that is open to intervention but has no proven connection with delinquent behaviour' (1984, p. 302). The indeterminate interventions which are claimed to be essential for treatment to take place frequently justify greater intervention, for example by keeping children in secure conditions, than would be merited by considerations of conduct alone.

Critics of the justice model would raise similar issues on the adequacy of an alternative approach. If official delinquent conduct is *associated* with social disadvantage to what extent is it just to punish? If the majority of young offenders admit guilt, how relevant is a full-blown adversarial system? If intervention is to be proportionate to the offence committed who should determine the issue of proportionality? If children who offend do have welfare needs how should they be met?

The aim of this chapter is not to adjudicate between the various models. What is clear, however, is that the past five years have seen an open discussion of the principles upon which delinquency control may be based. The unquestioned adoption of welfare (or at least welfare-oriented) systems has meant that issues of rights have remained dormant. That can no longer be — each jurisdiction is in the process of reconsidering the equilibriuim between the two sets of assumptions.

(b) Discretion — professional judgement or routine action?
The second area of debate which has contributed to a reconsideration of the operation of juvenile justice systems relates to the nature of professional decisions that are made in the child's 'best interests'. As we have noted, these decisions are discretionary, and as such deeply rooted in the professional autonomy and esoteric knowledge-base of those given the power to act. In fully developed welfare systems the bases of these decisions are obscured from view and to the uninitiated may seem arbitrary acts based on undefined criteria. In the United States the very identification of discretion as 'the problem' in the operation of the criminal justice systems and a thorough-going attack on discretionary practices, along with an awakening to the decline of the rehabilitative ideal and the demands for due process, formed the foundations of the development of the

justice model (see Bottomley, 1980 for a fuller discussion).

As we have seen, in the Republic of Ireland — the only one of the four jurisdictions which like the US has a written constitution — there are similar constitutional restraints on moving away from the justice model. In the United Kingdom research into delinquency control has been preoccupied with probing the soft centre of decision-making organizations which operate a welfare philosophy in the juvenile delinquency sphere (Parker and Giller, 1981). In relation to the police, for example, the 'net widening' effect of cautioning discretion (Ditchfield, 1976; Farrington, 1980; Farrington and Bennett, 1981) and the 'push in' effect of prosecutional discretion (Parker *et al.*, 1981) have been well documented. In relation to social workers, the vagaries of their decision-making (Giller and Morris, 1981) and the inappropriate use of their powers (Thorpe *et al.*, 1980) have similarly highlighted crisis points in the operation of professional autonomy. Finally, in relation to the juvenile court, the inconsistencies of decision-making and the serious political implications of unfettered direction have been shown to produce a setting in which 'injustice' has frequently been discovered and denounced (Parker *et al.*, 1981; Priestley *et al.*, 1977).

Alongside this body of work which has exposed the inconsistency of professional decision-making, however, there exists another exposing the bases upon which such decisions are made. Increasingly, empirical work into discretionary decision-making in a number of human service agencies (including those dealing with offenders) has demonstrated an apparent paradox — that those who are thought to operate discretion may well not and that professional decisions are frequently a range of routinized responses to categories of familiar 'problems' with which the organization must deal (see Smith, 1981).

In the area of juvenile court decision-making, evidence for this first came to light in the 1960s from the United States. David Matza's analysis (1964) of the *kadi* justice employed by juvenile court judges clearly documented how in a discretionary 'best interests' jurisdiction decision-making became possible by routinely utilizing, *sub rosa*, assessments of the seriousness of the offence. Moreover, Matza went on to demonstrate how the language of 'best interests' could obfuscate the nature of the discretionary decision — reinforcing the professional autonomy of the decision-maker while at the same time creating a sense of injustice in the recipient of the decision. Similar strategies were explained by Aaron Cicourel (1976) in his detailed ethnographic account of intake and probation workers' decision-making showing how categorizations of 'problem cases' were constructed by professionals and how routine responses to them emerged through the reports and recommendations they made.

During the course of the 1970s a series of publications began to provide similar demystifications of professional practice on this side of the Atlantic. Magistrates' decision-making (Parker *et al.*, 1981), social workers' decision-making (Giller and Morris, 1981), probation practice (Hardiker, 1977) and residential work with young offenders (Walter, 1978; Petrie, 1980), all became the subject of empirical investigation. Spencer Millham and his colleagues' work on children referred to secure units in the community home sector in England and Wales provides a useful illustration of the findings produced (1978). Millham found that despite the rhetoric of 'treatment', children placed in secure accommodation did not exhibit identifiable 'needs' which graphically differentiated them from those in the community home system generally. Selection for security was not found to be associated with any distinctive characteristics of the young people, but rather with the inability and unwillingness of other (open) residential establishments to absorb their troublesome behaviour. Millham's findings that 'the secure units provide a brief sojourn in an expensive anteroom to the penal system' raised doubts not only on the way in which a costly resource has expanded during the 1970s but also on the continuation of the autonomy of welfare professionals to determine how these resources were to be used in the future.

Legal control of welfare decision-making
The arguments advanced so far should not be taken to indicate that the systems for dealing with offending or other troublesome young people in the four jurisdictions are entirely 'lawless'. As we have seen in an earlier chapter each jurisdiction has a range of legislative and administrative (and, in the case of the Republic of Ireland, constitutional) regulations which govern, with a greater or lesser degree of specificity, the operation of judicial and welfare bureaucracies. The aim of this section is to comment upon the use of these various regulations at different points in the operation of the local systems and to highlight similarities in their application and outstanding problems which legal regulation alone may not attack.

The primary right which safeguards all young people from entry into the juvenile justice system in each of the jurisdictions is the age of criminal responsibility. As has been noted, the precise setting of this 'gate' is largely arbitrary — and differs between the jurisdictions — but it is critical in any consideration of children's rights in respect of their criminal conduct. It must be stressed, however, that intervention in the lives of young people otherwise non-responsible for their conduct because they are below the age of criminal responsibility can frequently be achieved by other forms of regulation (for example civil proceedings, the use of mental health facilities or education facilities or by way of voluntary admission to public or charitable authorities). Indeed in those European countries with high minimum ages of criminal responsibility elaborate secondary networks of socialization exist to meet the full range of deviant conduct. What is important for this discussion is to note that these other forms of regulation may be identical in *content* to those that would be applied if the young person could be formally adjudicated as a delinquent. The history of the development of the welfare ideology on young offenders is characterized by this coalescing of services for all children deemed in 'need' irrespective of their presenting problem or their formal entry procedure — the assimilation of the depraved and the deprived. While this practice had been widely endorsed officially since the end of the Second World War (Morris and Giller, 1979; Dingwall *et al.*, 1984), this policy of commingling did come under fire with the use of secure accommodation in England and Wales during the course of the 1970s. Interestingly, it was a DHSS working party on the legal and professional aspects of the use of secure accommodation that wrote:

> we feel it is contrary to natural justice that children who have been placed in care on a voluntary basis without a court order should be locked up . . . (1981a).

Similar criticism was voiced in the United States during the 1970s on the mixing of status offenders with adjudicated criminal juvenile offenders in institutions. In the United States the Juvenile Justice and Delinquency Prevention Act 1974 attempted, with little apparent success, to address the problem (Krisberg and Schwartz, 1983). In Northern Ireland the Black Committee, much persuaded by these arguments, also suggested proposals to tackle the problem. Already many of the committee's proposals appear to be rejected rather than implemented.

Any consideration of children's rights (perhaps more properly termed 'protections') in respect of the minimum age of criminal responsibility may be irrelevant to the operation of parallel systems of control with different formal entry requirements. The possibility of abuse of mutually inclusive grounds of referral between criminal and civil jurisdictions based on juvenile misconduct, and the lack of accountability over the operation of other systems of control (medical, educational, voluntary), have been the major targets of attack for those who wish to regulate discretionary welfare agencies. .

The four jurisdictions under review do seem to share a common feature concerning the recognition of children's rights in the application of the criminal justice system. Broadly speaking, fewer rights

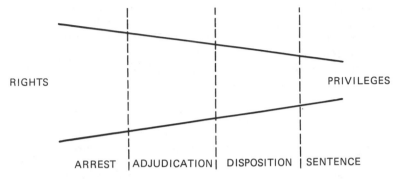

RIGHTS   PRIVILEGES

ARREST | ADJUDICATION | DISPOSITION | SENTENCE

are afforded to young people as one moves from the arrest to the sentence stage of the criminal justice process. As one penetrates the system young people move from being the subject of intervention to its object, and greater professional autonomy is given to those in charge to determine the appropriate procedures to be applied. Legally enforceable rights become replaced by discretionary rules and ultimately administrative codes of practice and privileges which may be unenforceable. The visibility of the basis of decision-making becomes more obscure as one moves through the system, and con-comitantly the basis upon which to challenge decisions becomes more uncertain.

At the arrest stage, for example, young people have rights akin to adults in such matters as making statements and being interviewed. Indeed frequently they are afforded greater rights, with special rules regulating the taking of photographs and fingerprints which may not apply to adults. Concern with rights at this stage of system intervention is understandable given the wider civil liberty issues which are involved — issues which in no sense are age-bounded. Moreover, these wider civil liberty issues have implications for the way in which other aspects of the system operate. In the Republic of Ireland, for example, the Criminal Justice Act 1984 gave new powers of detention without charge to the *gardai*. These changes were seen to so challenge established civil liberties that by widespread demand an amendment was adopted removing children under 12 from their scope. However when the more general issue of raising the age of criminal responsibility was discussed by the taskforce in their overall review of provisions for children in the Republic, the majority resisted such a change on the basis that it would create 'widespread public unease'. It remains to be seen whether or not a *de facto* increase in the minimum age of criminal responsibility will take place when the new provisions are implemented.

At the adjudication stage the mediation of rights over welfare considerations becomes more evident. In essence a tribunal with the twin powers of adjudication and disposition runs the risk that the decision-making basis becomes conflated. Perhaps the best recent statement of the problem is still to be found in the Ingleby Committee Report reviewing the legislation in England and Wales in 1960:

> The court remains a criminal court in the sense that it is a magistrate's court, that it is principally concerned with trying offences, that its procedure is a modified form of ordinary criminal procedure and that, with a few special provisions, it is governed by the law of evidence in criminal cases. Yet the requirement to have regard to the welfare of the child, and the various ways in which the court may deal with an offender, suggests a jurisdiction which is not criminal. It is not easy to see how the two principles can be reconciled: criminal responsibility is focussed on an allegation about some particular act isolated from the character and needs of the defendant, whereas welfare depends on a complex of personal, family and social considerations. (1960, para. 60).

The available evidence would suggest that, in practice, this reconciliation is by no means easy to achieve. In the United States, for example, during the course of the 1960s many juvenile court judges had given up the balancing act and adopted wholesale a welfare orientation. In one celebrated case the following judicial statement was made:

> An infant need not be warned that the truth will be used against him ... the truth will be used to help him. ... To deny the attention he needs because the police erred in obtaining evidence of that need may not be the parental thing to do. (In the Interests of Carlo, 48, NJ, 224 at 245-6)

Reaction to this imbalance of rights and welfare led to a readjustment of the position. The President's Commission on Law Enforcement in 1967 reasserted the importance of legal rights and due process in the juvenile court at the adjudication stage. In the same year the US supreme court handed down its famous judgement *In re Gault* giving defendants in the juvenile court rights to counsel which ensured that at least the formality of legal procedures were to be complied with, even though they might have marginal impact on the decisions made.

In England and Wales numerous research reports have demonstrated that a variety of adjudicatory practices have been adopted and, concomitantly, a variety of responses to the issue of legal formality. This is perhaps best illustrated by reference to the literature on legal representation (Giller and Maidment, 1984). Here research shows that the role lawyers play in the juvenile court and the impact they make depends very much on the orientation adopted by the bench. An adversarial ethos cannot be imposed on courts which view themselves primarily as agencies of social welfare. Consequently, adversarial techniques (such as insisting upon rigorous application of the rules of evidence) will be seen as inappropriate by the tribunal and not only less efficacious but unacceptable to the extent they are seen to question the basis of the court's action (see Anderson, 1978; Parker *et al.*, 1981). As such, quantitatively greater legal representation may have only a marginal impact on juvenile court decision-making unless the content of that representation is understood and accepted by all the participants involved. It is for this reason that the decision of *In re Gault* in the United States has had less dramatic impact on the decisions made in juvenile courts than anticipated (see Stapleton and Teitlebaum, 1972; Clarke and Koch, 1980). As one American commentator has written:

> To advocate representation without delineating the nature or mode of that representation may be to advocate a hollow right. (Bersoff, 1976, p. 34).

The provision in the Irish constitution that 'no person shall be tried on any criminal charge save in due course of law' governs juvenile justice in the Republic of Ireland. The phrase 'due course of law' has been held to 'require fair and just treatment of the person so charged.' It includes the accepted principles of criminal justice in the common law would but is always subject to further elaboration by the higher courts. For instance in Healy's case discussed by Duncan (1984) the right to legal representation was established. This case 'is also significant for its recognition that the youth or immaturity of an accused are factors influencing the degree of procedural protection required by the Constitution.' (Duncan, 1984).

Under the Irish constitution there is a right to trial by jury for all offenders, except in the case of 'minor offences' which 'may be tried by courts of summary jurisdiction'. 'Minor offence' is not defined in the constitution but the courts have held that the principal test is the severity of the penalty which the offence attracts. In relation to detention the courts have refused to accept a distinction between a prison sentence and a sentence to St Patrick's Institution (formerly a borstal institution).

> It can scarcely be contended that a sentence to a period of detention in St. Patrick's Institution is not a punishment even if the punishment

may produce more beneficial results by way of reform or rehabilitation in the offender than would an equal period in an ordinary prison. The deprivation of liberty is the real punishment. (Kelly, 1980)

The provision in the Children Acts in the Republic of Ireland that a youthful offender may be detained in a reformatory for not less than two years and not more than four years has never been tested constitutionally. It is arguable that committals by children's courts under this provision are unconstitutional (Shatter, 1977). More generally the constitution undoubtedly has implications for juvenile justice which have never been fully explored. If they were, the resulting guidelines and practice would be of interest throughout the two islands.

At the dispositional stage the issue of children's rights becomes even more extended as 'best interests' decisions come unequivocally to the fore. In Scotland the incompatibility of the same tribunal dealing with both issues of adjudication and disposition was squarely confronted by the Kilbrandon Committee in framing the 1968 legislation. The isolation of the hearing system from issues of guilt or innocence means that the tribunal may pursue the 'best interests' doctrine without the philosophical confusion seen in the tribunals of England and Ireland. But what of legal rights? Certainly Lord Kilbrandon would have nothing of formal *legal* representation at the hearing:

> The doctrine is a concomitant of the accusational or adversary system of criminal procedure. Certainly we hear nothing about 'due process' in the nursery or the schoolroom where it would be totally out of place. (1968: p.2)

Nevertheless, there are a number of rules and statutory requirements under the Social Work (Scotland) Act 1968 which must be adhered to by panel members during the course of a hearing; for example explaining the grounds of referral to the child, explaining the decisions of the hearing and its reasons, and informing the family of the right to appeal to the sheriff. However, the available evidence suggests that 'the standards of procedural compliance ... both can and should be improved upon' (Martin *et al.*, 1981, p. 111).

In England and Wales procedural safeguards at the disposition stage have also been found to be in need of improvement. For example, on the issue of presentation of background reports, both social enquiry and school reports, there is little consistency in the form and content of reports (that is, the extent to which they should comply with rules of evidence) and even less regarding who should receive, read and be able to challenge reports (see NACRO, 1984). Indeed, indicative of the confused state of the art in England and

Wales is the fact that many social enquiry report writers are with-drawing reports because of the appreciation that in some instances they may expose young people to *greater* intervention than would otherwise be the case if a report was not produced (Tutt and Giller, 1983).

Overall the very discrepancy on decision-making at the disposition stage (hallowed by those promoting the 'best interests' doctrine as reflecting the uniqueness of each individual case) makes it virtually impossible to articulate the principles of disposition decisions and with them details of how safeguards to produce greater consistency may be achieved. Recent criteria introduced in England and Wales by the 1982 Criminal Justice Act, for example, attempt to delineate greater consistency in sentencing decisions. But lack of specificity of the criteria and their mechanistic application by the courts means that procedural regulation of sentencing has been advanced without any review of substantive sentencing decisions. As shall be seen later, until this latter issue is addressed little will be achieved by legal regulation alone. The absence of a juvenile jurisprudence on disposition decisions in any of the jurisdictions under review demon-strates the lack of interest, importance and relevance accorded to this issue.

Finally, the issue of rights at the sentence service stage of the criminal justice process is the least well articulated of all in any of the jurisdictions. The recently introduced secure accommodation regulations in England, Wales and Scotland are primarily concerned with criteria and procedures on *entry* into security rather than the rights of the young person so detained. Ironically, the most detailed legal regulation of rights during the service of sentence comes in the custodial sector, for example, the detention centre, youth custody centre, and prison rules in England and Wales. These establishments — unequivocally at the penal end of the sentencing range — osten-sibly recognize inmate rights far more than do their welfare counter-parts. This is not to say that establishments in the welfare sector do not have regulations and codes of practice — rather that the machinery to ensure their enforcement and compliance is not well established. It is to be hoped that more may be done to articulate rules and practices which may be enforceable for those who find themselves in such compulsory welfare settings.

Rights and legality — answer or question?
Clearly justice and welfare considerations may be seen as competing ideologies. In pure form they posit flatly non-complementary systems of delinquency control. At the level of debate they cause policy makers and practitioners alike to question taken-for-granted assump-

tions and resuscitate dormant issues of rights, due process and the nature and form of legal and welfare interventions. To date none of the four jurisdictions has abandoned one set of assumptions in favour of another. Rather each of the four jurisdictions has borrowed from both sets of assumptions to modify, in policy and practice, existing arrangements for dealing with young offenders. The most recent example of this 'borrowing' can be seen in England and Wales with the implementation of the Criminal Justice Act 1982. We have previously noted that this legislation introduced judicial review of what was previously a decision unequivocally in the welfare professionals' domain, namely the use of secure accommodation for children in care. (A similar provision with a comparable breach into the welfare philosophy can be observed in the secure accommodation regulations which now apply in Scotland.) Further encroachments on welfare decision-making have been made in respect of care orders for offences. These may now only be made where the court is satisfied that the offence is sufficiently 'serious' to justify such intervention and that the child is demonstrated to be in need of 'care or control'. Again the introduction of care orders for offenders with 'charge and control conditions' enabling the juvenile court magistrates to restrict named parents, guardians, relatives or friends from having charge and control over a young offender in care for a period of up to six months fundamentally alters the balance of professionals' decision-making and makes concerns of the community — as expressed and perceived by the court — override 'best interests' considerations.

The continued decline in the use of care orders since the 1982 Criminal Justice Act came into force and the virtual non-implementation of the charge and control provisions (30 orders were passed in 1983) should not be taken to demonstrate the efficacy of legal safeguards on welfare decisions. Indicative of this are the findings of the Children's Legal Centre on the use of the secure accommodation regulations on implementation of the Act. While the overall number of children in secure accommodation fell, where applications for orders were made to court 98 per cent were successful. The 1982 Act did nothing to limit either the variety of juvenile justice philosophies which have continued to underpin the system throughout the decade of the 1970s or the juvenile court magistrates' role in determining the applicability of welfare services. Rather the 1982 Act emphasized three procedural principles of decision-making while in substance giving magistrates greater powers to intervene *directly* in the lives of young people on the basis of their offending behaviour. The three procedural principles which were emphasized in the Act were as follows:

(1)   that juvenile court proceedings were essentially adversarial
       — illustrated by those provisions which give young people
       greater rights to legal representation and appeal;

(2)   that juvenile court sentences ought to be determinate
       interventions — illustrated in the demise of the semi-
       determinate detention centre and borstal training sen-
       tences;

(3)   that juvenile court sentences ought to be proportionate
       to the offence committed — illustrated by the introduction
       of statutory criteria relating to 'seriousness', and 'public
       protection' which must be satisfied before certain dis-
       position can be imposed.

Some have argued that these changes to the English system reflect
the adoption of a 'justice model' to juvenile crime control. Con-
comitantly, as early sentencing returns indicate more young people
entering custody from court since the change of legislation, some
have argued that one is witnessing a failure of that model. By divorcing aspects of due process or procedure, however, from a through-
going review of the substance of the decisions being made in respect
of young people, the weaknesses of legal control on discretionary
decision-making is exposed. As Alder and Asquith have written:

> Judicial control of discretionary decision-making in welfare can mean,
> at least, that the procedural rights of the individual concerned are
> offered greater protection but it cannot lead to any significant improve-
> ment in the conditions and circumstances in which they find them-
> selves.
>   The dangers of a return to legality are that, by focussing on the
> procedural aspects of decision-making more subtle forms of control
> are left unexamined, and by introducing an ideological veneer of
> equality, equity, fairness and justice, attention may be deflected away
> from basic social and structural inequalities. (1981, p. 21)

According to this perspective, legal regulation and the recognition
and institution of rights is clearly not the answer to the problem
(Asquith, 1983). But the issue of rights and legality in systems of
delinquency control are not necessarily ends in themselves. More
importantly the issues enable us to pose fundamental questions on
the nature of our justice system and the operation of secondary
mechanisms of socialization in general and, in particular, on the
appropriate role of those systems when children come into conflict
with them.

5   A census of children in custody

Objectives and methods

The original intention of the Study Group on Children in Custody was to make a comparative analysis of children in custody within child care, penal and health services in the four jurisdictions of the British Isles, using existing research and statistical sources. It soon became apparent that this method was unlikely to produce a satisfactory result. Not only are there no readily comparable standard statistical sources showing the total numbers of children who are held in secure conditions in the three sectors within the four jurisdictions, there are no standard official statistics at all on juvenile patients in mental hospitals. Some prison statistics show age groups but only insofar as they relate to specific sentences, like youth custody for under-21-year-olds in England and Wales. Again, there are no standard official statistics about the total numbers of children of any given age who are in penal institutions for whatever reason, over any given period. Even in the child-care sector the position is not much clearer. Government departments in each jurisdiction could tell us how many beds in residential establishments they had designated as officially secure, but not how many children were actually in these secure units at any given time, and certainly not how many children may have been locked up in ordinary residential homes.

None of the jurisdictions seems to attach sufficient importance to the position of children in custody to record how many there are in state institutions — penal, child-care or mental health — within their own boundaries. It might have been thought that an assiduous researcher could piece together what was going on in each sector in each jurisdiction and work out an overall picture, and this is what the study group had originally intended to do. But there are two insuperable obstacles to this approach: among the four jurisdictions of the British Isles there is no common notion of childhood, and no agreed defintion of custody, so it is impossible from official sources to enumerate children in custody.

The social construction of childhood, and how this relates to ideologies of welfare and punishment, has been discussed in Chapter 4. Chapter 2 has documented the confusion of age thresholds that feature in the legislation of the four jurisdictions. For a definition of childhood which could be applied to all four jurisdictions we took the highest age at which a person can be received into care (16 in England and Wales, and Northern Ireland), and the lowest age of criminal responsibility (7 in the Irish Republic). So for the purposes of this comparative study, a 'child' is a person aged under 17. The minimum age is less significant, as no 7-year-olds were found, but it had the effect of excluding very young children who may spend some time in custody with their mothers, where the mother is the target of intervention, not her baby.

The definition of 'custody' adopted by the study group was intended to reflect the restrictions experienced by a person whose freedom is curtailed, rather than the motivation of custodians.

Custody: means any situation or device which is intended, for whatever reason and for however short a period of time, to remove or significantly restrict a young person's freedom of choice to leave.

The method chosen for identifying children in custody was a head-count census survey which gives a snapshot of the overall situation on a particular day: Wednesday 12 September 1984. With limited resources of money and time, priorities had to be decided within our broad ambition to find all the children in custody in all settings. Effort was concentrated on the penal system and designated secure child-care accommodation, as these are the settings where children are officially held in custody, and are recognized as such by the government departments concerned. Even here there were some problematic areas. One government refused access to its open prisons on the grounds that because they were officially open (though still prisons!) they should not be regarded as custodial.

The study group was also concerned to gather evidence about children held in 'hidden custody', outside the formally designated secure settings. The survey has provided information about the circumstances under which children are prevented from leaving residential homes which are officially open establishments, and about juvenile patients in mental hospitals. This is valuable as qualitative, rather than quantitative data. It highlights the issues involved, and points to directions for future research, but because we can still only estimate the scale of the problem it would not be valid to make statistical comparisons between what is going on in the different jurisdictions, and between the formal and hidden custodial settings. So the findings on hidden custody are presented separately, in Chapter 8.

The survey was aimed at workers in the residential establishments, and the questionnaires were designed to be completed by staff who knew the children concerned. We wanted to find out what was known about these children in the institutions where they were held, by the staff who were actually working with them, and what the staff thought about the use of custody for children. However, it would not have been acceptable just to write direct to the residential homes and institutions, nor could we have expected much of a response had we proceeded in that way. Many preparatory stages had to be gone through first.

Organizing the survey

It would not be helpful to describe the organization of the survey in tedious detail. But it is important to convey the complexity and volume of work involved in conducting a survey of this sort, whose purpose is to gather information about specific state services which governments have not made openly available. The comparative dimension of the survey was a complicating factor throughout. The questionnaires had to be worded so that they were applicable to recipients in the four different jurisdictions, and would elicit comparable responses which could be analyzed together. Yet the accompanying explanatory papers had to be specific to the situation in each separate jurisdiction.

At the first stage, approval had to be sought from the central government departments responsible for prisons and child-care services. Several interested parties were involved in each case and the whole process was multiplied by four for the different jurisdictions (plus the Welsh office within England and Wales). On the whole the various civil servants were helpful and gave valuable advice. Similarly, negotiations were held with the professional associations representing senior managers of the services concerned — such as the Association of Directors of Social Services and the Association of Chief Officers of Probation in England and Wales — and again the process was multiplied by four. The fact that these associations all gave the survey their good will must have contributed substantially to its success. Next, advance approval was sought from each individual authority — 140 social services (and similar) departments and 58 probation services. Altogether, and including the separate survey of the health service which is reported in Chapter 8, contact was made with 458 authorities during these preliminary stages. Meanwhile the questionnaire was piloted in establishments run by two English social services departments, to check that it would work and that the questions made sense to the people who were asked to fill in the forms.

Only two social services departments (one in outer London, one in Wales) refused to take part in the survey, and as neither managed approved secure accommodation their cooperation was not really necessary. No probation authority refused cooperation. As time was limited, the request had been worded in such a way that the survey could proceed without an advance response having been received from every authority. As it turned out, we were quite justified in assuming that silence did not mean unwillingness, because 45 per cent of the returns which were subsequently received in the 'penal survey' came from penal institutions served by probation authorities which had not replied to our earlier contact and, similarly, 31 per cent of secure units making returns were managed by authorities which had made no advance reply. Prison service management had been separately circulated in advance by the relevant central government departments in each jurisdiction.

The questionnnaires for the two sectors, penal and child-care, differed only in terminology and matters of detail; they were designed to be compatible. Both were in two parts: part one was about the institution, its staffing and services, and the overall numbers of under 17-year-old inmates or residents on the survey date. Part two was about individuals, and separate returns were requested for each child held in security. In the penal sector, where some institutions such as junior detention centres hold large numbers of under 17-year-olds, respondents were invited to return a graded sample where there were numbers over 20. Such samples have been weighted in data analysis, to give an accurate overall picture.

Responses and basic findings

The response rates to the surveys in the penal and secure child-care sectors were unexpectedly high. The rate of response from potentially relevant penal institutions was nearly 100 per cent; only one youth custody centre and two adult local prisons, all in England, did not reply, and the Home Office has kindly provided the basic information on numbers of under 17-year-olds who were held there on the census day, thus ensuring an accurate total figure for the penal sector. Seventy-three insitutions gave positive responses, and a further 42 (mainly adult prisons and senior detention centres) said they had no under 17-year-old inmates on the date in question, nor during a previous three-month period. Not every single institution had been circulated, only those where it seemed possible that there could be juveniles; not, for example, maximum security prisons receiving only prisoners on long-term sentences nor adult open establishments where only prisoners serving sentences would be sent after allocation.

The response rate from designated secure child-care accommodation was 94 per cent. There were positive responses from 54 establishments where children were held in security. A further five establishments with secure beds for up to 24 boys and 7 girls did not reply. It has been possible to learn some basic details about them from other sources though not, of course, about the individual children held there. Twenty-one approved secure units (26 per cent of the total, all of them in England and Wales) were found not to be in use for this purpose; they will be discussed briefly below. It is worth noting here that no usable returns were received from privately managed establishments, though several were contacted. One which was known (through Children's Legal Centre publicity) to prevent children from leaving said that it was not relevant to our survey because it was a 'mental nursing home', although called a school. Presumably this was meant to suggest that the establishment came outside the scope of the secure accommodation regulations, as the matter was under discussion within the English DHSS at the time. Very few voluntary organizations run secure units, and those that do are included in the data analysis.

As far as can be ascertained, at least 1,688 under 17-year-olds were officially locked up in penal and secure child-care establishments within the four jurisdictions of the British Isles on the census day. Including the likely number of children in the child-care secure units which did not reply (at the prevailing rate of occupancy), the true total was probably in fact around 2,000. Basic details of total numbers of children in official custody are compared in Tables 5.1–5.3. Four-fifths of the children were in penal institutions. Only one in twenty were girls, and over three-quarters of these were in secure child-care accommodation. Eighty-five per cent of the total juvenile population in custody were locked up in England and Wales. Points of comparison between the two sectors and the four jurisdictions will be discussed at length in Chapter 8. In England and Wales, the number of under 17-year-olds in penal institutions represents 10 per cent of the total penal population aged under 20 on an average day in 1984, while the number in secure units was probably around 1 per cent of the total of children in residential care (Home Office, 1985, pp. 8, 14, 15; DHSS 1984, p.11).

Within these overall figures which delimit the juvenile population in custody, detailed personal information was provided on 1,096 individuals which, with weighting in data analysis to account for sampling, gives a response rate of 93 per cent on the overall population. The only significant omission is the two main remand homes which serve London, one a prison department remand centre, the other a secure assessment centre, with probably 48 children between them on the census date. Neither sent returns on individuals due, apparently, to pressure of work as the senior probation officer attached to the remand centre explained:

It is not practical for even a sample of forms to be completed on individual inmates — mainly because it is very much a 'transit camp' for young offenders so that most of the staff are out daily as escorts both to Courts and to other prison establishments. We have only one part-time Probation Officer employed at the Remand Centre.

The questionnaire forms on the establishments and the individual children in both sectors were very largely completed by practitioner-grade workers, as had been intended. The survey would not have been possible without their cooperation because we were seeking not only 'facts' which could be copied from records but, more importantly, interpretation and opinions which must have taken a considerable time to compile. Practically all of the returns on children in penal institutions were made by practitioners: 93 per cent of them by seconded probation officers or social workers, and in many cases they had obviously interviewed the children to get their account of their past history. In secure child-care sector again 93 per cent of the form-fillers were residential workers or unit heads, the rest being field social workers or management. As the researcher who inflicted all this extra work on so many people, I am most grateful for their efforts.

Table 5.1.   Total numbers in the two secure sectors within the four jurisdictions

	Sector		Total
	Penal	Secure child care	
Jurisdiction			
England and Wales	1,207 = 84% = 90%	231 = 16% = 67%	1,438 = 85%
Scotland	97 = 65% = 7%	52 = 35% = 15%	149 = 9%
Northern Ireland	23 = 50% = 2%	23 = 50% = 7%	46 = 3%
Irish Republic	18 = 33% = 1%	37 = 67% = 11%	55 = 3%
Total	1,345 = 80% = 100%	343 = 20% = 100%	1,688 = 100%

Note:
See Table 9.1 (p. 211) for relation of numbers in custody to total comparable populations in each jurisdiction.

Table 5.2   *Total numbers of boys and girls in the four jurisdictions*

| | Sex | | |
	Male	Female	Total
Jurisdiction			
England and Wales	1,365 = 95% = 85%	73 = 5% = 92%	1,438 = 85%
Scotland	143 = 96% = 9%	6 = 4% = 8%	149 = 9%
Northern Ireland	46 = 3%	–	46 = 3%
Irish Republic	55 = 3%	–	55 = 3%
Total	1,609 = 95% = 100%	79 = 5% = 100%	1,688 = 100%

Table 5.3   *Total numbers of boys and girls in the two secure sectors*

| | Sex | | |
	Male	Female	Total
Sector			
Penal	1,327 = 99% = 82%	18 = 1% = 22%	1,345 = 80%
Secure child care	282 = 82% = 18%	61 = 18% = 78%	343 = 21%
Total	1,609 = 95% = 100%	79 = 5% = 100%	1,688 = 100%

N.B. Any discrepancies between overall numbers shown in these tables and figures cited in subsequent chapters are due to incomplete returns on individuals having been received from some establishments, and to the effect of weighting samples.

Pressure and change

There was a pervading impression from the survey returns of pressure and change in the social work services of both sectors where children are officially held in custody.

Policy undercurrents

The survey in local authorities was about secure units as residential institutions, the opinions of staff and the background of residents who were held in custody. It was not about the authorities' policies and range of services for difficult adolescents, nor about the practices of magistrates in granting secure accommodation orders. Similarly, the penal survey was concerned with the circumstances and backgrounds of inmates, and the opinions of probation officers, not the sentencing habits of courts. Nevertheless, some important broader policy issues emerged in both sectors.

Some interesting comments were received even from authorities which did not themselves manage secure accommodation. Several local authorities in England and Wales, and Scotland have made explicit policy decisions neither to manage nor use secure accommodation, or to stop doing so as soon as possible. One such metropolitan district in the North West had only one child in its care placed in a secure unit run by another authority, but there were four secure establishments, all managed by other authorities, located within its boundaries holding between them 24 children in custody, who were in care to different authorities around the country. The 'host' authority presumably has no control over what others do within its boundaries.

Some local authorities, particularly shire counties, manage secure units which are occupied mainly by children from elsewhere; implications of this will be discussed in Chapter 7. The authorities concerned seem to regard it as a source of income. User authorities who are likely to be from the same children's planning committee region, will 'lease' secure beds — an annual fee of £25,000 in 1983/84 was mentioned, whether or not the bed was occupied — and then sub-let to yet further authorities if the bed was not actually required. Saving having to pay 'rents' of this sort has been a consideration for some of the authorities which have made policy decisions to avoid using secure accommodation.

The director of an English shire county social services department wrote that 'strict criteria' had been approved by his committee for the use of secure accommodation, going far beyond Section 21A of the Child Care Act 1980. Accordingly, no children in care to that authority were placed in secure units 'ex County' on the census date and the authority had no approved secure accommodation of its own. But 14 children with home addresses in that county turned up in penal institutions, and 8 of them had been in care immediately before they were admitted to custody. We can only conjecture that the authority's rejection of secure accommodation meant that children received penal sentences when they might not otherwise have done so. Of course, it is a matter of value judgement whether children are better off in secure accommodation or in penal institutions. One thing is clear: an authority's level of involvement in the secure child-care sector does not necessarily have a direct inverse effect on the likelihood that its children will receive custodial sentences. High use of secure accommodation does not in itself guarantee a low incidences of penal sentencing for under 17-year-olds; the overall effect may just be high numbers in custody in both sectors. (This is illustrated at a regional level in Table 9.1, p.211 and Table 7.5, p.159). Another shire county which itself ran four secure units at the time of the census and had 15 children in its own and other authorities' secure accommodation, also produced 25 children in penal institutions, 21 of whom had been in care. Something in the practice of social work in this county, the behaviour of children in its care, or the sentencing habits of the local courts seems to be directing an unusually large number of children towards custody in both the child-care and the penal sectors.

Closure and openings
It came as some surprise that more than a quarter of all the establishments which were on the various government departments' lists of approved secure accommodation (or equivalent in Ireland) were not actually operating as such. As all of these unused establishments were in England and Wales, they in fact amounted to nearly a third of the secure units which were listed as being approved by the DHSS at the time when the survey was being organized. Twelve units — 6 assessment centres and 6 community homes with education — had been closed after functioning for a time as secure units. Nine, mostly assessment centres, had been approved but were not yet open, being still at the planning stage or waiting for a full quota of staff to be appointed. More than half of the 21 closed units were managed by county councils. Geographically, they were spread around the country but the largest concentration was in the South East including Greater London. Nearly all (18) were located in the same authority as that which owned and managed the establishment — a relatively unusual situation, as we shall see later on. This suggests that they would have been smallish units with an in-authority, local catchment area.

Reasons for closure among those which had once operated as secure units were varied and included: the expense involved in converting an old unit to meet the standards required under the regulations which came into force in 1983; a policy decision by the authority against looking up children (one former secure unit was being used as semi-independent accommodation for adolescents leaving care); a decision to save the cost of maintaining and staffing this relatively expensive form of residential care in the face of continuing under-use. We were told that some other establishments which were operating as secure units in Scotland as well as England and Wales at the time of the survey were due to close, for reasons such as these. This threat of closure may have influenced one or two of the non-respondents to the survey.

A degree of under occupancy was evident in all types of secure child-care accommodation. The 59 establishments which were operating as secure units at the time of the survey had a total capacity of 543 beds, that is an average of 9 or 10 children each. The 54 establishments which responded (with a capacity of 512 beds) contained 343 children, that is 6 or 7 children each on average. This represents an occupancy rate of 67 per cent overall, so a third of the available beds were not in use. The national occupancy rate for all community homes with education (CHEs) in England and Wales is very similar (68 per cent) but much higher for assessment centres and all other types of residential child-care establishments (CIPFA, 1986, pp. 43-7).

Management distrust?
Awareness of this relative under-use of secure accommodation, and of the high cost of staffing the secure units, may have been behind the somewhat strained relations between unit staff and departmental management which could be detected in some of the survey returns.

One of the questions which authorities were asked, when their advance approval for the survey was sought, was whether the staff in residential establishments or institutions who were being asked to fill in the forms could be approached direct, or whether the papers had to be sent via headquarters. Half of the social services (and equivalent) departments who managed secure units and who responded at this stage specified that the survey had to be conducted through management. But in the comparable survey of penal institutions only the authorities in Northern Ireland and the Irish Republic, where the administration is more centralized than in Great Britain, made this requirement. No probation service in England and Wales nor social work department in Scotland insisted that we communicated with practitioners working in the penal institutions, through management. This suggests that management of the two sectors have different attitudes to their practitioner-grade staff, and that some social services departments may be less likely to trust their staff to present acceptable views to an outside researcher, even though confidentiality was assured. This could, of course, be a consquence of the general fear of public criticism which social services departments have developed in response to child abuse enquiries. A number of letters and telephone calls were received from senior managers complaining about the survey and anticipating that its findings would be critical; no such reaction came from probation services. Whatever the reason, there was evidence that some survey returns which had been completed by residential staff had been 'adjusted' by the hand of management before being forwarded. When it was still possible to read the original, the offending remarks seemed quite innocuous and not worth repeating!

Many of the residential workers in secure units clearly felt under some pressure to justify their relatively favourable staffing ratios and command over resources, compared with other residential child-care staff, and also to justify what they did in their work with children in custody. This latter point relates to professional objections which have been expressed to locking up children, and which can hardly have failed to influence staff in secure accommodation. These will be discussed in Chapter 7.

Withdrawal from penal institutions
The pressures on social workers[1] in penal institutions are of a different nature. Since 1983, it has been Home Ofice policy that 'in detention centres and youth custody centres ... Prison Department staff will have responsibility for the administration of through-care for individual trainees during sentence.' (Home Office, 1983, para. 8). This means that prison officers should be concerned not only with containing and disciplining young inmates in custody, but also with their daily welfare and with any personal or family problems which might arise. This policy was introduced for England and Wales in the Criminal Justice Act 1982 and seems to have resulted from the earlier May Committee Report on working conditions in the prison service and the running of penal institutions (Home Office, 1979). The implication is that the probation service assumes a minimal role in penal institutions for under-21-year-olds. The aim is eventually to withdraw probation officers altogether from working inside such institutions, and this had already happened in one youth custody centre which responded to the survey only sixteen months after the Home Office circular was issued.

The probation officers who remain seconded to institutions,

usually just one basic-grade officer or a senior, sometimes part-time, are supposed only to liaise with the local probation service in an inmate's home area, and they have time to do little else. The National Association of Probation Officers (NAPO), has endorsed this policy because it 'believes that a better and more effective through-care service to prisoners will be provided if seconded officers are withdrawn from prison department establishments' (NAPO, 1984, para. 1.1). However, some of the comments made by probation officers who responded to the survey suggested that so far a vacuum has been left by their colleagues' departure and that the personal needs of vulnerable under-17-year-olds are neglected by a system which relies on the involvement of supervising officers who may be based a long distance away. This situation seems to be a source of strain for some probation officers who are still left in the institutions.

Note
1. In England and Wales and both parts of Ireland, probation officers are seconded to work in penal institutions. There is no separate probation service in Scotland, where the penal institutions are served by social workers seconded from regional council social work departments. As probation work is normally regarded as a form of social work, both probation officers and local authority social workers seconded into penal institutions and generically referred to as social workers.

6 Penal institutions

Describing the institutions
Figures about children in prison can convey little about the circumstances which led to them being sent there, and their surroundings and quality of life in the institution. But figures provide the 'factual' framework within which this more qualitative information can be presented and interpreted.

There were 76 penal institutions in England and Wales, Scotland, Northern Ireland and the Republic of Ireland where under-17-year-olds were held on 12 September 1984 or, in a couple of instances, not actually on that date but during the previous full quarter — April to June. The commonest type of institution was the youth custody centre and similarly named equivalents, including senior detention centres in Scotland, or youth annexes to adult prisons, both used specifically to imprison young people aged mainly under 21. Sixty-one per cent of the institutions were of this sort, and 48 per cent of the children reported on the census date were imprisoned in them. There were only seven junior detention centres, all in England and Wales, but as they are totally dedicated to the imprisonment of under-17-year-old boys, they accounted for 38 per cent of the census population. Thirteen per cent of the child inmate population was in remand centres (or locally named equivalents) which were nearly all for mixed age groups. The remaining 1 per cent, 18 boys and 1 girl, were dispersed around eleven different adult prisons in England and Scotland.

Only the detention centres held just one type of inmate, those serving sentences. Otherwise child inmates remanded for trial, remanded for sentence and serving sentences (including those awaiting allocation) were to be found in every kind of institution. The survey did not cover the detention centre at Heathrow Airport, but there was one boy in an English remand centre waiting to be deported under immigration legislation. Within England, nearly half of the penal institutions containing under-17-year-olds were concentrated in just two regions out of eight: the South East and the East Midlands. The origins and distribution of their inmates will be discussed later. Altogether over four-fifths of the penal institutions containing juveniles in England and Wales were in shire county

Table 6.1   *Types of penal institution holding under-17-year-old in the four jurisdictions (showing numbers of children on census date)*

	Jurisdiction				
	England & Wales	Scotland	Northern Ireland	Irish Republic	Total
Institution					
For only under-17s	513	—	—	—	513 = 100%
(junior detention centre)	= 42%				=38%
for young people*	547	51	23	18	639 = 100%
	= 45%	=53%			= 48%
remand centre etc.	142	33	—	—	175 = 100%
	= 12%	= 34%			= 13%
adult prison	6	13	—	—	19 = 100%
	=1%	= 13%			= 1%
Total	1,208 = 90%	97 = 7%	23 = 2%	18 = 1%	1,346
	= 100%	= 100%	= 100%	= 100%	= 100%

Note
*Includes senior detention centre, youth custody centre, young offenders' institution, young offenders' centre, youth custody etc. annex to adult prison.

areas rather than the main conurbations. Few of these were open institutions: only 16 per cent were open, all of them youth custody centres or similar. These contained less than 10 per cent of the census population. It seems that juveniles are thought to require the formal structure of a closed institution. There may, of course, have been some under-17-year-olds in the Irish Republic open prisons to which we were denied access, but probably not many.

Regimes
Respondents were asked whether the institution where they worked operated any sort of distinctive regime. The replies from those who answered this question fell into two main categories, reflecting conventional penal regimes and those with a more overtly welfare orientation. Seventy per cent of the institutions were said to have distinctive penal regimes mainly involving training and discipline. Less than a third of respondents mentioned welfare aspects such as availability of counselling to individual inmates, or a general therapeutic programme.

It is probably true to say that the main objective of any penal establishment is keeping the inmates in order, and this was reflected in descriptions of regimes. 'A certain amount of discipline is imposed' wrote a senior prison officer in a youth custody annex to an English local prison. One of the Irish young offenders' institutions was said to have:

> A disciplined regime with some emphasis on physical exercise and facilities for the longer stay inmates to learn some occupational and social skills. . . . The regime is brisk at the reception stage, relaxing as the young prisoners move round the system towards their release.

Accounts from remand centres and adult local prisons placed consistent emphasis on keeping order: 'They are held here on remand awaiting court disposal. If held on unruly certificate, i.e. under 16, they are located in the prison wing. If over 16 held in the remand wing. They are subject of same routine discipline regime as prisoners under sentence' (prison officer Scottish prison). 'The regime is disciplined and geared to produce activity for inmates to an optimal level, rather than inactivity' (deputy governor, English remand centre). 'The regime is geared primarily towards holding and producing women and young men in Court' (probation officer, English remand centre). 'Remand centre regime — overcrowded and understaffed. Extremely high external commitment to Courts. Long hours locked in cells' (senior probation officer, English remand centre). 'Total absence of facilities — containment only' (prison officer, youth custody wing of English prison). 'Lack of activity. We have no workshops — a very restricted education programme — no evening activity. We have three wings and only one can have association in the evening. Less activity at weekends' (senior probation officer, English remand centre). One Scottish prison kept order through using a 'grades system — earning privileges.'

There was evidence of more variety and sense of purpose in the regimes of institutions which held children and young people under sentence, rather than on remand or for allocation. The inmates of such institutions are officially called trainees rather than prisoners. 'The aims of a YCC [Youth custody centre] are to provide work, training and instruction of a kind that will assist offenders to acquire or develop personal resources, interests and skills. Being an open establishment there is a *relaxed* regime. Lads are encouraged to take personal responsibility' (senior probation officer, English youth custody centre). 'Full working day. Controlled atmosphere but not oppressive. Hopefully trainees can learn and feel some sense of purpose' (probation officer, English senior detention centre which occasionally receives under-17-year-olds). 'Emphasis on training — flexible routine, with trust an important feature' (social worker, Scottish youth offenders' institution).

The senior probation offier in an English junior detention centre which had not yet been told to implement a 'short, sharp shock' regime wrote enthusiastically that his institution ran a:

> Brisk but *not* tough regime. Excellent educational facilities, gymnasium (not punitive, P.E. proficiency awards of all kinds taken), remedial education/life and social skills for all trainees/bed-sit survival course/ numerous evening class facilities/workshop/market garden/adventure training — hikes/visiting groups for religious worship. First two weeks 'induction party' mainly cleaning (and education for schoolboys). The regime for the young people concerned seems surprisingly relaxed.

Besides exercises in the gym, which seem to be a common feature of penal institutions for children and young people, the training facilities here seem to be an unspecified workshop and a market garden. In another English detention centre, children received 'instruction in machine shop practice, arts/crafts, building trades, including bricklaying, plastering and painting and decorating', but only if they were over 16: 'for trainees of compulsory school age, 90% of time is spent in education.' The senior probation officer in an English youth custody centre said it was a 'standard YCC — training courses mainly related to construction industry.' Another probation officer in a youth custody centre wrote that his institution provided 'education and trade training rather than industrial based.' A further youth custody centre was described as 'very agricultural — largest holding of land of any Prison Department establishment. Shire horses etc.'

Only a few institutions claimed to operate a regime with an overtly therapeutic orientation. One English detention centre (mixed junior and senior) had what sounded like a treatment regime, but the fact that the senior probation officer who worked there himself put quotation marks around this passage suggests that it represented policy rather than reality: 'remedial treatment. To provide for the trainee an experience which can enable him to take stock of his lifestyle: to at least look at his faults and weaknesses; and to be made aware of the opportunities for continuing any useful or reward-ing activity experienced at the detention centre.' A senior prison officer in a Northern Irish institution for female young offenders wrote that, 'our aim is to provide a therapeutic regime with the minimum discipline required for the maintenance of good order.' A senior probation officer wrote similarly from an English women's prison: 'assessment process, leading to sentence planning. This is aimed to be therapeutic and caring, to provide the inmate with relationship opportunities. Social skills courses, life relationship group. House system and personal officer scheme.'

Two English youth custody centres still have a specialist therapeutic function. The senior probation officer from one of them described what this was supposed to mean, again quoting from the official account:

> This youth custody centre will operate a psychiatrically supported regime in most of the establishment, although to the extent that there are vacancies it will still also take some ordinary trainees. . . . So far as its specialist role is concerned, [the YCC] takes trainees who are in need of full-time psychiatric oversight or treatment or who require medical treatment. In addition to the normal facilities of a youth custody centre, it has particular resources in the education, medical and psychiatric fields which enable it to specialise in the care and treatment of trainees who suffer severely from psychiatric disorders, alcoholism, drug misuse, epilepsy, psycho-sexual disorders, personality disorders and physical disabilities.

There were 16 boys aged under 17 in this youth custody centre on the census day.

In rather more institutions it seemed that while no special regime was operated, welfare services were available for inmates to use if they wanted, or on a personal basis by special request. An example from an English senior detention centre was: 'Life and social skills groups are aimed at improvement in self image and sense of achievement.' The senior probation officer in a small English youth custody centre wrote that 'there are no specialist support services available for young people under 17. They receive the same range of services that all inmates receive. . . . The regime here is intended to allow inmates to utilise any facility available *if they wish*. Prison staff are involved actively with inmates and the regime is relaxed.'

One English youth custody centre still had a 'Central Casework Unit' instead of a more common 'singleton' liaison probation officer post. This institution was said to operate

> a fairly open regime designed to identify specific needs of trainees in the areas of work experience, JTC courses, education life and social skills, drugs, alcohol or homelessness and attempt to remedy before discharge, or provide information for the supervisory services to enable on-going casework. More emphasis would be given to the needs of any under 17-year-old when the sentence plan is formulated, they would be given first access to available resources.

A probation officer from another long-term youth custody centre reported a 'shared social work scheme, personal officer scheme, a caring regime with sympathetic management set-up'. A probation officer in an Irish Republic young offenders' institution wrote that, 'the Welfare Department engage in a counselling role for tried prisoners and refer these out to the field officers.' But the 'singleton' senior probation officer in an English youth custody centre described the more general pattern in English and Scottish penal institutions for children and young people:

> Prison officers are required to offer 'casework' to lads as part of their (the prison officers') task list . . . Probation officers in the medium-term YCCs are not responsible for the carrying out of the day-to-day social work task with the inmates. Prison officers do this. The senior probation officer at medium term YCCs is a singleton post and is responsible for liaison with outside agencies and acts as a consultant to prison officer and governor grades in the establishment.

In view of societal attitudes to youth as impressionable, corruptible and likely to be led astray by older bad company, one might have expected to find some segregation of under-17-year-olds within penal institutions, particularly where older adults were also accommodated. But this seems not to be the case. None of the regimes which have been described above was specific to juveniles. The only exception now is the 'short, sharp shock' or special 'tougher' regime which at the time of the census was operating in a few senior and one junior detention centres. Shortly afterwards it was extended and applied to all junior detention centres in England and Wales, despite Home Office research evidence of its ineffectiveness in reducing the likelihood of reconviction (Thornton, *et al.*, 1984).

It is ironic that the current British response to children in prison is not to protect them nor to make their experience of custody less harsh than for adults. Instead, the British policy is to ensure that child prisoner have it even 'tougher' than adults. Penal custody seems to be regarded as insufficient punishment in itself for juvenile offenders. Children must be sent to penal institutions not just *as* a punishment, but *for* punishment.

Only in junior detention centres were under-17-year-olds sure of sharing their living quarters with others of the same age; because no one over 17 was imprisoned there. More than half of the youth custody and similar institutions which hold under-21-year-olds serving sentences provided single-cell sleeping accommodation; but this applied to all inmates and was no special arrangement for juveniles. Separate single accommodation was described by at least one youth custody centre as a dubious advantage, because it meant isolation at night when the inmate was left alone with his thoughts. That particular instition had a policy of putting new arrivals in with another prisoner for their first night, when they were thought to be most vulnerable to depression and despair. The single accommodation provided for potential suicides in another youth penal complex, at Glenochil in Scotland, seems to be isolated and 'safe' to the point of sensory deprivation (Chiswick, 1985).

Children who were in remand centres or adult prisons, and particularly those who were remanded in custody and not yet convicted or sentenced, were the least likely to receive special consideration because of their age. The reason seems to be pressure on cell space; when an institution was already overcrowded, any new arrival would be allocated to whatever accommodation was available. When it came to day-time activities, special services or arrangements for under-17-year-olds were available in only 12 per cent of institutions. Practically all claimed to provide education for children under school-leaving age, but it was usually unclear what this amounted to. Presumably schooling would be provided on a systematic basis only in institutions where there was a consistent population of under-16-year-olds. Elsewhere, it would be a matter of formally attempting to meet minimum requirements of schooling for children under school-leaving age. One Scottish assistant prison governor managed to make this sound like a punishment in itself: 'The regime for under 16s both convicted and untried is different to that for the 16-21 age group within the institution. Under 16s receive full time education on a compulsory basis. Over 16s cannot be compelled to work if untried although some volunteer to do so and are employed on domestic duties.' In an English prison, the probation officer said 'YC inmates are out of their cells in the classroom block from 1.30-4.30 p.m. every day', but she did not say what they did there. Just escorting children to a classroom can be a problem for overworked staff in adult prisons and remand centres. The deputy governor of an English remand centre wrote: 'under 17s and inadequates are located, as far as possible, in a separate wing. Slightly higher staff ratio. Education facility available when staffing permits.' And the senior probation officer in an English local prison confirmed the uncertainty: 'If still of school age, they are provided with a full education programme where possible during their very short stay here. Otherwise they are with under 21s in workshops and gymnasium.' There were 3 under-17-year-olds in that prison on the census date.

The children in prison

Two-thirds of the children in penal institutions on the census date were aged 16. The youngest were 14-year-old boys, of whom 73 were reported. The great majority of all age groups were boys. Details of the ages of children in the different jurisdictions are given in Table 6.2. Eight per cent were from racial minority groups, mainly Afro-Caribbean, concentrated in England and Wales. This is consistent with Home Office findings about the 'ethnic origins' of the prison population in general and youth prisoners in particular (Home Office, 1986).

In Scotland, where there is a policy of not sentencing children to penal custody, and adulthood begins at 16, all of the under-16-year

Table 6.2   The children's ages in penal institutions*

	Jurisdiction				
	England & Wales	Scotland	Northern Ireland	Irish Republic	Total
Age					
16 years	680 = 85% = 65%	84 = 11% = 90%	21 = 3% = 96%	14 = 2% = 88%	799 = 100% =68%
15 years	304 = 98% = 29%	4 = 1% = 4%	1 =4%	2 = 12%	311 = 100% = 26%
14 years	68 = 93% = 7%	5 = 7% = 5%	—	—	73 = 100% = 6%
Total	1,052 = 89% = 100%	93 = 8% = 100%	22 = 2% = 100%	16 = 1% = 100%	1,183 = 100%

*The data in Tables 6.2–6.4 are based on census returns on individual children. The figures are slightly different from the overall totals given in previous tables.

olds were on remand. Most had been imprisoned under unruly certificates, a practice which has come under scrutiny in Scottish Office funded research (Denham, 1984). There is no such restriction on the imprisonment of under-16-year-old boys in England, as the numbers clearly show, but the Home Office has announced that criteria for remanding them in custody are to be tightened (*Hansard*, 1986).

Where they come from
As such large numbers of children were imprisoned in England, it has been possible to make a geographical analysis of where they had previously lived and relate this to where they were imprisoned — with some interesting results. Nearly half of the children in English penal institutions came from the big conurbations, mainly metropolitan districts. Nearly two-thirds had home addresses in what could broadly be called the north of the country, including the four regions of the North West, Yorkshire and Humberside, the North and the West Midlands (in descending order of frequency). As mentioned earlier in the chapter, the penal institutions containing under-17-year-olds were concentrated in shire county areas and in the East Midlands and the South East. These two regions, and the South West (with large numbers of children in a few institutions), were indeed where about two-thirds of the English children were imprisoned. So it is not surprising that only 11 per cent of English childrn were imprisoned in the same local authority area as their home address, and that well over half of those who were imprisoned near home lived in the three regions which contained the institutions: the

South East, East Midlands and South West. More than two-fifths of all English under-17-year-olds in penal institutions came from metropolitan districts such as Manchester, Liverpool and Newcastle upon Tyne, yet only 3 per cent of these northern city children were imprisoned within their home districts. So the general trend was for children from northern cities to be given custodial sentences and imprisoned in penal institutions situated in the rural or suburban southern half of England. With the end of specialist functions for borstal institutions, which were intended to meet perceived needs on a national basis, young trainees were supposed to be sent to an institution located within their home region. It seems that this is not happening.

The situation is very much the same in Scotland, with young Glaswegians being distributed to institutions in other parts of the country. In the Irish Republic, the opposite happens; children are sent from home areas around the country to an institution in relatively prosperous Dublin. Only in Northern Ireland are a majority (53 per cent) of children imprisoned in the same town where they live: Belfast. The variant there is that a more detailed analysis of the children's home addresses would show that they tend to come from Catholic, not Protestant, districts of the city. Overall, in the four jurisdictions, only 13 per cent of children were imprisoned within the same local authority area as their home. The movement was from homes in the poorer and more deprived regions of each jurisdiction into institutions situated in the more prosperous areas. This confirms the general truism that those who fall foul of the law and order system tend to come from relatively disadvantaged sections of the country's working-class population. Their punishment is removal from their own community into a custodial institution, which is also likely to be at a distance far removed from their home. The expense and inconvenience of a long journey makes maintaining family links through visits all the more difficult.

Two-thirds of the children had been living with their parents or other relatives immediately before they were taken into custody. For just over two-fifths of this group — comprising 27 per cent of the total population — this was the first time they had been removed from their parental home. Practically all of the remaining third were living in residential child-care establishments when they were taken into custody, or were 'on the run' absconding from residential homes. Nearly a quarter of them were in secure accommodation, often having been remanded there by the court.

Their previous history
As 27 per cent of the under-17-year-old population of penal institutions had never lived away from home before this means that

conversely, 73 per cent had previously been removed from their families. Most commonly this was into residential child care provided by local authorities (or equivalent); three-quarters of this group were known to have been in residential care.

However, nearly half of those who had been removed from home before had already served at least one custodial sentence, mostly in a detention centre. This means that out of the whole population of under-17-year-olds in penal institutions on the census date, more than a third already had a previous conviction which had resulted in custody: 30 per cent had been in a detention centre at least once before and 11 per cent had been in a youth custody centre (or equivalent) including an overlapping group of 5 per cent who had already been in both — some achievement by the age 16! It does not seem to have been a matter of automatic progression from detention centre to youth custody, along a tariff of sentencing. Only just over half of those who were in a youth custody centre (or equivalent) on the census date had already been in a detention centre, while 9 per cent of the detention centre census population had already been in a youth custody centre, even though the Criminal Justice Act 1982 should have ruled out this possibility. This lends support to the impression that sentencing to youth custody has increased after the 1982 Act, in preference to the shorter detention centre sentence.

Respondents' main source of information on the children's previous custodial sentences were prison department records held in the institution. For information about other aspects of the children's background, they used social enquiry reports where these were available, and particularly interviews which they conducted with the children for the purpose of completing the survey forms. At least 55 per cent of all the under-17-year-olds in penal institutions were known previously to have been in residential care, but the general incidence of contact with the child-care services was higher. Only 17 per cent overall were said not to have been the subject of statutory social work intervention of some sort. Forty-eight per cent had been under a care order (or equivalent) when they were admitted to custody, and a further 23 per cent in the recent past. Twelve per cent were under probation supervision when they received their custodial sentence; some of these had earlier child-care experience but they tended rather to be relatively late first offenders. Eighteen per cent of the children overall had at some time been under probation supervision and 47 per cent had received local authority (or equivalent) social work supervision.

Of course, these statutory categories tend to merge in the experience of an individual child. Social work supervision, with the child living at home 'on trial' may precede a care order with admission to a residential establishment, or voluntary supervision at home may continue after a formal care order has been revoked. And for children of this age group, social work supervision and probation supervision may be virtually indistinguishable, particularly when either can be ordered by the court following an offence, and even more so in Scotland where there is no probation service separate from the local authority social work department.

The *Review of Child Care Law* has reported that there are more than twenty different routes into care in England and Wales (DHSS, 1985, para. 2.4c), and the juvenile justice 'system' in particular has become an esoteric and complex area of academic study for enthusiasts. We should not be surprised that many of its nuances are lost on the children who receive the services and sentences. They seem equally unfamiliar to many of the seconded probation officers in penal institutions; details about care orders and reasons for admission were given in only a third of relevant cases, and are therefore of little use. One senior probation officer working in a youth custody centre in the South East wrote that a 16-year-old from East London had been in 'Stanford [sic] House — I am not sure what that is — neither is subject'. Stamford House is, of course, a large assessment centre with secure accommodation which serves as a remand home for the London area; many inmates of the youth custody centre must have been through it. The bold question 'Have you been in care?' may mean little to a 16-year-old in a youth custody centre, or the probation officer interviewing him, but what the child at least does know is the various establishments where he has been placed. Much of the data about the children's backgrounds has been pieced together from quite specific pieces of information like that, obtained in interviews with the children. As the senior probation officer in a youth custody centre explained: 'We have no idea how the various residential child care establishments classify themselves and often we only know that they *were* in some form of residential care', so information based on social enquiry reports alone would not have been sufficiently accurate.

It is likely that the details given relate only to current or most recent care episodes and that earlier incidents in the children's past have not been mentioned. In support of this supposition, no information about early social work contact was given for the 12 children who had been adopted, although there must have been some formal child-care intervention during the adoption process. Also, the number of children who were said to have been fostered was relatively low (only 5 per cent), and this is a form of service likely to be used for pre-teenage children. If earlier care episodes have generally gone unreported this does not necessarily mean that a higher proportion of children in total have experienced social work intervention, but it would mean that some of the complexity is missing from the life histories of those who are known to have been in care.

Among those who had been through residential care, more than half had been in an open assessment centre, two-fifths in an ordinary children's home, and nearly half in an open community home with education (CHE), List D school or training school. About a third had been in secure accommodation, just over half of them for purposes of assessment or remand. On the whole, the children identified by the census seem to have come from working-class backgrounds, but occasionally there was evidence of middle-class alternatives to residential care. A 16-year-old from the South East, serving six months youth custody for three burglaries, theft, 'taking and driving away' and 'obtaining by deception' had previously been sent by his parents to a private boarding school, an adolescent psychiatric unit and a clinic for gamblers. When arrested he was under a 2-year supervision order to social services, with intermediate treatment, but had never been in residential care.

Even though these may have been only the children's most recent care episodes, a lot of disruption and movement was involved: nearly three-quarters of those who had been in residential care had been moved five or more times since they first left their parents' home. Only about half of them had returned to live with their parents again in the meantime, often for a short time after a previous period in custody. No attempt was made to chronicle changes within the children's families, as this was felt to be too demanding for a postal questionnaire. However two institutions, an English junior detention centre, and a Scottish senior detention centre, volunteered this information systematically. It was no surprise, from previous research on the family background of young offenders (see for example West, 1973), to find that about half of their under 17-year-old inmates were from 'broken homes' where the parents had separated and often formed new relationships introducing a step-parent. A 15-year-old from the North West had lived with his mother, at the time a single parent, and 'various cohabitees and husbands' for the first ten years of his life. He was the subject of a matrimonial supervision order when he was 4. After the age of 10 he lived with his mother and a stepfather until a care order (unspecified) was made when he was 14 and he spent the next eighteen months in an assessment centre. He was serving a 6-week sentence in an East Midlands detention centre for burglary.

A tenth of those who had already been removed from their parents' home had been placed in the care of a relative, usually a grandmother or older sister. A 14-year-old from the North West of England serving three months for theft in an East Midlands detention centre, had lived with his mother in London for only four years, between the ages of 9 and 13. Before that, from birth, he was cared for by his grandmother, and afterwards lived with an uncle and aunt. At the time of his arrest he was back with his grandmother again. He had never been in care, but was in contact with child guidance for a year when he was 8.

Some children experienced a high level of disruption over quite a short period. A 16-year-old girl from the South East, serving six months youth custody for property offences, moved from a children's home to an open CHE to secure accommodation in a CHE and was then fostered. Thereafter the probation officer said that she 'has oscillated at twice weekly intervals between mother and foster parents'. All this happened between 28 November 1983 when a care order was made 'because of offending' and 11 June 1984 when she was put into custody.

For many children a major cause of disruption is their own attempts to escape from residential establishments where they do not want to be held, or to avoid living with their parents. The recent career of a 16-year-old Irish boy from Cork was described:

> Parental home up to age 13. Three weeks in secure accommodation in assessment centre. Sent by court to industrial school for two years. Did not settle, frequently absconded. Age 14 sent by court to reformatory school for two years. After eight months, released from reformatory and returned to reside at parental home. Indicated that he subsequently spent about eight months in parental home, followed by three months with a brother in England. Then he stated he returned to Ireland, slept rough in Cork for two months then returned to parental home and finally arrived in the Institution.

In the meantime he had also breached a 2-year probation order, but his twelve-month sentence was for two minor asssaults. Some children survive quite long periods of homelessness with 'no fixed address' (NFA), whilst absconding or trying to live independently. Four per cent were NFA immediately before they were admitted to custody. Indeed having no address to give in court may have been a factor in their receiving a custodial sentence on the argument, sometimes heard, that prison is better for children than being on the streets with no home to go to. Discounting those children whose current sentence was taking them away from home for the first time, at least 10 per cent overall had been NFA on their own at some time during their lives.

Details about non-residential services which the children had received were rather patchy, a few institutions returning no information at all. Probation and social work supervision have already been mentioned. Twenty-eight per cent of those who had been under a supervision order to either agency had also received intermediate treatment (IT), comprising 18 per cent of the overall population. There were no details about the type of IT scheme involved. Around 45 per cent of the children had been through an attendance centre (sometimes more than once) or on a community service order, the latter depending on local availability. At least 9 per cent had received 'special' education, at a unit within an ordinary school or more frequently at a separate day school or boarding school for educationally subnormal or maladjusted children. The great majority of these pupils had subsequently gone into residential child-care establishments.

What they had done
Details of offences were given in 95 per cent of cases including, unrequested, the charges facing many of the children who were on remand. Over half the children were charged with only one or two offences, over a quarter with three or four, and the remaining 17 per cent with five or more. A quarter of the children had been charged with offences which involved some degree of violence, but less than a fifth of these (5 per cent of the total) have been classed as most serious: murder, or attempted murder, rape, grievious bodily harm, arson, and firearms offences. Most offences against the person involved assault or actual harm. Robbery or 'mugging' as an offence involving both person and propery was mentioned in only 4 per cent of cases. There was nothing that sounded like 'football hooliganism'.

Predictably, the great majority of offences involved property only: 87 per cent of the children were charged with property offences. By far the most common was burglary (61 per cent), then theft (37 per cent), and 'taking and driving away' or other variants on theft of a motor vehicle (21 per cent). All this seems to be consistent with previous findings (e.g. Thornton, *et al.*, 1984, p. 20; DHSS, 1981b).

A third category of public order and other victimless offences applied to 14 per cent of offenders. Mainly involved were secondary offences involved in the theft of a car — driving without a licence and insurance, both 'status' offences for under-17-year-olds who are too young to have a driving licence. Breach of the peace, obstruction and the new English offence of interfering with a motor vehicle were also mentioned, and possessing (but not using) an offensive weapon. There was only one boy charged with possessing drugs.

Finally, 7 per cent of children were charged with offences against the criminal justice system such as breach of probation, breach of bail and resisting arrest. Sometimes this and some minor public order offence were all that the child was said to have done. Probably a number of others could have been charged with breaking the condi-

tions of a supervision order following their recently previous detention centre or youth custody sentence, which would not have had
time to expire before they were charged with the next offence.

No satisfactory methodology has yet been developed to rank the
perceived seriousness of offences independently of sentences
received, and link the two together taking into account the number
and range of different offences with which one person may be
charged, and the effect of their known background and any previous
convictions on tariff sentencing. In the absence of an appropriate
method, speculation about regional inconsistencies in sentencing and
about whether the severity (or lenience) of sentences seems to be
deserved by the nature of offences as described, is probably inadvisable.

But bare descriptive details can make an incident sound rather different to the image associated with the formal charge and more easily
understood in relation to the child's social world. 'Burglary', apparently
the most popular offence, is popularly associated with house-breaking
and stealing valuable goods for financial gain, but entering private dwell-
ing houses was only involved sometimes. Taking another kid's bike
from a 'lockfast' garden shed would be classed as burglary, so would
'theft of a pedal cycle and C.B. radio' from a shop. 'Criminal damage'
carries an image of wanton destruction, wrecked telephone boxes; it
was more likely to involve 'graffiti on school walls'.

Sometimes offences are associated with a specific personal
problem. Thus a probation officer in a remand centre wrote about
one 16-year-old from Yorkshire who was charged with two robberies,
two burglaries (house), and two 'taking without consent' (car theft):
'Has a problem of gambling on the one-armed bandits — nearly
all his offences are to get money to gamble. It's the process he
seems to be obsessed with.' He had already been in secure accommodation in an assessment centre, broken a 2-year probation order
and served three detention centre sentences, the last one ending
the same day as he was sent to the remand centre, 'It was a gate
arrest.'

The implied social context of an incident can provoke speculation
about what was going on. If a child is charged with 'allowing himself
to be carried in a stolen car', this can suggest that he is thought
to have fallen into bad company. A charge of 'theft and possession
of arms and ammunition' against a Northern Irish 15-year-old who
had been in residential care since he was 4, including a period in
a psychiatric hospital and 6 years in a training school, suggests that
he had become involved with a para-military organization whilst
in care. It is difficult to know how to interpret a charge of 'throwing
petrol bombs and riotous behaviour' against a 16-year-old from
Derry, also a former training school resident; it sounds serious, but

Table 6.3   Unremitted sentences of penal populations in the four
jurisdictions

	Jurisdiction				
	England & Wales	Scotland	Northern Ireland	Irish Republic	Total
Sentence					
3 months or less	326 = 92% = 35%	29 = 8%	1	—	356 = 100% = 35%
4–6 months	324 = 96% = 35%	9 = 3%	2	4	339 = 100% = 34%
7–11 months	103 = 96% = 11%	—	2	2	107 = 100% = 11%
Over a year	172 = 86% = 19%	11 = 5% = 22%	7 = 4% = 58%	10 = 5% = 63%	200 = 100% = 20%
Total	925 = 92% = 100%	49 = 5% = 100%	12 = 1% = 100%	16 = 2% = 100%	1,002 = 100%

he could just have been a member of a crowd. The ambient level
of violence in Northern Ireland is high compared with the other
three jurisdictions: the province accounted for three out of the six
charges of murder or attempted murder in the whole of the census
penal population for the British Isles. On the other hand, sentencing
in the Irish Republic, for mainly property offences and minor
assaults, seems to be relatively severe. Tables 6.3 and 6.4 compare
length of unremitted sentences in the four jurisidictions and the
length of time already spent inside.

Helping objectives
Respondents in the institutions were asked whether they were
involved with the child inmates (individually) in a helping capacity,
and what objectives they were trying to achieve. This was put as
an open-ended question, with no prompts to suggest what replies
were expected. Probation officers (it was mainly them rather than
prison officers) in contact with only just over a fifth of the children
in penal institutions replied positively, describing specific objectives.
Others explained why they were not involved with the child in question, and I shall return to these reasons later. The helping objectives
which were described have been grouped into seven categories. Most
respondents specified only one, but some mentioned two or three,
as in the case of a Scottish 16-year-old in a detention centre: 'Examin-

Table 6.4   *Length of time already spent in penal custody, in current period**

	Jurisdiction				
	England & Wales	Scotland	Northern Ireland	Irish Republic	Total
Time inside					
Under a month	476 = 89% = 46%	50 = 9% = 54%	5 = 1% = 31%	6 = 1% = 38%	537 = 100% = 46%
1–3 months	463 = 90% = 44%	33 = 6% = 35%	11 = 2% = 69%	6 = 1% = 38%	513 = 100% = 44%
4–6 months	86 = 87% = 8%	7 = 7% = 8%	—	4 = 4% = 25%	97 = 100% = 8%
Over 7 months	18 = 86% = 2%	3 = 14% = 3%	—	—	21 = 100% = 2%
Total	1,043 = 89% = 100%	93 = 8% = 100%	16 = 1% = 100%	16 = 1% = 100%	1,168 = 100%

*Includes children on remand.

ing attitudes and behaviour. Developing increased responsibility. Planning for release — accommodation, employment, seeking support for drug addiction on release. Counselling on addiction whilst in custody.' The seven categories are, in order of frequency:

(1) facilitating insight, self-control or maturity;
(2) providing support, advice or counselling in response to children's expressed problems;
(3) enabling the child to receive remedial education or work experience;
(4) trying to improve relations between the child and his family;
(5) helping with financial, housing and employment problems anticipated on release;
(6) developing social skills;
(7) assessing the child's needs and planning future help.

Helping clients to achieve insight into their behaviour and self-control is a common objective in social work practice, and one which was expressed frequently by probation officers and social workers in these penal institutions, usually in general terms within the penal context, but sometimes over something more specific to an individual child. Inmates would be helped to think about why they had committed the offences which led to their custodial sentence: 'To help him understand better the circumstances leading up to his offences — and how to organise his life so that he does not offend again.' 'Knowledge of pattern of offending in past related to means of avoiding trouble in future, linked with leading a constructive life.' 'To help him look at the situations leading up to the offences and the circumstances of his life which he regards as unsatisfactory with a view to him being able to organise things differently in the future so that he doesn't return here.' And about a Welsh boy who had been in residential care since he was 11 and had been moved at least ten times, including stays in a youth treatment centre, a secure assessment centre and a detention centre: 'In view of his institutional background, discussion of future opportunities and problems and avoidance of repetition of offending pattern.'

Frequently the objective was to enable an inmate to take stock of his/her personal development: 'To enable him to modify and adjust his present antisocial behaviour. Family strengths and support are poor with history of mental ill health. . . . Casework should be geared toward improving his self awareness and level of functioning.' 'To get rid of his resentment and hostility towards authority. Encourage more positive and constructive thinking.' 'To adjust attitudes towards socially acceptable behaviour.' 'To adjust to realities.' 'To promote self awareness at what damage he is doing to his life. Thereby encourage some self discipline'; this related to a 14-year-old from the North West who was in care under Section 7(7) of the Children and Young Persons Act 1969, and had already served a previous detention centre sentence.

The senior probation officer in a women's prison wrote about a 16-year-old girl who had been sentenced to six months' youth custody for abducting a baby, that her aim was 'to get her to examine her apparent sophistication versus her immaturity and irresponsible behaviour.' Another 16-year-old girl was in care under Section 3 of the Child Care Act 1980, and had received four months' youth custody for breach of the community service order, was said to have 'no accommodation, drink or drugs problems. She admits to being anti-authority. She has been frightened by her first penal custody. I am trying to help her work on her authority problem because it was that that created the problem with Community Service and led to her being here.' About another 16-year-old girl from the South East who was in care as being beyond control and was serving a four-month sentence for arson, it was said: 'It is obvious she needs help with learning to express her feelings in a less volatile way. This is being done during the frequent group sessions on her house.' A 14-year-old boy who had been in care under Section 2 of the 1948 Children's Act since he was 8, and had been convicted of robbery and assault, was said to be receiving 'supportive therapy, i.e. not allow his present situation to deteriorate any further while he matures to his next phase of development and hopefully he will gain more sense and learn from his past experience.'

A major reason for offering support to inmates of penal institutions, of whatever age, is to enable them to cope with the experience of imprisonment, particularly if it is their first custodial sentence or is likely to be a long one. This form of social work help scarcely featured in the survey responses from residential workers in secure units, and this will be discussed in the next chapter. A reason for this difference may be that while residential staff in secure accommodation are the custodians as well as the helpers of children in custody, probation and social workers in penal institutions have a separate role and are normally able to distance themselves from the custodial purpose of the institution. Thus they are better able to appreciate that the experience of custody itself, just being locked up, may be the main problem for most inmates.

Many probation officers wrote about this aspect of their work. Three seniors in remand centres and a local prison were responding to children's first admission to custody on remand: 'Recent reception into custody. Assistance given in adjusting to custodial experience.' 'Given the limited period of time he will remain at this local prison on remand, my work, as prison social worker, involves meeting immediate needs and giving advice/support in adapting to incarceration.' 'To cope with the remand period — the frustrations caused by time taken to negotiate acceptable bail address by home Probation Officer'; it took over two months to arrange a bail address out of London for this 16-year-old boy from inner London, as required by the court.

Other probation officers were concerned with mitigating the effects on children of sentences, often long-term, imposed for crimes of violence; 'Support him at this stage of his sentence. Offer him hope by helping him to plan his future ahead and make the best use of the time he spends in custody' (16-year-old boy from the North West of England who had already served one year of a life sentence for murder). 'Helping adjust to difficult environment in difficult circumstances' (16-year-old Irish boy charged with attempted murder and indecent assault). 'To help him come to terms with the remorse and shame he has suffered' (15-year-old boy from a mining town in the North East, serving a sentence for indecent assault). 'Coping with long sentence. Keep family contacts alive' (16-year-old from the North West who had received a sentence of 3 years nine months for burglaries, his first offence). 'General assistance in adjusting to custody during anticipated long wait for trial' (16-year-old boy from the North East charged with rape).

In other cases, support or counselling was directed at particular problems which had been presented by children, for example about a 15-year-old boy from the North West: 'This young man needs counselling to come to term with his parents' divorce.' Work on improving relationships between children and their parents has been identified as a separate, specific objective: 'General support and assistance in maintaining family contacts and relationships.' 'To encourage him to attend psychology sessions aimed at helping him to look at family relationships.' 'Maintain links with offender's family due to parent being seriously ill.' 'Re-establish satisfactory relationship with family.' Maintaining or improving family relationships could be particularly difficult when the children were imprisoned far from home.

Substance abuse and compulsive behaviour, such as gambling, were mentioned as the focus of counselling in a substantial minority of cases. A senior social worker's aim with one 16-year-old from a Scottish new town was to 'examine difficulties which have led to present predicament. Counsel regarding drug/alcohol/solvent abuse.' With another boy from the West Midlands, a probation officer intended 'to look at problematic drinking patterns'; and with another from the North West: 'Encouraging him to discuss his drug problem and give information regarding available facilities, etc., but he will only remain here for a matter of weeks.'

In longer-stay institutions addiction problems could be the subject of social skills courses, which in one women's prison were 'mandatory'. More usually such help was just available: 'This young person will participate in an alcohol education programme as his offending is drink-related' (in an Irish Republic young offenders' institution). 'He admits to sniffing solvents and this has been the main problem between him and the rest of his family. He has now consented to seek medical attention for his glue sniffing and is getting support in his intention to stay off glue in the future. Assistance is also being given to him to try to improve his social skills.' Sex education was also provided in some institutions, as an aspect of social skills. For example, a 16-year-old boy from Yorkshire, charged with indecent assault, would be helped, 'to come to terms with his sexuality — increase his social skills — help him to be more at ease with girls — understand more about relationships.'

Education, beyond compulsory schooling, was more usually seen in terms of preparing children for employment. The 'sentence plan' for one 16-year-old who would be returning to a community home in the West Midlands, was to 'improve employment skills'. A boy

from the East Midlands, who had never before left his parents'
home, was to be encouraged 'to think about family relationships
(hitherto problematic), and to take advantage of work experiences
available at this establishment' (a YCC). The aim with another boy
from the same institution was 'to encourage him to complete a
bricklaying course whilst here.'

Remedial education was mentioned in some cases. A senior probation officer in a women's youth custody centre wrote about a
Welsh 16-year-old that 'a primary aim is to provide encouragement
to seek the education avoided during the latter part of her schooling.
Unfortunately efforts in this direction have been limited by the fact
that she arrived at the commencement of the school summer holidays
and is due for release in October.' It was said of another 15-year-old
girl that 'the problem revealed on initial interview was truancy from
school. Any education she has missed should be remedied at least
partly now that she is receiving full time education here.' The visible
skin complaint psoriasis may have been a contributory factor to
her truancy, and it had also caused her to lose several months'
schooling in hospital.

In these last two cases the objective was to compensate for perceived educational disadvantage. Sometimes there was a positive
hope to 'encourage educational achievement', as with a 15-year-old
boy from Yorkshire. Sometimes a special project could be arranged,
as for a 16-year-old girl from the South East of England: 'This
young woman's energies and talent have been directed towards helping others by a three week placement at a City Challenge Project . . .
and for her own benefit by a nomination for a YTS course post
release.'

Responses to children's material problems, to do with lack of
money, accommodation and job prospects on release, related both
to practical improvements and to helping children to come to terms
with, and make the most of, an impoverished home environment.
Practicalities involved: 'Liaising with field social worker to obtain
accommodation, supported or otherwise'; 'Planning of future existence on basis of his intention to live independently of his parents
in a different town'. 'This man is homeless and has been given
advice on getting accommodation through the home social work
department.' Three of the cases just cited were from Scotland, where
16-year-olds are classed as adults, who are entitled to live independently. Another Scottish social worker was involved in 'sorting
mainly financial (fines) problems and ensuring that boy begins to
help himself.' In England, a remand centre probation officer was
concerned to give a 16-year-old boy from Yorkshire 'some understanding of how to resolve the problems of drink, no job, very little

money — without breaking the law.' About another boy she wrote: 'Says he has had enough custody. Wants to sort things out differently. Am trying to help him increase his understanding of himself and how he can organise his life differently. He has the usual problems of many of the lads in here — no job — nothing he particularly wants to do — feels rejected — very short of money.

Not involved

Nearly four-fifths of the children in penal institutions were not receiving any significant help from the workers who responded to the survey, nearly all of whom were probation officers seconded to the institutions. In most cases respondents explained their reasons for not being involved in a helping capacity. These were either given in general terms, as applied to a whole category of inmates or, less frequently, as reasons specific to individual children.

A few children who had been interviewed by a probation officer were regarded as unlikely to welcome help or had explicitly rejected it. A probation officer in an English detention centre wrote about a 15-year-old boy from the North East: 'There is a long extended family history of burglary and persistent offending in this case and from an early age he has been indoctrinated that criminal activities are the norm. In my opinion the prognosis in this case is poor.' The boy had never been removed from home before, and there was no comment on how he had responded to a previous supervision order to the probation service, with intermediate treatment. A 15-year-old girl from the South East who had been in residential care since she was 12 and at a special school for educationally subnormal children for 3 years before that, was described thus: 'She has accepted that she will be returned to the children's home from which she came and seems to regard her time here as an unavoidable interlude in her life that is little different from being in the children's home. Seems unmotivated to change and hence there is little that can be done.' She was serving four months' youth custody for assaulting a teacher, and had already been in a secure CHE. Probation officers in penal institutions have no authority to 'force' social work help on unwilling inmates, unlike unresidential care staff in secure units who are expected to work with the most uncooperative children. It is possible that giving the residential staff a break from this girl was a reason for charging her with an offence which had been committed in a CHE.

Occasionally it seemed that the reason for non-involvement with child inmates was that the probation officer concerned had adopted the values of the penal institution and was not concerned with the social work helping objectives which were identified in the last section of this chapter. Thus a probation officer in a detention centre wrote that her objective with one boy was to 'deter him from further criminal activities', which is a formal purpose of imprisonment according to Home Office policy (Home Office, 1977). The same officer wrote about another 16-year-old from Yorkshire: 'Hopefully the experience of detention centre will make this client think hard before getting involved in crime again.' And again about a 14-year-old boy from the North East, that her aim was 'To prevent him from further criminal activities by giving him an unpleasant experience, i.e. separation from home and his appreciation of this'. Being a woman probation officer in a male penal institution may have affected her apparent incorporation into the prevailing penal ideology.

However the most common reasons for non-involvement were not particular to the child nor the probation officer concerned, but were due to the more general constraints which are experienced by probation officers working in penal institutions where there are young offenders. The constraints experienced by probation officers working in remand centres and adult local prisons are different from those imposed by Home Office policy in detention centres and youth custody centres in the UK, but their effects are similar: to prevent structured help for child inmates. In remand centres and adult institutions, including youth custody allocating establishments, the problem is that inmates of all ages, or children in particular, are supposed to be held there for only a short time before being moved to another institution or sent to court. Thus their length of stay is uncertain and there is thought not to be enough time to undertake any planned programme.

Many probation officers explained their non-involvement in these terms, for example from an adult prison in the North West of England: 'He will only remain here for a matter of weeks and the help offered to him tends to be superficial and in the main concerned with information giving prior to his transfer to a youth custody centre.' 'Because of transfer, time only to discuss social enquiry report' (remand centre attached to an adult prison). 'There are no specific goals in any work which might be done with this young man, as he will only be at [the prison] for a few days before he is allocated to a YCC.' 'Unfortunately he will be transferred within the next 6 days so little time to do any positive work, other than go through the SER with him and discuss the reasons for offending.' 'Brief intervention in case of immediate problems during short stay prior to transfer' (adult prison again).

> Seen on Probation Reception Board, any immediate problems dealt with. Made aware of what help etc. probation can offer whilst awaiting

court appearance. Advised to make application to see probation when necessary. No case work undertaken at this stage nor probation file made up. If he were to receive a sentence in excess of 18 months a probation file would be opened as he could remain at [the prison] for some time.

As suggested here, a child's temporary stay in an adult prison await-ing allocation can extend for some time. One 16-year-old boy on a ten-month sentence had been in that particular prison for 5 weeks already on the census date, but the probation officer wrote that there had been 'no contact with him other than when he first was received.' Another 16-year-old serving a four-month youth custody sentence had been in the same prison for about 6 weeks and was expected to remain for another 4 awaiting an appearance at the local juvenile court on a further charge of 'tampering with a motor vehicle'. Sometimes remands in custody can last for a long time, if an exceptionally busy juvenile court is involved or if there are delays in presentation of evidence by the prosecution. A 16-year-old boy from the West Midlands had already spent nearly six months in custody at a remand centre awaiting trial and then sentence on charges of taking and driving away motor vehicles and assaulting a policewoman.

The limits to the probation officer's role imposed by Home Office policy in UK detention and youth custody centres have been dis-cussed earlier in this chapter. Respondents variously described the effects of this policy on their work; some had virtually no contact with inmates, others only under restricted circumstances. 'Being a Senior Singleton Post at [the YCC] I have no direct contact with trainees due to the prison staff now carrying out the "welfare role". I am here in a liaison/advisory role only.' 'Since the day-to-day welfare problems have been undertaken by the prison officers under the personal officer scheme I am only called upon to see a trainee if the prison staff is unable to resolve the difficulty' (detention centre in the South West). 'I am a liaison officer for the YCC and have limited client contact with trainees.' 'My present role not to focus on direct casework, but only discharge arrangements, specific problems, as they arise' (detention centre in the South East). About a black 16-year-old who had been in residential care since he was 10 with at least eleven moves between establishments including two secure units and three other penal institutions, the probation officer in a South Western youth custody centre wrote: 'I only work specifically with longer term inmates and would therefore only deal with him by handling problem areas he presents to me — none so far.'

The senior probation officer in a youth custody centre in the

South West of England explained what the prison officer's role was supposed to be under the post-1983 policy:

> In this YCC a personal officer system operates for each trainee/inmate. The personal officer is a prison officer with particular responsibilities to assist a trainee during his period here. The personal officer (known as the unit training officer) will (a) get to know the trainee, (b) be available to advise on training courses, ocupation whilst here, and (c) assist with contact from family and home social worker/probation officer.

Similarly another senior probation officer wrote about a 16-year-old boy from the South East who was serving five months' youth custody for stealing £35: 'His unit training officer would know him in a helping capacity. This UTO will be responsible for advising him on a training plan and being attentive to welfare needs. Progress reports will be sent from UTO to the home supervising social worker/ probation officer.' Under such a scheme, a probation officer working in a penal institution seems to have no role beyond maintaining a token probation service presence from which the inmates are unlikely to benefit; it sounds an unrewarding job.

It is difficult to tell from this census survey what prison officers are making of their new welfare role. Although the questionnaire was addressed equally to prison officers and probation officers, and separate sets of papers were mailed to the two services in each institution in Scotland, Northern Ireland and the Irish Republic (in England and Wales it was agreed that papers for the institution should go through the probation office), very few returns on individual children were received from prison officers acting as personal officers under the new scheme. None of them suggested that the officers were giving personal help to the children in any recognizable social work sense of the word. Those comments which were received were of two kinds. In the first case, the relationship between prison officer and trainee seems to have been no different than before the new welfare scheme started. One officer wrote that he supervised a 16-year-old boy's employment as a cleaner in the work department of a youth custody centre, and referred to this as 'case work'. In the second type of response the personal officer had clearly found out quite a lot about the children's family background, but seemed to have interpreted this information at a rather superficial level. For example, one officer in a Scottish detention centre wrote about a 16-year-old boy from one of the Western islands:

> This man lives with his parents whilst his older brother and sisters live outwith the family home. There have been parental problems in the past with trial separations with [sic] father and mother. It appeared they are together again and the family situation is more stable.

His recent offences appear to have been concerned with thoughtless teenage pranks rather than of any criminal intent. He seems to have learned from his present sentence that he does not like being in the Institution and this could be a deterrent from him against criminal activities in the future. It does not appear that he needs any special counselling at present.

The boy had already served a previous custodial sentence, which puts the likelihood of deterrence in doubt; his current three-month sentence was for two charges of breach of the peace. The same officer reached a similar conclusion about another 16-year-old (and indeed about many of the boys in his charge):

> Parents separated five months ago and he will return to family home on liberation. He had been behaving well until this incident but does realise that he has been rather stupid and there is a possibility that this might be a solitary incident. He claims he committed the offence in order to get cash to return home to a sick mother whilst he was in the berry fields in the Blairgowrie area. Does not appear to require further counselling.

This city boy had been under a social work supervision order; his current offences were salmon poaching and jumping bail.

The new government throughcare policy, to phase out the involvement of institution-based probation officers and introduce the personal officer scheme for children in custody, relies explicitly on increased input from the social worker or probation officer who will supervise the child when he returns home (this is made clear in the relevant circulars, for example Home Office, 1983). There was a strong impression from the survey that the probation officers who remained in the institutions thought this was not happening, at least for the youngest age group of child prisoners with whom we are concerned. Because about half of them had actually been under care orders when they were taken into custody, it was likely that local authority social workers would have been responsible for supervising them on release as often as probation officers (in Scotland, of course, it is the same agency). Yet visits from social workers to the children in their care while they were in penal institutions seem to have been rare, particularly when the institution was some distance away from their home authority — and remember only 13 per cent of children were imprisoned near home.

Intervention from a distance by a future supervising officer on a child's behalf also seems to have been unusual, as a senior probation officer in an English youth custody centre commented: 'All trainees have a supervising probation officer or social worker who could, in theory, refer to specialist agencies, but in practice, I am not aware of this happening.'

Some quite critical comments were made about local authority social workers by probation officers who responded to the survey. Sometimes these were at a general level, for example: 'It constantly surprises me that social workers will recommend custody for clients subject to care orders in social enquiry reports, with the expectation that imprisonment will provide some form of treatment' (senior probation officer in an English youth custody and detention centre). Derogatory remarks were also made over individual cases. A senior probation officer in an English remand centre wrote that a 16-year-old boy under a supervision order after leaving residential care, 'has seen social worker about three times in past three months. Said social worker didn't make appointment. He just turned up at the house.' Another senior in an English youth custody centre said that his objective was 'facilitating contact with new probation officer — previous relationship with social worker was very bad.' The 16-year-old boy, from the North East, had been taken into care five months previously under Section 1 of the Children and Young Persons Act 1969, as being 'beyond control'. The YCC senior wrote: 'Care order revoked during present sentence. . . . Probation service will now supervise. No contact from social worker since sentence. Probation officer has recently written. . . . . Too short a sentence to be included in the long-term assessment and review procedures.' Such implicit accusations of bad practice may, of course, have been the result of inter-professional rivalry between probation and social workers. No detailed comments were made about probation officers who had previously supervised children.

Where would they go on release?
Most respondents would have regarded it as the responsibility of the child's supervising probation officer or social worker, not themselves, to make sure that he had somewhere suitable to live after leaving the institution. But many had clearly discussed the matter with the children and perhaps also with their future supervisors, and an unprompted answer was given in practically every case to the question of where the child would go on release. Two-thirds were expected to go and live with their parents. The only other sizeable group was where all concerned had no idea what would happen. Nine per cent were to return to open residential care, secure accommodation or foster care, or would be placed in some sort of supported accommodation. This latter solution, which applied to only 2 per cent of the whole population, represents the only genuine attempt to arrange after-care accommodation before the child was released from custody. The accommodation involved was

hostels, supported lodgings, or special leaving care schemes. The remaining individuals (another 2 per cent) were expected to make their own arrangements, usually in board and lodgings, or to become homeless.

These findings indicate that all but a tiny minority of children leaving penal institutions can expect little practical help with after-care arrangements before they are released. Of course action may be taken at the last minute when they are actually on the point of leaving, but there was no evidence from the survey to suggest that this was happening. It would not, in any case, have been a very satisfactory solution, involving a lot of avoidable uncertainty for the child concerned. It seems likely that a claim that a child can go and live with his parents is taken at face value, and that everyone waits to see if he gets there and how long it is before the arrangement breaks down. When it does, some temporary alternative may be arranged on an emergency basis.

Only children who had previously been in residential care had any advance arrangements made for them, and well over half of those who had been in care were expected to live with their parents. All of the children who had never been in care were said to be going back to their parents, or there was no idea what would happen. All of the children who had never been removed from their parental home before their current spell in custody were expected to return to their parents. How realistic were these expectations?

Because a child had not been in care and had never previously been removed from home, this did not necessarily mean that all was well at home and between him and his parents, ensuring a warm welcome back. Indeed, family disruption may well have been the precipitating factor in the child's offending which resulted in the custodial sentence. One 15-year-old from the North West, serving a three-month sentence for burglary, had never been removed from home before and was expected to return there. But earlier in the year his parents had divorced and they were still living together in the same house; a situation likely to cause domestic tension and pressure on the boy. Sometimes it was clear that there had already been conflict between a child and his parents. A 15-year-old from an East Midlands pit village, serving his first sentence for burglary, was expected to return home. But he had already run away from home before his arrest and slept rough for a while. The probation officer wrote: 'This young man is uncertain of his gender. He was transferred from a D.C. to a hospital unit of a Y.O.C. to assist him in his first custodial sentence.' There was no reason to suppose that the situation would be resolved by his time in custody.

Among those who had already been removed from home into

residential care, the question of why they had been received into care in the first place must be relevant to their prospects of settling in with their parents again. As already explained, insufficient details were provided of the statutory bases and reasons for care proceedings for analysis of this data to be used, though it can be said that reasons for original admission to care were by no means all to do with offending. Many children had been received into care at an early age because of inadequate home circumstances, abuse or neglect, or at their parents' own request. Others were said to be beyond their parents' control. Subsequent offending might lead an authority to seek parental rights when an interim care order had been made on other grounds. The care histories of many of these children suggest that relations with their parents had been too seriously damaged for all to be suddenly made right when they were discharged from custody.

This can be the case also when admission to care had resulted from more recent adolescent crises. One 16-year-old boy from a city in the North West had been the subject of a care order when he was 14 because he was said to be 'beyond control'. He had previously received a supervision order, intermediate treatment and an attendance centre sentence. In the space of less than 2 years he seems to have been through foster care, two children's homes, secure accommodation in a CHE, two detention centres and two youth custody centres. There is no reason to suppose that these experiences would have made him any more easy to live with than 2 years earlier when he was described as 'beyond control', yet he was to be returned to his parental home.

A 16-year-old girl from outer London, serving nine months' youth custody for property offences, had been the subject of a care order when she was 14 'because of difficulties at home but then made into "secure" order because of offending.' She 'went straight from home into residential care', and in just over 2 years had been through two children's homes, two open assessment centres and two secure units in assessment centres. She had absconded from all of the open establishments and 'lived in hotels for short periods' whilst on the run. (At age 15, her hotel room rent could not have been paid by social security benefits, so she was presumably being given money by adults.) The probation officer wrote,

> She says she is Afro-Caribbean. I would have classified her as Caucasian unless she told me. Seems thoroughly confused about her identity as a person. Am trying to help her have some sense of who she really is so that she does not need to live in a world of pretence.

She was about to be released at the time of the census: 'Now able to return home. Social worker reluctant to enforce care order and hopes girl will find own lodgings.'

Sometimes it seemed doubtful whether there actually was a parental home for the child to return to, as with one 15-year-old who came from somewhere in the South East. Before being sent to a youth custody centre (he had served a previous detention centre sentence); he had been living with his mother in a bed-and-breakfast hotel used for homeless families in Camden. The probation officer who filled in the survey form did not apparently appreciate the significance of this when he stated that the boy would be released to 'his mother's house'. It can take a couple of years for a homeless family to be rehoused in inner London, and no one seemed to have checked whether the mother was still living in a hotel room with her other children. This boy had already been through residential care, including secure accommodation, but he told the probation officer that an application for care order (by an unnamed authority) had been unsuccessful, so he would be supervised by probation on release.

Arrangements which children were expected to make for themselves sounded equally insubstantial. A Scottish 16-year-old who had just started remand in an adult prison was said to be 'returning home but thinking of looking for bed and breakfast accommodation. Mother and father separated two months ago. Stayed with father.' Under 18-year-olds receive a lower rate of supplementary benefit than adults, which make it difficult to pay for independent accommodation. Moreover, around the time this particular boy would have been finishing his anticipated sentence, new regulations imposed stringent cost limits and time limits (4 weeks in the city to which he was returning) on young people claiming benefit in board and lodgings. So his proposed solution could not have lasted for long.

There were, of course, exceptions and some children were receiving positive help towards resettlement after they left the institution. One Irish Republic probation officer wrote about a 15-year-old who was serving six months for 'malicious damage', that he had 'left home approximately three months prior to commencing current sentence. Stayed with various friends during this period and slept rough occasionally. The two nights prior to commencing sentence were spent in a probation hostel.' Shortly before leaving home he had spent a week remanded in custody, his first time away from his parents. He had completed two probation orders when he was 13 and 14. The probation officer in the institution said that she was 'working towards improving relationships between this young person and his family and arranging for him to return to his parental home when he is released from custody.' The social worker in a Scottish young offenders' institution wrote about a 16-year-old: 'Negotiation with parents to allow return home, on completing of sentence. Should be a possibility and is the most practical assistance that can be given. A Welsh 16-year-old, serving four months in an East Midlands detention centre for property offences, had previously lived with his parents but had spent some time in an open assessment centre, and had 'left home on two occasions for short periods', and slept rough. He was currently under a supervision order. It was 'not known at this stage' where he would go on release: 'He has stated that he does not wish to return home and efforts are being made to obtain alternative accommodation', so his wishes were being taken seriously. But with all the will and time in the world (which probation officers and institutions do not have), it would probably be quite impractical to make advance arrangements for appropriate after-care accommodation for all the under-17-year-olds leaving penal institutions who need it. Providing resources of this sort has not been a priority in any of the jurisdictions of the British Isles.

7 Secure units

Probably most readers will know what prisons look like. Some may even have been inside one to visit an inmate, or to admire its architectural features as an historic monument, as some are former castles or stately homes. But it is unlikely that you will ever have seen a secure unit. Compared with penal institutions, they are small establishments and tend not to advertize their presence in an area. So what are they like?

Describing secure accommodation
Most secure units, at least in England and Wales, consist of sleeping quarters, and associated day rooms, for a few children actually within, or attached to, an open establishment. The overall mean shown in the census survey was around 4 secure beds per unit. In England and Wales the 'parent' establishment is most likely to be an assessment centre. In the other jurisdictions they tend to be longer-stay establishments: List D schools in Scotland, and Irish equivalents (training schools, reformatories). Table 7.1 shows the types of establishment in the four jurisdictions.

Table 7.1   Types of secure unit in the four jurisdictions

	England & Wales	Scotland	Northern Ireland	Irish Republic	Total
	Jurisdiction				
Type of unit					
Assessment	26 = 90% = 55	2	—	1	29 = 100% = 49%
CHE etc.*	16 = 70% = 34%	4 = 17% = 50%	2	1	23 = 100% = 39%
Multi-purpose	3	2	—	—	5 = 100% = 9%
YTC	2	—			2
Total	47 = 80% = 100%	8 = 14% = 100%	2 = 3% = 100%	2 = 3% = 100%	59 = 100%

(N = establishments)
Note:
*Includes List D school, training school, reformatory.

However, some secure units, particularly of the CHE/List D school type, are much larger and more autonomous institutions. These may stand on their own as wholly secure establishments, or may have attached to them smaller open units where children are placed for a while as part of a programme towards being discharged. In this case the secure unit is the 'parent' establishment and any open accommodation is there for its use.

This contrasts with the previous example where the open 'parent' establishment can operate without actually using its attached secure unit. There the secure accommodation is intended to be a resource for the open establishment: somewhere to hold children who cannot be contained in an open unit. But in practice children tend to be referred from elsewhere to establishments like this specifically for the purpose of placing them in secure accommodation.

Numbers of secure beds in the larger, more autonomous units are higher. The maximum secure capacity found in the survey was around 35, depending on sex (secure units for girls only are much smaller, but those taking either sex are the largest of all). As these larger units are mainly of the CHE type, rather than for assessment purposes, this means that although half of the secure units overall (more in England and Wales) are in assessment centres, less than a third of the children are in this type of accommodation. The survey showed that two-thirds of the children who were locked up in secure child-care accommodation on the census day were in CHEs, List D and similar schools, and youth treatment centres. The details are shown in Table 7.2.

Forms of security
Descriptions of the lay-out of different secure units and what makes them secure can help to give us an impression of what they are like. The actual security precautions are quite complex, and in England, Wales and Scotland are subject to technical specifications drawn up for the government by architects (Blumenthal, 1985, describes these). Windows made of thick polycarbonate instead of glass, in narrow frames set into walls with reinforced metal girders, prevent children from climbing or literally breaking out. Doors are made of steel. Observation windows allow staff to see into every part of every room. Minimal bedroom furniture is built into the walls and floor so that it cannot be unbolted and used as a weapon. There is no inflamable bedding, nor any breakable material which could be detached and filed to a sharp point. Particular care is taken to avoid high ledges or hooks from which children could hang them-selves. Walking round a secure unit, it feels like a sensorily deprived

Table 7.2   Numbers of children in the different types of secure unit

	Jurisdiction				
	England & Wales	Scotland	Northern Ireland	Irish Republic	Total
Type of unit					
Assessment	97 = 92% = 43%	1	—	7 = 7% = 19%	105 = 100% = 31%
CHE etc.*	87 = 46% = 38%	50 = 27% = 96%	23 = 12%	29 = 15% = 81%	189 = 100% = 56%
Multi-purpose	10 = 4%	1	—	—	11 = 100% = 3%
YTC	34 = 15%	—	—	—	34 = 100% = 10%
Total	228 = 67% = 100%	52 = 15% = 100%	23 = 7% = 100%	36 = 11% = 100%	339 = 100%

(N = individual children on whom information was returned)
Note:
*Includes List D school, training school, reformatory.

environment, controlled by the routinized locking and unlocking of doors.

The survey questionnaire asked what made each unit's accommodation secure. The following quotations reflect the range of responses received from smaller units: 'Physical factors — e.g. locked buildings, window types, general design features' (English assessment centre with little-used secure accommodation for 4 children of either sex). 'Specially designed separate unit consisting of three bedrooms, lounge, bathroom and separate toilet. Small exercise yard. Quite separate from other living accommodation' (in a Welsh CHE). One small unit for two children which was 'due to be upgraded to comply with new regulations' already had 'bedrooms [with] armoured plate glass. Entrance door can be locked as can bedroom doors.' Another specified 'secure features, e.g. locked doors, polycarbonate windows, etc. Separate unit within the main complex with a high staff ratio.' This unit in a multi-purpose centre was described as an 'Intensive Treatment Facility'. Similarly, another was 'part of a purpose-built intensive care unit with secure provision.' Descriptions of the regimes in these two establishments gave no hint of what made their 'intensive care' different from practice in other units. A unit for girls in an English CHE sounded more familiar: 'Separate building with secure facilities and individual rooms. In school grounds close to main school.' An assessment centre unit in Yorkshire and Humberside was frankly described as having 'three locked separate cells.''

The larger secure units sounded more insular and self-contained but they also seemed to have more internal facilities, presumably because of economies of scale resulting from their size. Some sounded like classic total institutions: 'Each bedroom secure. Each bedroom designed to be locked. All bedrooms are locked at night. Living areas designed to be locked. Exercise area secure. School room secure' (an English assessment centre). 'Specially designed 30 bedded building. Three self-contained units of 10 beds each with living areas, plus a school block, gymnasium, playgrounds and provision for playing fields — all inside security' (Irish Republic). The emphasis in both these establishments was on physical security; a new English assessment centre with secure accommodation for 8 boys emphasized other factors:

> The Unit is purpose built with lounge, dining room, single bedrooms, recreational and educational rooms and outside recreational area. The staff team comprising a team leader, three group leaders and eight care staff are drawn from the main staff group and slowly rotated to gain experience in all parts of the Centre. Security is, therefore, achieved through a combination of human and physical resources neither of which are adequate independently.

Some of the largest secure units must be recognizable from the outside as custodial institutions, from their locked gates and high wire fences. One English establishment for 30 children was described: 'All three treatment houses have secure perimeters and almost invariably the front door remains locked. Young people from Houses 2 and 3 use the central studies block and refectory which are geographically separate from the units, which differs from House 1, which is totally self-contained.' A Northern Irish unit was in a 'building [which] was originally designed as a Grade "C" prison and used as a Borstal. Modified internally to meet our needs.' Twenty beds in this secure building were designated as official secure accommodation 'for immediate use' and we were given details about the 16 boys in them. But there were apparently another 50 beds 'for project use, e.g. secure remand provision', about which no further details were provided. If any children were in this other accommodation they would form part of the child population in hidden custody, incarcerated but not counted, which will be discussed in Chapter 8.

Extra restraints
Besides all the security precautions which have been described above, about four-fifths of the establishments which the survey identified used extra forms of restraint. A quarter of the boys and 43 per cent of the girls who were in secure units on the census date were subject to these extra forms of restraint. The clearly different treat-

ment of the sexes — unremarked upon by survey respondents — suggests that girls are regarded as more difficult subjects in security than boys. The forms of restraint used included: separation of the child in a room specifically intended for the purpose or in his or her own bedroom; intensive supervision by a member of staff, known as 'specialling' in the health service; withdrawal of 'privileges' or 'rewards' or, conversely, the imposition of specific punishments; use of drugs, or physical restraint. I shall give examples of each shortly. Many secure units had a written set of guidelines about permissible methods of restraining children. Sometimes these were rules prescribed by departmental management direct or through the social services (or equivalent) committee. Sometimes they were practice guidelines which had been developed within the unit itself, probably in consultation with immediate line management, usually as an integral part of a broader regime or therapeutic method to which staff were working. Regimes followed in security will be discussed later. In either case, it often seemed that a quite detailed tariff had been worked out, reacting to particular breaches of perceived good behaviour with predetermined responses. Others followed a more ad hoc or personalized policy, like an assessment centre in east London: 'Any form of constraint would be directly connected to client's action or inaction.' Several respondents specified forms of restraint which were *not* practised in their establishment.

Probably the most common method of controlling unacceptable behaviour is separation of the child(ren) concerned from the rest of the group. 'Some excessive behaviour causes removal from the group.' When this is done in a special separation room it is under conditions specified by the DHSS (in England and Wales) or the Scottish Office (in Scotland): 'A strictly regulated time-out procedure is available if a boy inflicts physical damage onto other people or the environment.' 'Young people can be placed in separation rooms, i.e. rooms other than their own bedrooms. This is monitored very carefully indeed and monthly returns are sent to DHSS.' However use of these special separation rooms is officially discouraged and they are apparently being phased out.

Confining a child to his or her own bedroom is much more convenient and, from the evidence of this survey, much more common. It is a practice which is, no doubt, as old as residential care, and as such is unregulated — though at the time of writing, the DHSS is considering introducing controls in response to a publicized incident (*Social Work Today*, 7 April 1986, p. 3). Respondents variously mentioned: 'Time out in bedroom in cases of physical aggression towards peers and/or staff'; 'Time out — isolation in bedroom constantly observed by staff.'

Types of action vary but generally follow the principle of remove child from group and try to talk out problem and reach an agreement about future behaviour. If no agreement is reached child may be placed in bedroom with team leader's consent. Member of staff involved stays with the child all the time till problem is resolved.

In these examples the bedroom is being used as a substitute separation room or observation facility. In other cases it is less clear what goes on: 'early bedtimes'; 'excluded from some activities, early bed'; 'early to bed, wearing pyjamas'. Does this mean that children are sent to bed early as a punishment, much as might happen to young children in their own home, so that they miss the evening's television viewing? Or could it mean that children are forced to spend extended periods of the day in their bedrooms in their nightclothes?

The social work press has reported the case of a teenage girl who was stripped and put in her room, who unsuccessfully sued the male worker concerned for assault (*Social Work Today*, 10 February 1986, 7 April 1986). As only the fact that a male worker had stripped a female client was at issue, this suggests that the practice itself is quite common.

'Specialling' as a method of restraint was used rather less often, perhaps because of its staff-intensive nature. Respondents referred to: 'occasional individual supervision for example, with repeated absconders.' 'Young people may be placed on constant supervision, i.e. they must stay with a member of staff at all times.' 'Very occasionally, to prevent the use of more secure conditions, a child will be placed under individual supervision of a staff member. This permits in depth, one to one, work with a very disturbed child.' 'For severe behaviours — staff may be allocated to supervise on a one-to-one basis — depends on staffing levels and is variable. One case required one-to-one supervision for nearly two years.'

Withdrawal of 'privileges' or 'rewards' was sometimes done on an ad hoc basis: 'Sanctions can take form of loss of some privileges, for example, use of record players, television.' More often it was done as a systematic response, involving loss of a positive reinforcer, in a behaviour modification programme: 'Lower levels of access to reinforcers in the Centre if behaviour does not meet desired level.' 'Positive reinforcement. Points system used — privileges can be earned.' 'A points based levels system is operated as part of a sequential treatment model in order to give positive reinforcement to children who display appropriate behaviours.' 'Behaviour modification: Token Economy approach to treatment programmes for individuals in security.' 'Unit operates a Tier System whereby behaviour is assessed and recorded on a card for each period of the day, i.e. range from 15 mins. to 1 hour. The Tier System is based on "privilege" earning.' Some establishments seemed to take a straight-forward sentencing approach: 'Fines for destruction or vandalism'; 'restitution to damage (all or part)'; 'extra housework.' 'Targets (which include completion of specific tasks) are imposed for gross inconsideration to others, i.e. disruption of class, absconding, etc., both defined to help young people to recognise consequences of action.'

Use of physical restraint to control children was mentioned by two respondents: 'Only when needed to stop young people hurting themselves or others.' Drugs also seemed to be used infrequently, but were not unknown: 'The use of medication is strictly regulated within the Centre and would only be utilised if it was a "treatment of choice" agreed by the medical officer. No boy may be prescribed medication which is intended to overtly control his behaviour without the agreement of the Social Services Committee.' 'Medication is not used but sedation has on occasions been necessary and is possible within our policy. There is one recorded use of sedation during the last twelve months.' 'Medication — reluctantly used — only upon prescription from Doctor — child may refuse.'

An equal number of respondents stated categorically that drugs were never used in their unit: 'The use of medication for purposes of control is explicitly prohibited'; 'Medication has not and never will be used.' One indicated that the use of any extra forms of restraint would be regarded as a sign of defeat: 'Being a relatively high staffed secure unit, we never have to use medication for control purposes and seldom resort to withholding privileges (such as they are in security!).' Some units which run token economy behaviour modification programmes made it clear that negative reinforcers were not used and some things were regarded as a child's inalienable right: 'No reduction allowed in earned privileges, or home leave or contact'; 'Young people have fundamental rights of access to family, social workers, food, bed, etc.'

Regimes

As in the questionnaire to penal institutions, respondents were asked to describe any distinctive features of their unit's regime; an open-ended question which received a wide range of answers. Most units did seem to operate regimes which were based on explicit principles, though some rejected the idea. Behavior modification systems have already been mentioned, and this was the most clearly standardized form of regime, whose principles are described in turn by the officers in charge of a large Irish secure unit and a regional assessment centre in London:

The secure unit operates on a sequential system, all admissions being through the first unit, progressing via the second unit to the third unit and discharge. The orientation of the school is behavioural and the programme operates broadly on the principles of social learning theory. A Token Economy system is in operation with points as the currency.

The methods used are based on social learning theory and recognise the interdependency of assessment and treatment. The approach therefore, is essentially prescriptive and based on functional analysis, identifying treatment objectives and appropriate methods of achieving them. The methods essentially focus on reinforcement of appropriate behaviour and teaching new skills utilising modelling, behaviour rehearsal, token reinforcement, social skills teaching, contingency contracting, counselling and group work methods. The programmes adopted are essentially sequential commencing with a basic programme focussing on response to simple and clear expectations with token reinforcement and graduating to personal targets with token reinforcement to contingency contracting progressively phasing out specific reinforcement strategies. Each boy has a keyworker who is responsible for the collation of reports and the boy's general welfare during his placement.

In the first example the sequential system was applied to 30 children in a closed, secure institution. In the second example the secure accommodation for 8 children was one stage within a wider, largely open system. There were other examples of social learning theory being applied to just a few individuals. As behaviour modification systems treat the individual as a commodity progressing through the system, presumably they can be applied to just one person.

The therapeutic community, a rival method to behaviour modification, was very much less in evidence. Its theoretical base is psychotherapeutic group interaction, as described by the director of a 'mixed secure residential establishment operating a psychodynamic treatment philosophy. The strands of the treatment are the warm, supportive milieu; the emphasis on individual counselling; the group work which is central to the treatment; and the intensive family work.'

A common type of regime emphasized individual programmes for children directed towards discharge, often combined with attempts at participative democracy: 'Regime attempts to maintain sufficient flexibility to meet the needs of individual children. Children involved in decisions regarding their treatment and future combined with facility to express opinions.' 'Emphasis is always placed on solving the problems which brought the child here, and on achieving re-integration to an appropriate placement which is usually within the child's own family or community. Preparation for reintegration is continuous and is based on Social Skills Training' (a CHE in the South West of England). 'Pattern of treatment based on individual treatment and educational plans, reviewed monthly or three monthly. Full girl participation in planning, discussion and reviews. General environment of Good Order, sound adult/girl relationships based on small group living, key workers, individual counselling, weekly girl staff meetings and some girl committees' (a Welsh CHE). The policy paper sent from a new secure unit in a London CHE recognized that,

> We are asking staff to undertake a task that is highly complex and arduous .... It is intended that each girl admitted will have an individual programme which will take into consideration the emotional, social and educational factors in her life. The programme will aim to develop the girl's realisation of her own worth, assist her in experiencing satisfaction through achievement, to develop self-discipline and the ability to postpone immediate gratification, and to help her acquire socially acceptable behaviour and habits and to appreciate the needs and feelings of others.

While that unit was just opening, a multi-purpose children's centre in Scotland seemed to have decided not to use its 2-bedded secure unit, with no residents in security on the census date and none admitted during a previous three-month period; 'The most distinctive feature of the regime is our willingness to attempt to prepare an individual, community oriented treatment programme to meet a child's specific needs. The programme for each child is monitored closely at 4-6 week intervals. We deliberately eschew long term residential care.'

A number of regimes were frankly eclectic, such as one large secure unit in a CHE in the North of England which used 'a variety of behaviour modification, counselling and group treatment methods.' The principal of an assessment centre in the East Midlands wrote: 'Notwithstanding security procedures we are keen to retain good care practices and would use any technique or social work strategy to advance the needs of an individual child. Natural relationships developed to encourage growth in a non-repressive structure. We would like to describe ourselves as progressive but not permissive. Structured but not rigid.' Eclecticism seems there to have been a deliberate choice, but in the account from a CHE secure unit in the North West it was difficult to comprehend any clear rationale: 'The infrastructure of the Unit's philosophy is security and care which underpins a plethora of individual rehabilitative programmes which in turn are underscored with ongoing programmes of familial interaction/preparing for life.'

Some regimes could be characterized as liberal: 'An accepting, warm and permissive regime within a physically secure perimeter';

'an easy, gentle management of the children as a prelude to multi-faceted assessment of their condition' (both English assessment centres). 'High level of tolerance to absconding and other forms of acting out aggressive and violent behaviour. Good staffing levels, good support to staff, good general conditions for children and staff and a pleasant living environment' (Scottish multi-purpose centre with 2 secure beds). 'The climate is non-repressive, youngsters are encouraged to voice their feelings, thoughts, anxieties and fears as much as they are encouraged to retain and develop their identity and personality. There is an air and sense of doing something prevailing. Relationships are based on honesty and accountability. Cultural compatibility also helps' (a multi-purpose centre in Wales).

Others explicitly rejected this sort of liberal image: 'Whilst we aim to have a high degree of consideration for girls and develop the individual's ability to make decisions for herself, it is *not* envisaged that the regime will be permissive. All growth involves conflict, constraint and restraint and this can be painful, but firmness is often necessary so that we may support a girl through difficult and emotional times until she is able to support herself' (London CHE). Two units, both in English shire county assessment centres, sounded rather repressive: 'It is a Regional resource dealing with a high number of boys deemed unmanageable in other establishments. Regime is structured and controlling.' 'We do not have a "regime". We have control and structure as we believe that one cannot have care if the former do not exist.' The officer in charge of this unit in the East Midlands believed that the main drawback to secure accommodation was that it was 'too comfortable'.

A few establishments responded in unexpected ways. Staff in one Northern assessment centre with 3 secure beds seemed to have lost sight of any positive purpose to their work with children in security, and wrote in bureaucratic terms about the regime;

> Follows strictly the spirit of the 1969 Act with regard to good professional practices, also the recommendations of Local Authority Circular (75)1 with respect to children in Secure Accommodation. A *daily* review of child held in security and a bed in the open unit for every child held securely, i.e. we do not accept a child in the secure unit *unless* we also have a bed in our open unit.

This may have been a defensive reaction to insecurity within their own organization; this particular unit had recently been investigated by outside researchers. In emphasizing the generic nature of their establishment, a couple of respondents seemed to gloss over the fact that children were locked up in security. For example a senior social worker from a large secure establishment in England wrote of 'active community based programmes, including youth training schemes, family placement, etc.' The principal of a multi-purpose centre in the South East wrote:

> [this] is a multi-function Centre providing a range of services both residential and non-residential for children and their families. Non-residential activities at the present time include I.T., fieldwork, foster care and adolescent placement. In addition to residential work there is a small educational facility although most children go to outside schools. The Centre has been very successful in integrating field and residential work. Within the total residential facility there is a small intensive facility for 4/5 children which operates within secure conditions.

Finally, some of the smallest secure units with only 1 or 2 beds, used occasionally, clearly regarded security as peripheral to their work. For example the respondent from a young persons' centre in the South East of England wrote, 'our secure unit is only used for emergency admissions and for holding young people until such suitable accommodation as deemed necessary is found elsewhere.' Its 2 beds were empty on the census day and had been used for only 5 children during the past year, for a few days each.

The children in security

Among the children in official secure accommodation in the four jurisdictions, boys outnumbered girls by more than five to one, but nearly all the girls were in England and Wales where they formed a quarter of the population (none in either part of Ireland). One in ten overall were from racial minorities, again nearly all in England and Wales. No particular racial minority group predominated. Nearly two-thirds of the children were aged under 16. Very young teenage girls were less likely to be locked up than boys; only 18 per cent of girls were aged 14 or under, compared with 30 per cent of boys. Table 7.3 shows the details. In many respects the age distributions within the four jurisdictions were remarkably similar, with the exception of Northern Ireland: two-thirds of Northern Irish children were aged 16, against the general trend. The figures are set out in Table 7.4. Nor were there any under-14-year-olds in Northern Ireland. The very youngest children, two boys aged 10 and 11, were locked up in the Irish Republic. Of course, all of these children were even younger when they were put into secure units, if only by a few weeks or days. The differences were in fact considerable. More than three-quarters of the children overall were aged under 16 when they went into secure accommodation, and nearly two-fifths were 14 years or less.

Table 7.3   Sex and age of children in secure accommodation

| | Sex | | |
	Male	Female	Total
Age on census date			
16 years	93 = 83%	19 = 17%	112 = 100%
	= 36%	= 36%	= 36%
15 years	85 = 78%	24 = 22%	109 = 100%
	= 33%	= 45%	= 35%
14 years	47 = 90%	5 = 10%	52 = 100%
	= 18%	= 9%	= 17%
13 years or less	30 = 86%	5 = 14%	35 = 100%
	= 12%	= 9%	= 11%
Total	255 = 83%	53 = 17%	308
	= 100%	= 100%	= 100%

Table 7.4   Ages of children in secure accommodation in the four jurisdictions

| | Jurisdiction | | | | |
	England & Wales	Scotland	Northern Ireland	Irish Republic	Total
Age on census date					
16 years	70 = 63%	17 = 15%	14 = 13%	11 = 9%	112 = 100%
	= 35%	= 33%	= 66%	= 31%	= 36%
15 years	75 = 69%	19 = 17%	3 = 3%	12 = 11%	109 = 100%
	= 38%	= 37%	= 14%	= 33%	= 35%
14 years	29 = 56%	10 = 19%	4 = 8%	9 = 17%	52 = 100%
	= 15%	= 20%	= 19%	= 25%	= 17%
13 years or less	26 = 74%	5 = 14%	—	4 = 11%	35 = 100%
	= 13%	= 10%		= 11%	= 11%
Total	200 = 65%	51 = 17%	21 = 7%	36 = 12%	308
	= 100%	= 100%	= 100%	= 100%	= 100%

Where they came from

As so many children in secure units were from England (nearly two-thirds of the total), it is useful to make a more detailed geographical analysis of where they came from, as was done with the penal population in the last chapter. Nearly half of them were from the big conurbations, mainly metropolitan districts — just like the

Table 7.5 *Children in secure accommodation related to total numbers*
in care within England and Wales

Region (home address)	In care per 1,000 pop. under 18	Total care all ages	In Secure accom. all ages	As % of total in care
North West	8.17	13,513	56	= 0.41%
North	7.64	5,984	24	= 0.40%
Yorks. & Humberside	7.56	9,435	13	= 0.14%
East Midlands	6.91	6,820	11	= 0.16%
South East*	6.62	28,504	75	= 0.26%
West Midlands	6.57	8,864	14	= 0.16%
South West	6.35	6,450	15	= 0.23%
Wales	6.21	4,387	8	= 0.18%
East Anglia	4.88	2,595	8	= 0.31%
All England	7.05	82,165	233	= 0.27%
*incl. Greater London	9.92	15,278	41	= 0.27%

Source: DHSS (1984) *Children in Care in England and Wales, March 1983,* DHSS.

children in penal institutions. And again there was a concentration on the North of England, though less marked this time, with exactly half having had home addresses in the four regions of the North West, the North, the West Midlands, and Yorkshire and Humberside (in descending order of frequency). The North West stands out in particular, with more than a quarter of all the English children in secure accommodation coming from that one region alone. The South East including Greater London accounted for a third of the total, with only 16 per cent coming from homes in the remaining three regions of the South West, the East Midlands and East Anglia combined. Table 7.5 shows how these figures for secure accommodation relate to the numbers of children in care in each region.

When we look at where these children had been placed and were held in custody, the picture becomes complicated. Three factors are likely to be important to a geographical analysis and have to be taken into account: where is the secure unit actually located, that is within which local authority's boundaries? Which authority is responsible for its management? And finally, which authority is responsible for the care of the child? It is quite possible for these to be different authorities in the case of any one child, and all different again from the authority covering the child's home address.

It should be mentioned here that within England there were in official existence umbrella organizations called children's regional planning committees (CRPCs) which were supposed to coordinate major child-care services, including secure accommodation, for small groups of local authorities notionally sharing access to these services. The 12 CRPCs have not been used as a basis for geographical analysis for two reasons. Firstly, at the time of the census they seem effectively to have been defunct except for the one covering the London boroughs, so taking them as point of reference would not be useful. Secondly, because they relate to quite small groupings of local authorities which may, between them, manage only a couple of secure units, it could be too easy to identify individual establishments run by particular authorities. This would breach the undertaking of confidentiality which was given when the survey was conducted. For these reasons English local authorities have instead been grouped into the eight standard economic planning regions used by the Department of the Environment and other central government departments for analyzing social trends.

Among the 59 operational secure units in England and Wales, Scotland, Northern Ireland, and the Irish Republic, just over two-thirds were managed by the same local authority as the one within whose boundaries the unit was located. A quarter of those whose management and location were not the same were run by a central government department or a voluntary organization, that is by an agency which is not directly accountable to local government.

This was the case for all four secure units in Ireland, both north and south, and for three of the five units in Scotland. All four secure units in Wales were local to their managing authority. But in England while only two of the 43 secure units were managed by a central government department and one by a voluntary organization, more than a fifth were 'out-county', that is located within a different local authority to the one which managed them. Nearly two-thirds of the units in Greater London were in this position, and half of those in the North West. In part this is a legacy of the changes in local authority boundaries in 1966 and 1974 respectively. It probably also has something to do with differential property prices in urban and suburban or rural areas; inner-city authorities have tended to look for buildings to use as residential homes further out of town. Only a tenth of units managed by shire county council social services departments were located 'out-county', and these would all have been in the same authority before local government reorganization.

This distribution of secure units 'in' and 'out of county' is complicated enough, but the confusion really starts when you try to fit the children into the pattern. There is one rational factor: unless a court had made them the responsibility of a central government department (as under Section 53 in England and Wales, or Sections 206 and 413 in Scotland, for example) nearly all were in care to the same local authority as where they, or their parents, had lived. Only 4 per cent were the responsibility of a different social services (or equivalent) department to their home authority. That covers one of the factors which were identified above as being potentially important for geographical analysis. The other two were 'where is the secure unit located?' and 'which authority is responsible for its management?' In both cases what was happening to the children seemed to bear little relationship to the pattern of distribution already described of secure units among local authorities. Overall, only just over a third of the children in security were placed near home in an establishment located in the same local authority area as their home address; in England and Wales it was only a quarter (this distorts the position in the other three jurisdictions in each of which the majority of children were placed near home). This is a higher proportion than among the penal population which was discussed in the last chapter (that was just over 10 per cent). But remember that while the forces of law and order are responsible for allocating a child to a penal institution, as a punishment, it is normally the child's own care authority which makes the decision to place him or her in a secure unit, ostensibly in the child's best interests. Less than a third of the children were in a unit managed by the authority responsible for their care. (The comparable national figures for England and Wales are two-thirds for all CHEs and nine-tenths for all assessment centres: CIPFA, 1986, pp. 43-7). Altogether less than a quarter of the children in secure accommodaton in the four jurisdictions were in a unit which was both near home and managed by their own care authority.

Coming from a region where there was a lot of secure accommodation did not necessarily mean that a child could expect to be placed within the same region, even if it was in a different local authority. Less than two-fifths of children with home addresses in London were placed within the Greater London area. The rest had been sent out of London; another fifth to the counties in the South East and the remainder all over the country. Nine-tenths of the children in secure units in the North West came from the same region. But these were not all the children with home addresses in the North West. A quarter of the children who came from that region were dispersed around the country, including London. A logical explanation for this situation could be that the displaced children were being sent to specialist units far from home because it was only

162 Children in custody

there that their particular needs could be met. We shall see later whether this was likely to be the case, in discussing the reasons given for placement in secure accommodation.

Their previous history
One might have expected that the residential staff in secure units would have had information on record about reasons for each child being in care, to enable them to give appropriate help. That this was not the case may have been due to most of the children being referred from another authority, as I have just shown, and it may reflect the relatively low status of residential establishments within the social services hierarchy. One unit head commented that it seemed to take a very long time for children's files to reach him, but even then they were likely to be incomplete. Other researchers of secure accommodation have noticed this too (e.g. Lathaen, 1984; Millham *et al.*, 1977). Respondents were able to state the legislative provision under which the child was in care (Section and relevant sub-section), in 65 per cent of cases, with some less precise information for all but 9 per cent. Comparable full details relating to first admission to care were given for only 44 per cent, with no information at all on 29 per cent.

Forty-five per cent of all the children in secure accommodation were currently in care specifically for offending. In 10 per cent of cases the reason was not to do with offending but involved voluntary admission, being 'beyond parental control', abuse, moral danger. For more than a third it was unclear what reason lay behind, for example, a full care order under Section 3 of the Child Care Act 1980, or exactly which sub-section was involved of Section 1 of the Children and Young Persons Act 1969. Seventeen per cent of the children in secure accommodation in England and Wales were known to be in care under Section 7(7) of the 1969 Act, and a similar proportion had been remanded under that Act. Twenty-four children were in care for a serious offence, under Section 53 of the Children and Young Persons Act 1933, or the Scottish equivalent Section 206 of the Criminal Procedure Act.

At least 21 per cent of those on whom information was given had originally been admitted to care 'voluntarily' under Section 2 of the Child Care Act 1980 (previously Section 1 of the Children's Act 1948), or Section 15 of the Social Work (Scotland) Act. At least 29 per cent had originally been admitted under provisions specifically to do with offending, and offending was mentioned as a precipitant factor for 53 per cent. Beyond that, it is difficult to make a clear statement. The ages reported when children were first said to have been admitted to care were probably unreliable, insofar as they usually related to the date of a full care order, rather than the initiation of proceedings. It is likely also that much of the detail which follows about experiences of residential care relates only to the child's current care episode, earlier episodes not having been recorded in the same file. Unlike the probation officers in the penal institutions, secure unit social workers seem to have filled in the survey forms from case records and their general knowledge of the child; they did not do special interviews.

In exactly half the cases, some information was given about offences which children were said to have committed (the remaining half would have included an unknown number of non-offenders, as well as others for whom no details were given). Where offences were specified, in 57 per cent some level of violence against the person was involved, of a serious nature (including arson) in about a third of cases. There were more murderers and rapists in secure child-care accommodation than there were aged under 17 in penal institutions, but they should not be given undue emphasis; there were only 30 individuals in both sectors combined. Property offences were still the most common, but only just, and straight theft rather than burglary or taking vehicles was the commonest single offence, committed by nearly one in five. These were, of course, offences which related to their current 'sentence' or period of remand in secure accommodation.

In the past, usually before their first admission to residential care, the majority of these children had been subject to helping interventions on a non-residential basis. More than a fifth of the total were known to have been clients of the child guidance service, representing over two-fifths of the sub-group on whom such information was given. More than a third of this group had been under social work (or occasionally probation) supervision, over half of them with an intermediate treatment order attached. Special day education and family therapy also featured frequently. Some children had clearly gone straight into residential care with no previous intervention, but is is likely that others had also experienced these forms of help although it did not appear on their current case record.

Only 22 of the children in secure units had never been removed from their parental home before. The English *Review of Child Care Law* has commented on the practice of locking up children on reception into care, and has recommended limitations (DHSS, 1985, paras, 7.24, 7.25). Mainly those children who went straight into secure accommodation were remanded under the 1969 Act in England and Wales, or were under detention orders in the Republic of Ireland. Half of the children had been moved at least 4 times during their time in care; over a third had been moved more than 6 times. Nearly three-quarters of these children had previously been in open assessment centres, over half in open CHEs (or equivalent) and nearly half in ordinary children's homes. Only 15 per cent had ever been fostered. About two-fifths had already spent time in secure units, sometimes more than once. Twenty-nine per cent had already been in a penal institution, most commonly a remand centre, but nearly a fifth had served a detention centre or youth custody sentence. Thirteen per cent of those who had been removed from home before had been in-patients in a psychiatric (or occasionally mental handicap) hospital or adolescent unit, nearly always before admission to residential care. A similar number had been in 'special' boarding schools, usually also before admission to care. Altogether, 27 per cent of the under-17-year-old population of secure units had received 'special' education services for subnormal or maladjusted chlidren, on a day or boarding basis.

It seems that once these children in secure accommodation had been admitted to residential care, they tended to remain there; only a fifth had been 'home on trial' with their parents after their first removal from home. Half of the children had been in open residential care immediately before their current placement in security. Nearly a quarter had been in another secure unit, and another substantial group were in penal institutions, meaning that over a third of the total had been moved from one secure setting to another. In many cases it was not entirely clear where the decision to place a child in secure accommodation had originated. Some 17 per cent of placements were made at the instigation of the police or the court itself, formally the Secretary of State, because of the seriousness of the offence involved. Nearly a fifth of decisions to seek a secure order clearly originated with residential care staff. In nearly two-thirds of cases the order was said to have been made by a court (or children's panel in Scotland) following a social work recommendation. But it was unclear whether this was entirely a decision by the child's field social worker or whether she had been prompted by police pressure, or by residential staff from the home where the child was previously placed.

The standard length of a secure accommodation order in England, Wales and Scotland is three months,[1] like the usual detention centre sentence. But a secure accommodation order is not really comparable to an unremitted penal sentence. While the latter is a maximum which can be reduced for good behaviour, the former can actually be extended or renewed by further application to the court. A more realistic comparison can be made by looking at the lengths of time which children had already spent in custody in secure units. Table 7.6 shows this, for each jurisdiction, in periods which are comparable

Table 7.6   *Length of time already spent in secure accommodation, in current period*

	Jurisdiction				
	England & Wales	*Scotland*	*Northern Ireland*	*Irish Republic*	*Total*
Time inside					
Under a month	83 = 78% = 37%	13 = 12% = 25%	I	9 = 9% = 26%	106 = 100% = 32%
1–3 months	74 = 72% = 33%	15 = 15% = 29%	10 = 10% = 43%	4 = 4% = 11%	103 = 100% = 31%
4–6 months	23 = 51% = 10%	11 = 24% = 21%	5 = 11% = 22%	6 = 13% = 17%	45 = 100% = 13%
Over 7 months	44 = 55% = 20%	13 = 16% = 25%	7 = 9% = 30%	16 = 20% = 46%	80 = 100% = 24%
Total	224 = 67% = 100%	52 = 16% = 100%	23 = 7% = 100%	35 = 11% = 100%	334 = 100%

with Table 6.4 (p. 132) relating to penal institutions. While nearly half the children in penal institutions had been there for less than a month on the census day, with proportions declining in three-month bands to only 2 per cent who had been there for over seven months, the pattern in secure accommodation is towards longer periods. Nearly a quarter of the children in secure units on the census day had already been there for over seven months, half of them over a year — on that occasion, discounting any previous periods in security. A third had been there for less than a month, another third for one to three months. The residential staff were asked how much longer they expected each child to remain in security. Half of all the children were expected to stay locked up in the same establishment for over seven months, including a third of the total for over a year. Only one in ten was expected to leave within a month. As the recommendation of the unit residential staff would be influential in any application to renew a secure order in court, these predictions should probably be taken seriously.

Secure units in Scotland and the two parts of Ireland all tended to keep children longer than those in England and Wales as Table 7.6 shows. In Ireland this is consistent with the tendency in the penal sector to give relatively long sentences. In Scotland, it may be associated with the type of establishment in which secure accommodation is located: nearly all of the secure beds are in List D schools, which are comparable to the English CHEs. Table 7.7 shows the distribution of periods spent in security among the different

Table 7.7   *Length of time already spend in security in different types of unit, in current period*

	Type of unit				
	Assessment centre	*CHE etc.*	*Multi-purpose*	*YTC*	*Total*
Time inside					
Under a month	58 = 55% = 56%	39 = 37% = 21%	8 = 8% = 73%	1 = 3%	106 = 100% = 32%
1-3 months	38 = 37% = 37%	58 = 56% = 31%	3 = 3% = 27%	4 = 4% = 13%	103 = 100% = 31%
4-6 months	8 = 18% = 8%	34 = 76% = 18%	—	3 = 7% = 10%	45 = 100% = 13%
Over 7 months	—	57 = 71% = 30%	—	23 = 29% = 74%	80 = 100% = 24%
Total	104 = 31% = 100%	188 = 56% = 100%	11 = 3% = 100%	31 = 9% = 100%	334 = 100%

types of secure unit. While more than half the children in secure accommodation in assessment centres and multi-purpose centres had been there for less than a month on the census day, more than half of those in CHEs and equivalents and youth treatment centres had been there for over four months, over two-thirds of them for more than seven months. Where this type of unit is available, it is likely that children will be held for longer periods in security.

Reasons for placement in security

The questionnaire asked the reasons for placement in secure accommodation in the case of each child. So as to invite a more useful response than merely restatements of the criteria under the current secure accommodation regulations applying to England, Wales and Scotland (quoted below) suggestions were given which included both these formal reasons and others which seemed likely to be important. Some of these proved not to be significant, and others were added by respondents. Ten reasons for placement in security were identified. Up to three reasons were cited in three-quarters of the cases, and the most listed for any one child was eight. They are listed in descending order of frequency:

(1)   Absconding.
(2)   Nature of offending.
(3)   Violence by the child against others.
(4)   Aggressive or abusive behaviour.
(5)   Substance abuse.

(6) Inappropriate sexual behaviour.
(7) Damage to property.
(8) Self-injury or violence against the child by others.
(9) Breach of residential rules.
(10) Mental state.

Absconding was a factor with over two-thirds of the children. It was predictable that a child's pattern of absconding would be a significant reason for seeking a secure placement, because it is the key criterion in the secure accommodation regulations:

> the criteria which must apply before a child in care may have his liberty restricted. . . are that:
> (A)   (i)   he has a history of absconding and is likely to abscond from any other description of accommodation; and
>   (ii)   if he absconds it is likely that his physical, mental or moral welfare will be at risk; or
> (B)   that if he is kept in any other description of accommodation he is likely to injure himself or other persons. (DHSS, 1983, para. 8; criteria for Scotland are similar).

What does require comment is that absconding seems *not* to have been a factor with nearly a third of the children. While placement reasons applying to non-absconders covered the whole range of the list just given, the nature of the offence was emphasized for more than one in three. As secure accommodation serves as an alternative to penal custody for a relatively high proportion of serious offenders, this emphasis on the nature of the offence is not surprising and reflects the further criteria for placement in security under the regulations applying to England and Wales:

> (a)   where the child is charged with or convicted of an offence imprisonable, in the case of a person aged 21 or over, for 14 years or more, or
> (b)   where the child is charged with or convicted of an offence of violence, or has been previously convicted of an offence of violence, and in either case it appears that accommodation other than that provided for the purpose of restricting liberty is inappropriate because that child is likely to abscond from such accommodation, or to injure himself or other people if he is kept in any such accommodation. (DHSS, 1983, para. 26).

Non-absconders tended to have less experience of being in care, with fewer previous residential placements: less than 40 per cent of them had had four or more moves in care compared with nearly 80 per cent of absconders. Twelve, 13 and 14-year-olds were marginally more likely to be identified as absconders than were younger or older children; 16-year-olds were marginally more likely to be placed in security because of their offending. Substance abusers were concentrated in the 14- and 15-year age groups, where there was a tendency for absconding, glue-sniffing and repeated offending to be linked. Reported 'inappropriate sexual behaviour; was gender-specific in that it was confined to girls or to boys who had been in contact with older homosexual men. Most remarkably, this category was not applied to the 19 boys who were said to have committed the offences of rape or indecent assault, so by implication their (hetero)sexual behaviour was not regarded as clearly abnormal.

Discharge criteria
The survey questionnaire included an open-ended question about what criteria would be used to decide when a child should be discharged from the current placement in secure accommodation. Nearly all of those who replied (15 per cent did not) gave just one or two criteria from the range listed in descending order of frequency:

(1) Child responds to treatment programme.
(2) Child stops behaviour which led to placement decision.
(3) Court or other external agent will decide.
(4) A new placement is arranged.
(5) Natural family accepts the child.
(6) Sentence completed or age reached for leaving care.
(7) Child gets a job.
(8) Source of danger is removed.

This is a motley collection of criteria which involve qualitatively different considerations. The first two, which were cited in about two-fifths of all cases, do clearly relate to the reasons for a child's admission to security and to the work being done there. However the same cannot be said of the others: a second group of criteria including numbers (3) and (6) involve arbitrary events or developments outside the control of both the child and the residential staff. Numbers (4), (5), (7) and (8), forming a third group, are reasons for transfer or discharge which could apply in any residential care setting and are not specific to discharge from security. Indeed, gaining family acceptance and obtaining a job seem less attainable as objectives for a child in security than for one from an open residential establishment.

When discharge criteria from this third group alone were being used, it sometimes seemed that keeping the child in security was actually hindering progress, particularly where family rehabilitation was the goal. For example, a 15-year-old Scot who would be in a secure List D school for a year following 'serious involvement with heroin abuse', was expected to complete a successful home leave programme, but the woker remarked that 'possibly difficulties at home will be reinforced due to his absence'. Family therapy had already failed three years previously. Another 15-year-old boy, from the North West of England, was expected to return home from five months in a CHE secure unit where he had been placed because of committing burglary and arson, after the staff were satisfied with 'successful family therapy. Successful rehabilitative programmes.' But again it was noted that, 'from a base of security we are endeavouring to achieve improved familial interaction. Too long a stay in secure conditions would only serve to negate the positives.'

A 13-year-old Scottish girl had to demonstrate 'success of the programme of reintroduction to home and acceptance and success at her local school. Acceptance by parents of her returning home and her acceptance of the conditions laid down for her at home.' This was expected to take seven months. The condition for a 15-year-old Northern Irish boy leaving security was, 'that the boy's family are willing to have him return to the family home and that there is a full understanding by all parties concerned of the possible problem this reunion may pose.'

Sometimes it appeared that the parents were required to show change before their child would be released from security, as in the case of a 15-year-old boy from the South East who was under a Section 2 care order and in a secure assessment unit because of his aggression, absconding and glue-sniffing. 'Greater involvement of family' was reported as an objective, and the boy would be discharged home-on-trial when his 'parents feel able to impose their authority.'

No respondent explained how children were supposed to find a job or a youth training scheme place in their home area while they were locked up in secure accommodation, particularly when the majority had been placed in units which were far from their homes. A 15-year-old Scottish girl would be allowed out of a List D school secure unit after nine months 'to work from home... if the present rebuilding of relationships at home is maintained. If she gains a full time job/job creation scheme.' The expectation of finding a job was more common in Scotland and Ireland (both areas of high youth unemployment) than in England and Wales, and it was likely to be a requirement for the child's release on licence from a sentence imposed by a court. The same List D school head wrote about a 15-year-old boy who was serving a 2-year sentence under Section 413 of the Criminal Procedure (Scotland) Act for the Road Traffic Offences, and for possessing an offensive weapon: 'We expect to get him full-time employment before he leaves and ensure that he has a period of successful employment before he is released. I would expect him to be released on licence after a year. This will be on condition that his current leave programme is successful and that he is in employment.' A secure Irish Republic establishment had an apparently standard condition of release for many children such as one 16-year-old who would be allowed out after eighteen months for larceny on condition 'that he is in gainful employment. That he lives at home.' Another Scottish 16-year-old in a List D school secure unit two regions away from his home town had to, 'find a job that will offer employment on a full-time basis. He must continue his successful leave programme. It is hoped that he will be released on licence within the next four weeks. If he can keep his job and not fight with his stepfather his chances are good. If he re-offends he will move into a Penal Institution.'

Respondents' use of the second group of discharge criteria which has been identified, when an arbitrary date is reached or an external agent makes the decision, tended to reflect lack of a positive attitude towards the child concerned. Sometimes this was because secure child-care accommodation was merely being used as an alternative to remand in custody, with no clear expectations of social work intervention and therefore a minimal response on the part of the residential staff. For example, a 16-year-old alleged rapist from the North West was said to have been remanded to an assessment centre on the recommendation of 'social work staff under court pressure.' The objectives for his stay were 'nothing other than satisfying the court that society is being protected', and the criterion for discharge would be 'that he has been safely delivered to Crown Court for trial', which would probably happen, after four months. This boy's presence in a child-care establishment seems to have been resented, perhaps because of the emotive nature of his offence. The head of another small secure unit in an assessment centre in the North was clearly ambivalent about the way his unit was used by the local court. He wrote about a 15-year-old boy already under a Section 7(7) care order who had been sent there as a 'police requirement to prevent remand in custody for serious burglaries':

> It became apparent to staff manning the unit that the open unit (having been tested out) was suitable for this young man, and that it was therefore unlawful to restrict his liberty. In effect, it was no longer to his benefit to have his liberty restricted and we resisted the court's desire to remand him back to this unit. He is a difficult boy who has chosen a way of life, rather than drift into it, and has resisted almost every effort to get him to change or even conform. He should be returned home, and work should be done with him and his family in the community, but he will probably get a Youth Custody Order because of his offences and his record.

In other cases, respondents' negative comment and reliance on external factors or agents to decide the point of discharge from

security were based on discouraging experiences of working with
the children concerned: 'The expiry of a court order if made will
be the main criterion, as no short term rehabilitation scheme would
work with this individual. This boy may return to his family or
possibly stay in residential care. Whichever happens I feel it will
be a very long time before this boy stops offending.' He was said
to be aged between 11 and 14, from a travelling family in the South
East, and was charged with 'burglary (several) usually against old
people.'

Another 13-year-old from the South East had to, 'satisfy social
services that he is able to manage living in an open unit without
reoffending, endangering people through reckless driving. The courts
may decide to release him before the above criteria [sic] is met.
I feel this boy will spend many periods of differing lengths in penal
institutions.'

Three Northern Irish boys were described in similar terms: 'He
will probably stay here till his 19th birthday because of lack of
resources in N.I. and G.B. He will then go home to live with his
father (cannot be held here after 19) — prognosis v. poor.' This
was a 13-year-old with severe *grand mal* epilepsy. A 16-year-old
who had been in care since he was 4 had been put in secure accommodation after being caught 'engaged in fellatio' with another boy:
'He will remain here until his Training School Order is up. Prognosis
very poor. Hostel/boarding house/flat. Probably future involvement
with law (on wrong side of it).' A third boy was said to be 'an
absconder at present. He will be 17 in January. The law will probably
take its course and he will end up in the YOC. Very poor prognosis
at present. This boy is entrenched in the sub-cultural delinquent
influences found in his home environment.' Similar misgivings were
expressed about a 16-year-old from the South West of England.
His discharge from security would be:

> at the court's discretion. It is likely that he will serve a further detention
> period. Given his previous history of offending, pleading a case on
> his behalf and remaining credible will not be easy. What happens
> beyond this depends on the support available within the community
> in a heavily urban environment. One wonders whether this support
> will be forthcoming, or whether the subject will accept it even if it
> is.

The first and major group of criteria for discharge from secure
accommodation related most directly to the reasons for placement,
and to the work being done with the child. These involved the
child responding to a treatment programme, or ceasing behaviour
which had brought about admission to security. Some children had
to demonstrate proven ability to cope in an open setting, a difficult

task when they were actually locked up. One establishment assumed that this would be achieved automatically by its behaviour modification system:

> In keeping with the School Policy this boy will have to complete satisfactorily his progress through the tier system which operates on the basis of marks rewarding acceptable behaviour. Provided this boy continues his progress through the tier system and completes his various periods of leave at home successfully, he will probably be discharged after six months in secure accommodation.

His referral had been for absconding from an open school.
In some cases the initiative was left with the child:

> He must show some success with his leave programme and give some indication that he can live in his home area without offending or abusing solvents. At present he cannot do this (Scottish 15-year-old).

Another Scottish 16-year-old would be released 'if the Secretary of State is satisfied that he has modified his behaviour so that he can cope with living in the community without offending'. In other cases, the children's behaviour was systematically tested out:

> Regular weekend leave will take place over the next few months and once he has experienced greater freedom his responses will be judged so that a decision on release from security could be taken from there.

A 14-year-old girl from London would be released, 'if she does not attempt to abscond from unit or while out with staff on purposeful visits or projects.' Other children were encouraged to develop social skills intended to equip them for life outside: 'That he develop social skills which would allow him to cope with and live in an open environment'; 'That he has acquired sufficient control and skills to live in a hostel.'

A 16-year-old boy from London had to show 'development of social and self help skills; reduction in hyperactivity; improved appreciation of consequences of offending.' Showing self-insight into behaviour and motivation to change were common requirements, as with a 15-year-old girl from the East Midlands: 'Some acknowledgement of the self-destructive life style which she has adopted. Realisation that her parents still love and want her.' And a 15-year-old boy from the same region: 'Successful extended boundaries and some wish to live a normal life.' For a 14-year-old Scottish boy: 'A variable plan for his future. Some sign that he is willing to participate in such plans.'

The commonest requirement under this group of criteria for discharge from security was that the child should show self-control, maturity and a change in attitude. Often this involved stopping some particular undesirable behaviour pattern: 'Reduction in aggressive/ violent behaviour'; 'Proven ability to control her temper tantrum'; 'That his constant talk of involvement with crime and criminal activity ceases and that he learns alternative subjects of conversation'; 'Positive response to temper control programme; positive response to counselling on glue sniffing and solvent abuse'; 'Child's ability to control the drug and alcohol abuse to a non-dangerous level'; 'Absence of the need to "slash wrists" etc.' Otherwise, change of a more general nature was expected: 'Modified behaviour and attitude'; 'Calm and controlled behaviour'; 'A coming to terms with the areas of stress in his life'; 'When he demonstrates that he can cope better with internal and external pressure'; 'When he demonstrates that he is capable of disciplining himself more effectively'; 'Control over own behaviour rather than all controls having to be externally applied'; 'Modification of inappropriate behaviours; able to behave in a more mature and sensible fashion'; 'Developing maturity and appreciation of the inappropriateness of dangerous behaviour.'

Where would they go on discharge?

In contrast to the juvenile population of penal institutions, a definite answer was made for four-fifths of the children in secure accommodation to the question of where they would go on discharge. However, this may have had more to do with the relatively younger age distribution of children in the secure child-care sector, and the fact that practically all were still under full care orders, than with any positive planning for what was to happen to them on leaving care. The largest single group, a third, were to move into open residential care. Fourteen per cent were being transferred into other custodial settings, penal institutions or different secure units. Only 7 per cent were expected to benefit from a hostel, supported accommodation, or some other special leaving-care scheme. The second largest single group, over a quarter of all the children, were to go back to their parental home direct from secure accommodation. It is likely that this could involve the sort of problems which were discussed in the last chapter, reviving family tensions between parents and children which may have precipitated admission to care in the first place. The very fact that these children had ended up in secure units suggests that their behaviour problems had not actually been solved. And residential workers often felt that apparent improvements while a child was in security would be jeopardized when s/he was returned to the pressures of the home environment.

Attitudes of residential workers

One objective of the survey was to discover what residential care staff thought about the use of custody, both at a general level and in relation to each individual child. To this end, respondents to the first part of the questionnaire, about the establishment, were asked to describe what they considered to be both the constructive value and the negative aspects of secure accommodation in residential child care (no prompts). Then in the second part of the questionnaire, relating to individuals, they were asked what they expected or hoped would be achieved by the child's being in security and what they expected or feared might be the damaging effects (again, open questions). Thus the workers' objectives with individual children were tested against their general attitudes to working in security. Usually both parts of the questionnaire were completed by the same member of staff: the unit head or another senior worker with direct involvement in the running of the unit. When the respondents were different, as in the largest units where the child's key worker would complete Part 2, the test of comparison was no less valid. The general statement in Part 1 by the unit head could reasonably be held to represent agency policy to which all members of the staff team would be expected to adhere. Replies to both pairs of questions have been analyzed and grouped to show a summary of content.

For and against security in general
Nine positive points of value about secure accommodation were identified, the 59 respondents proposing up to five each. Twenty-two per cent made no positive suggestions. Eleven different negative aspects were mentioned, of which respondents gave up to nine each. A similar proportion (29 per cent, mostly the same people) made no negative suggestions. The two groups of replies are shown, listed in descending order of frequency.

Positive
(1) The child is retained.
(2) Behaviour and relationships can be regulated in an ordered way.
(3) Prevents further damage to the child's health and safety.
(4) Further offending, or admission to penal custody, is prevented.
(5) Other residents or members of the public are protected from the child.
(6) High staff ratio.
(7) Relieves staff problems of control.
(8) Rescues the child from moral danger.

(9) Relieves pressure on the child's family.

Numbers (6) to (9) were each cited by less than 10 per cent of respondents.

Negative
(1) Its availability invites inappropriate use.
(2) Makes children dependent or institutionalized.
(3) Attracts prestige or stigma to children who are locked up, or facilitates contamination.
(4) An artificial environment.
(5) Deprives child of social and educational stimuli.
(6) Response to staff inadequacy.
(7) Incarceration has a disturbing effect on some individual children.
(8) Interrupts the child's normal development.
(9) Bad effect on staff attitudes.
(10) Difficulty in placing children afterwards.
(11) Unhelpfully focusses attention on legalities and absconding.

Numbers (5) to (11) were cited by less than 10 per cent of respondents.

Objectives and fears for individual children

Turning now to the second part of the questionnaire relating to the 339 individual children, respondents identified twelve positive objectives which they were hoping to achieve, up to six being mentioned in relation to any one child. For 11 per cent of the children no positive objectives were identified. The possibility of harm resulting from their current placement was recognized by workers for only half of these children in secure accommodation. Eight grounds for concern were mentioned, up to four in relation to any one child. This pair of questions about objectives and fears was left unanswered for only 9 per cent of the children, and among these non-repliers silence was often tantamount to denying the possibility of harm. For example, a letter received from the principle of a large regional secure facility in the North of England stated that 'for children undergoing assessment, it is not sensible to ask what the damaging effects may be. Hence the answer to [that question] is left blank.' The two groups of replies are shown, listed in descending order of frequency:

Objectives
(1) Insight, self-control, maturity.
(2) Control over child's behaviour.

(3)   Contain the child and stop absconding.
(4)   Provide education.
(5)   Prevent further offending.
(6)   Assessment.
(7)   Protect others from the child.
(8)   Improve relations between child and family.
(9)   For the child's personal safety, protection.
(10) Develop positive relationships with adults.
(11) Improve child's physical health.
(12) Provide intensive care.

Numbers (9) to (12) were each cited in relation to less than 5 per cent of children.

Harm feared
(1)   Dependency, institutionalization.
(2)   Stigma, prestige, contamination.
(3)   Child losing contact with natural family.
(4)   Support and opportunities provided are unrealistic.
(5)   Social and educational development will be disrupted.
(6)   The objectives will fail.
(7)   Stress on the child.
(8)   The child will think s/he is being punished.

Numbers (7) and (8) were each cited in relation to less than 5 per cent of children.

Comparison between positive and negative attitudes to the use of secure accommodation in general, and between objectives and fears in work with individual children, shows some consistency but also some contradiction. Emphasis on the general value of retaining children and regulating their behaviour is consistent with the specific objectives of controlling and containing the child and preventing him from absconding and offending. And the main detractions from secure accommodation, in both general and specific terms, were thought to be first the likelihood of institutionalization and creating dependency, and secondly 'deviancy amplification' through attraction of prestige or stigma and the risk of contamination by association.

However, in their accounts of work with individual children, workers expected a stay in security to provide the opportunity to give a child education, while also recognizing that normal social and educational development would be disrupted because of isolation from peers and lack of facilities. They hoped to improve relations between a child and his family, but feared that the child would lose contact with his natural family while he was locked up far from home. They expected that a child in secure accommodation would be prevented from offending, but also that he would learn new criminal skills from other more delinquent children in the unit. One criticism expressed in both general and specific terms (No. 4 in each case) was that secure units are an artificial environment with support and opportunities available which will not continue outside in the 'real' world. Learned ability to cope in such an environment, which can be demonstrated through success in behaviour modification programmes, gives no guarantee of success in life thereafter.

Note

1   Secure accommodation orders in England and Wales are made for fixed periods. In Scotland the only limit imposed is a requirement to review, which is initially after three months and thereafter nine months.

8   Hidden custody

The census survey has provided authoritative data on children in official custody in the child-care and penal sectors within the four jurisdictions of the British Isles, because of its comprehensive cover and high rates of response. The same cannot be said about the data on children in what has been called 'hidden custody': unofficially secure settings where children are prevented from leaving, but their position is not registered in any national returns, nor are they protected by any special regulations.[1] The unofficial, informal nature of this hidden custody makes it almost impossible to quantify, for lack of agreed definitions and the absence of any lists of relevant establishments. Nevertheless, we tried, and the results are a fairly clear impression of what is going on but without the backing of hard quantitative evidence that has been presented in the two preceding chapters. Investigative forays have been made into two sectors — local authority open residential child care and the mental health services — where it seemed likely that children were being held in custody according to our adopted definition: *'Any situation or device which is intended, for whatever reason and for however short a period of time, to remove or significantly restrict a young person's freedom of choice to leave'*. Because of the incompleteness of the data, and equally importantly because of the particular vulnerability felt by some of the respondents to this part of the survey, and their concern not to be identifiable, no specific comparisons are made between the four jurisdictions.

Semi-secure child care

While it seemed unlikely that residential care staff had stopped locking children up and otherwise preventing them from leaving officially open establishments just because there were new regulations restricting their power to do so, it was a chance event which prompted me to try and demonstrate this. During the final stages of organizing the main part of the survey, a basic grade residential child care worker who was a certificate in social service (CSS) student, wrote asking for information for his project about working in security. He said this project was related to the assessment centre where he worked, but it was not an establishment registered as having approved secure accommodation. The research officer for the social services department concerned confirmed that groups of children were indeed prevented from leaving that assessment centre, and another in the county concerned, both of which had wings used as remand units for children referred from the local courts. In the end that county did not respond to the survey, but its arrangements proved to be quite typical of many others, particularly in authorities which no longer manage approved secure accommodation or never have done. In this respect, hidden custody in child care is a local alternative to official secure units, and is recognized as such at a local level. As one officer in charge put it: 'This centre does *not* have an "Approved Secure Accommodation Facility", but we are required to receive children from Sheriff Courts, Petitions, and Place of Safety, Detention Warrants, and from the Children's Panel Hearing System Detention Place of Safety Orders 27.4 and 40(7).' In such circumstances it was expected that residential staff would prevent children from leaving.

Attempts were made to contact relevant establishments in the four jurisdictions, for example by asking cooperative managements to identify them or to pass on sets of survey papers. More underhand methods were rejected as being both unsound and impractical. As a result of this very limited exercise, usable responses were received from eleven establishments in Scotland and four regions of England, though evidence was found of the practice of hidden custody by our definition in all of the jurisdictions including Northern and Southern Ireland. Several refusals were received on grounds such as: '[the school] claim they had no one in security on the survey date, however the external doors of the establishment are permanently locked. It therefore meets your criteria but will not acknowledge as is formally an "open" establishment.'

The forms of security employed were not as elaborate as in the secure units designed to official standards. One assessment centre described as 'Not a secure establishment, however the outer doors are normally kept locked' was also in a 'remote rural location'. It held 2 boys on residential care orders and 19 remanded in care. The officer in charge of another assessment centre wrote: 'No beds are registered as "secure" but all children are subject to such supervision that will inhibit, if not actually prevent, unofficial departure. All were "discouraged from leaving", i.e. subject to maximum supervision although not locked in', on the survey date. Another assessment centre was 'dependent entirely on presence and awareness of staff. The secure element offered is facilitated by (a) the routine, and (b) close supervision by staff. Each day is carefully organised and staff work, and play, with small groups. We do not have any facility for locking up boys.' Ten boys were held there on remand on the survey day. The assistant head of a CHE gave a similar account: 'We have facilities for up to 23 remand places for boys aged 13–18, non-secure in the strict sense. Only secure in the sense that they are supervised at all times, but not locked in.' This is like the 'specialling' which was reported as an extra method of restraint in secure units. More than half of the hidden custody establishments which responded to the survey were assessment centres, though this is not necessarily representative. Two establishments had originally been contacted from official lists of approved secure accommodation, but were not currently operating as such: one was de-registered and the other's secure facilities were not yet open. About three-quarters of them were in-county, located within the boundaries of their management authority, a somewhat higher proportion than among secure units.

Many establishments were said to operate distinctive regimes similar to but less developed than those of the secure units: 'As opposed to just O & A [observation and assessment] the Centre is now largely based on group care dealing with remands, place of safety, long and short term care. Privilege system is used within the establishment based on good and bad behaviour.' The regime of another assessment centre was said to be, 'fairly structured in as much as there is always planned work and activities for children. Thus there is little opportunity for boredom.' Nearly all establishments specified particular forms of restraint used, again of a familiar sort: 'withholding privileges, "specialling" (one to one staff/child supervision)'. 'Constraints within establishments are: (1) withdrawal of time allowed out of establishment; (2) restriction of participation in activities; (3) fines for damage; (4) short periods of time spent in own room (usually as a method to allow child to "calm down").'

Respondents' general attitudes to keeping children in custody were very similar to those of workers in official secure units. Unprompted they emphasized the same positive advantages, and mentioned the same range of negative aspects to security. On the positive side: 'It allows for control of a boy who may otherwise run away or abdicate personal responsibility. Once control is established then a programme can be made to deal with the boy's problems. No boy, no programme. Control first, self development, personal progress later.' An assessment centre principal wrote: 'Whilst I naturally abhor the "locking-up" of juveniles, experience has proved that secure facilities are necessary (a) for the protection and treatment of the young person, and (b) for the safety of the community. Treatment cannot be effected unless the clients can be held.'

Another assessment centre head saw security as, '(1) Opportunity for child to relate to people. (2) Opportunity for child to be their "age" [sic] and not have to conform to peer group demands and expectations.' Another said: 'It allows treatment plans to be carried out with persistent absconders. Prevention of absconding, resulting in the commission of further offences. Very useful as a "time out" situation, both as protection for the boy himself and the other group members.'

The dilemma of balancing the positive and negative features of security was expressed: 'The constructive aspect, in my view, is the opportunity to work in a constructive way with the child and thereby reduce the risk he presents to himself and the community. The negative aspect, in my view, is how one reconciles the above principle with the need for a child to remain a member of his community.' Other respondents, from a CHE and two assessment centres, mentioned: 'A boy may become dependent on this type of control'; 'Often difficult transition from stage of dependency to community living, if flexible system not provided. Stress from concentration of individuals undergoing personal crisis. Lack of privacy.' 'Easy way out for staff. Often seen by children as part of the status process.'

The children in semi-security

Information was provided on 72 children who had been prevented from leaving seven 'open' residential establishments on the census date. White boys predominated, even more markedly than among the population in approved secure accommodation which was discussed in the last chapter. The age distribution was very similar if marginally younger. Much higher proportions were placed in a residential establishment near home, located within their home authority and managed by their own care authority (over four-fifths in both cases). A third of the children were currently in care because of offending, though only about a fifth had originally been received into care for that reason. At least half of them had recently been found guilty or were charged with offences, the same proportion as among the population in official security. However, in the detail of the offences committed there were significant points of similarity with the population of children in penal institutions. Less than a third had committed offences which involved some element of violence, serious in the case of only three individuals. Eighty-nine per cent of the children had committed property offences, with burglary being by far the most common (half of all the offenders were burglars).

These children in hidden custody had significantly less experience of the child-care system than their counterparts in official secure accommodation. Just over a third were away from their parental home for the first time. However, nearly another third had been moved four or more times in care. More than half had been admitted to their current placement direct from their parents' or a relative's home. A third had previously been in a truly open residential establishment, or on the run from one. Thirteen per cent had been on remand in a penal institution.

At some time in their past, more than half of these children had been in residential care establishments, and two-fifths of them had subsequently been 'home on trial' with their parents. Nearly two-thirds of this group who had experienced residential care had been in open assessment centres; nearly half in CHEs; a quarter in special boarding schools. None had ever been in official secure accommodation, but three individuals had already served a detention centre sentence, and one youth custody.

Experience of non-residential helping services were apparently higher than among the children in official security. For example, more than a quarter had been through child guidance, and nearly two-thirds had been under social work (or occasionally probation) supervision, nearly two-thirds of them with intermediate treatment. Only a fifth of the children in official secure units were known to have been under supervision; they seem to have been more likely to go straight on to a care order.

Loss of liberty
Four-fifths of the children had been placed in the establishment, which they were then prevented from leaving, at the initiative of a court or children's panel. Most of the rest had been placed by a field social worker or through a case conference involving field and residential staff. On the census date nearly half the children had been deprived of their liberty for less than a month; a third for one or two months; and the remaining fifth for periods between three months and a year. More than a third were expected to remain as they were for at least six months, and less than a fifth could hope to be released within 4 weeks.

A similar range of reasons was given for deprivation of liberty as with the children in secure units. Up to five reasons were cited in relation to any one child, but only one in two-thirds of cases. They are listed in descending order of frequency:

(1) Nature of offending.
(2=) Absconding.
(2=) Aggressive or abusive behaviour.
(4) Truancy.
(5) Inappropriate sexual behaviour.

(6)   Violence by the child against others.
(7=)   Self-injury or violence against the child by others.
(7=)   Breach of residential rules.
(9)   Substance abuse.
(10=) Mental state.
(10=) Damage to property.

Numbers (6) to (10) were each cited in relation to less than 5 per cent of children.

The serious nature of frequency of offending was mentioned in over half the cases, particularly 15-year-olds, and was most likely to be the only reason given. Absconding was always mentioned in conjunction with another factor. Truancy was mentioned only in relation to children who were under 14 at the time of placement, all of whom had previously been living at home with their parents. Reasons for referring children charged with offences to semi-secure remand units were pretty straightforward, as with placements in approved secure units. For example a 16-year-old boy who was remanded under the Children and Young Persons Act 1969 but had previously been in residential care, was admitted direct from a penal remand centre. Charged originally with actual bodily harm, he had committed a burglary whilst on bail in an open assessment centre. The purpose of the current placement was 'detainment until case is dealt with', and a custodial sentence was expected. Another 15-year-old boy was charged with 'taking without consent' whilst absconding from a CHE. It was expected that the court would return him to the CHE to resume his 'training programme.'

The situation of another 15-year-old was more complex. Admitted under a place of safety order at his own request, he had been in residential care once before 'briefly during NAI investigation.... Child known to Social Services Department through prolonged involvement with an older sister.' He had recently been running away from home and there was a suggestion that his parents, who were separated, were fighting over possessing him. In this case security seems to have been for the boy's protection. A 14-year-old boy under a Section 7(7) order, who had been admitted to care voluntarily less than a year before, had been referred to a CHE which operated 'hidden security' by his care authority's secure accommodation admissions panel, apparently after they had failed to obtain a Section 21(A) secure order in the juvenile court. He had already served a detention centre sentence and was described as being 'out of control' and suffering from 'severe emotional deprivation'. His most recent aggressive behaviour had involved violence against staff in an open CHE. He was an absconder on the census date, so it seemed that semi-security was inadequate to contain him. Another 14-year-old who had been under a Section 7(7) care order since he was 11, was expected to end up in official secure accommodation on a long-term basis, or imprisonment. He had been placed in three previous open residential establishments and returned 'home on trial' between each placement. His present placement was in a formerly approved secure unit which had officially been de-registered. His offences apparently included over a hundred to be 'taken into consideration' of burglary, assault, taking without consent, criminal damage and arson.

In contrast to the residential staff in official secure units, workers in the semi-secure establishments relied heavily on external agents to decide when and to where a child would be discharged. The decision of a court or children's panel, or arrangement of a new placement by the child's field social worker, were to be the decisive factors in around four-fifths of cases. The only other consideration which applied to more than 5 per cent of the children in semi-security was that their natural family accepted them or became acceptable to the care authority. This situation probably reflects these establishments' general lack of pretension to being therapeutic, the workers rather regarding it as a holding arrangement while the children's destiny was being worked out by someone else.

Half of the children were expected to move on to open residential care; 13 per cent to their parental home. A fifth were heading for penal institutions and a further 5 per cent were to be placed in officially approved secure accommodation. As with the two formal custody sectors, very few children (only three individuals) were to be referred to supported accommodation which was intended to prepare them for leaving care. Absence of resources for making a suitable placement was frequently mentioned, for example:

> He has been considered by Adolescent Psychiatric Units in other regions but has not been accepted yet. Provisional placement arranged for next year. At present he is being considered for secure accommodation owing to continuing offences at List G School. Condition of 44(1)(b) requirement states that he will spend only weekends and holidays in assessment centre, while remaining at List G School on weekdays. It is hoped that he will be prevented from offending by being placed here at weekends. He is *not* being prevented from offending as he frequently absconds. I believe he requires more secure accommodation than we can provide.

That boy was 14. Another comment about the discharge criteria for a 16-year-old struck an equally depressed note: 'When next court appearance could provide custodial disposal; or when private housing/lodgings become available. No other resource exists. One of the above alternatives hoped for by the end of the year.'

Workers' objectives
The positive objectives in working with individual children and fears for harm which might occur were very similar among workers in semi-secure establishments to those of their colleagues in the formal secure sector, discussed in the previous chapter. And they were equally likely to deny the possibility that children would be harmed by the experience of losing their liberty: again, half the children were said not to be adversely affected.

No positive objectives were identified for 11 per cent of the children. For the rest, the twelve objectives were as in secure units, and are listed below in descending order of frequency. Up to four were cited in relation to any one child.

Objectives
(1) Control over child's behaviour.
(2) Contain the child and stop absconding.
(3) Assessment.
(4) Develop positive relationships with adults.
(5) For the child's personal safety, protection.
(6) Provide education.
(7=) Insight, self-control, maturity.
(7=) Improve relations between child and family.
(9) Protect others from the child.
(10) Prevent further offending.
(11) Improve child's physical health.
(12) Provide intensive care.

Numbers (7) to (12) were each cited in relation to less than 10 per cent of children.

Among the 46 per cent of children where the possibility of harmful effects was acknowledged, six areas of concern were identified, only one or two in relation to each child. These are listed in descending order of frequency:

Harm feared
(1) Social and educational development will be disrupted.
(2=) Child losing contact with natural family.
(2=) The objectives will fail.
(4) Dependency, institutionalization.
(5) Stigma, prestige, contamination.
(6) Stress on the child.

Numbers (5) and (6) were each cited in relation to less than 10 per cent of the children concerned.

The primary objectives of controlling the child and stopping him or her from absconding were expressed particularly in relation to older children aged 16 or 15. The other objectives were distributed throughout the age groups. Often the desired change was expressed in general terms: 'Stabilising his own life in a secure but supportive environment'; 'A reappraisal of his own situation in a supportive secure environment'; 'A stabilising of his present attitude to life so that he can begin to develop and mature effectively'; 'A stabilising of his situation so that control can be exerted and support may be given'; 'Control, engagement with adults to facilitate personality development.'

Sometimes the expectations were more specific, as with a 16-year-old girl who was said to have demonstrated 'inappropriate sexual behaviour' (unspecified) and to have committed theft: 'Control; provision of appropriate models of male–female behaviour. Introduction to work.' She 'eventually absconded'. A 15-year-old boy who had committed a 'second serious indecent assault in 12 months' was said to need 'diagnosis, and subsequently treatment of problems'. Another 16-year-old boy who had been aggressive to his mother was said to require 'separation' from her and 'engagement with males, social learning and emotional security.'

There were several suggestions that parents were a source of the problem, as with a 14-year-old boy charged with theft, with whom the objectives were 'assessment, control, stability. Parents have established pattern of heavy drinking, violence, and "nomadic" existence.' A 13-year-old who had been admitted to semi-security on an interim care order for truanting and being beyond parental control, was intended to benefit from 'assessment; separation from pressures at home and in the community (social stigma due to parent's homosexual associations); social learning in more supportive group context; appropriate adult models.' But it was acknowledged that he 'may find it difficult to adjust to school/children's home if kept here for several months.' This concern with reinforcing conventional gender roles appeared in several case histories, particularly relating to girls and Scottish boys.

Several respondents commented that the circumstances of semi-security were likely to worsen a particular problem rather than to remedy it, as with the last case example, where isolating a child from normal schooling was queried as an appropriate response to truancy. Another 13-year-old had been sent to a semi-secure assessment centre for up to a year in order to receive 'the supervision that child's mother was unable to provide', which was thought to have been the cause of his truanting. However, the residential worker wrote that the 'main disadvantage may be stigma. School peer-group, or school staff, may be prejudiced.'

A 16-year-old boy on a care order with a six-months' residential 'charge and control' condition was in semi-security to achieve 'reduction of dependence on glue sniffing. Building up of relationships between boy and his family. Deterence of criminal behaviour.' But the residential worker feared that the effect could be that the boy 'may become more introverted and become more self-destructive than before.' Similarly a 15-year-old also on a residential care order for 'continual T.D.A.' (taking and driving away) was placed in a semi-secure CHE 'where it is hoped that he will successfully complete his education and rehabilitation with his family will take place.' But the result expected was 'alienation from his family who tend not to visit, contact therefore limited to short, escorted visits.' Again it was feared that a 14-year-old Asian boy's stay in a semi-secure CHE would result in 'isolation from family — though their influence has not always been very positive.'

A 15-year-old who had committed offences of theft and housebreaking with whom the worker's objective was 'control' was said to have 'continued to commit offences whenever given freedom', so keeping him in semi-security had been ineffective. It was feared that another 14-year-old guilty of theft, 'could assume delinquent identity and lose motivation and autonomy, if kept for several months more.' He had already been in semi-security in the assessment centre for three months. Depriving a non-offending 16-year-old of his liberty for six months was expected to cause 'dependency; limited responsibility'.

Semi-secure accommodation was thought to be unsuitable for some children; in the case of an allegedly promiscuous 14-year-old girl, because it did not provide sufficient control. The worker feared, 'instability (in assessment centre setting) and opportunities for sexual misbehaviour ˙ because of *insecure* accommodation.' For other children, it was felt to be too oppressive or disturbing: 'Child is mentally handicapped (mildly) — he could experience aggravation of aggressive feelings if under stress from peers with whom he cannot compete.' Aged 14, he had been placed in semi-security after being the 'victim of assault by other residents' in a special boarding school. 'Nothing which could not be achieved in children's home or foster-care', was expected for another mildly mentally handicapped 8-year-old girl: 'Unsettled group does not provide child with helpful relationships.' She had already spent nearly six months in semi-security under a residential care requirement after a fostering breakdown and having to leave a special boarding school: 'Parental home unsuitable because of NAI [non-accidental injury] register.'

Conclusion

In cases like these last two, semi-security seems to be compensating, inappropriately, for inadequacies in the mainstream open sector of residential child care. For rather more children with particularly difficult behaviour, it is probably a precursor to placement in formally approved secure units. For a larger group of non-dangerous juvenile offenders who would not satisfy the criteria for a secure accommodation order in court, semi-secure remand units offer an alternative to remand in custody in the penal sector. Only a minority of the children in this position were expected to receive a custodial sentence. So the others were kept out of penal institutions and without the stigma of a secure accommodation order which could subsequently be held against them in tariff sentencing for a future offence.

Undoubtedly the smallness of the sample in this survey of hidden custody under-represents the extent of semi-secure child-care accommodation in the British Isles. If returns from seven establishments run by six local authorities have revealed 72 children in hidden custody, it is likely that the semi-secure sector (if it can be regarded as a discrete sector) is overall as large as, if not larger than, the officially secure sector in residential child care. Although this part of the census survey does not claim to be systematic in its geographical coverage, there seems no reason to suppose that it distorts the structure of the population of children held in semi-security in England and Scotland (also in both parts of Ireland, as already explained). Indeed, the fact that it has consistently identified many points of similarity and some of difference between both the characteristics of the children and the opinions of the workers in the secure and semi-secure sectors, suggests that it can be regarded as a reasonably reliable starting point for any further research.

Children in mental hospitals

Besides residential children's homes and penal establishments, the other state institutions where children are generally known to be held are mental handicap and illness hospitals. Children, like people in any other age group, would be officially in custody as patients only if they were held under a section of the Mental Health Act, and it has already been shown in Chapter 2 that mental health legislation in the British Isles gives no special protection to juveniles. But the first report of this Mental Health Act Commission says that formal detention of child patients in mental hospitals is 'rare'. Generally they will have been volunteered by their parents, guardian or care authority. Nevertheless they may still end up in a 'de facto detention' in a locked ward or room or otherwise prevented from leaving should they wish to do so (Mental Health Act Commission,

1985). Children in this position are in hidden custody within our definition. Attempting to locate them using a postal questionnaire was the most difficult part of the census survey.

Organizing the survey
Permission to conduct this part of the census survey was sought from the five central government departments responsible for mental health services in the four jurisdictions of the British Isles, and from the four sections with responsibility for special hospitals. Only the special hospitals section of the English DHSS did not cooperate. Approval of the Royal College of Psychiatrists was sought, but a final reply was never received. Authority to make the relevant contacts in social services (and related) departments had already been received in connection with the child-care part of the survey.

A questionnaire was designed which was specific to the health service yet compatible with those used in the child-care and penal sectors. Questionnaires with accompanying letters and other papers were sent to the senior administrators of 243 lowest-tier health authorities in the four jurisdictions. A further 158 sets of survey papers were sent to named hospitals or units which could be identified, for example from the *Health Services Year Book*, as providing a relevant service for children and young people (paediatric services were eliminated). All in this latter group also received individual letters explaining who else in their administrative hierarchy had been contacted. Thus 401 authorities and establishments were asked to participate in the survey. The actual number of sets of papers mailed out was nearer 500, as in many cases hospital administrators, consultants and social work teams required their own sets. This survey of juveniles in hospitals generated a vast amount of correspondence in the form of 'phone calls and letters, and a lot of controversy, probably because it seems to have been the first time that any survey on such a scale has ever been undertaken, and because its assumptions and objectives were unfamiliar to health service workers. Resources made it impossible to respond adequately to all the queries, so in retrospect I thank all those concerned for their interest and effort.

Two hundred and eighty-five usable responses were received, but it is not possible to calculate what rate of response this represents without undertaking a level of systematic analysis which the data does not otherwise merit. To know what proportion of health authorities responded would be of little use, because while a few authorities have no in-patient facilities at all, others may have a dozen or more which are directly relevant. It seems that no one knows how many hospitals in any one of the jurisdictions contain under-17-year-olds under psychiatric or long-term care. Discovering how many such

Table 8.1   *Hospitals and other residential health establishments which responded to the census survey*

Establishment	Juveniles prevented from leaving	Juveniles allegedly not so prevented	Back admissions only	No juveniles	Unclear	Total
Mental handicap hospital	8	49	5	11	2	75
Psychiatric hospital	2	12	11	45	4	74
DGH psychiatric ward	—	5	5	11	5	26
Adolescent unit	5	17	—	—	1	23
Children's hospital/unit (long-stay or psychiatric)	2	10	—	—	—	12
Secure hospital/RSU (unspecified)	1	—	1	7	—	9
Mental hospital (unspecified)	—	—	—	4	2	6
Unspecified hospital (status unclear)	—	6	—	1	3	10
Total hospitals	18	99	22	79	17	235
Whole DHA	—	—	—	2	16	18
Home/hostel for mentally handicapped	4	27	—	1	—	32
Overall total	22	126	22	82	33	285

juvenile patients are prevented from leaving is even more elusive, and raises major issues about the status and options of juveniles in mental hospitals.

Basic findings

Table 8.1 shows the basic findings, based on a manual analysis of responses from 235 hospitals or in-patient units to questions about whether they had juvenile patients on the census day and whether these patients were prevented from leaving. Half of the 235 hospitals contained under-17-year-olds on 12 September 1984, and in 15 per cent of these hospitals it was recognized that some or all of the juvenile patients were prevented from leaving. Some further hospitals had a nil return for the date in question but reported that under-17-year-olds had been admitted and been discharged or reached 17 during a previous three-month period, making altogether 59 per cent of the hospitals likely to contain juveniles. By far the largest group of returns from hospitals with juveniles — 45 per cent overall — came from mental handicap hospitals, while psychiatric (mental illness) hospitals and psychiatric wards in general hospitals were relatively less likely to have juvenile patients.

Returns were also received from homes and hostels for mentally handicapped children and young people, some of which recognized that their residents were prevented from leaving. Survey papers had been sent to some such homes which were known to be run by social service authorities or (in the Republic of Ireland) by voluntary organizations in lieu of mental handicap hospitals. A few additional responses were received via district health authorities from homes for mentally handicapped children which had been established to provide substitute care for former hospital patients. This can provide only a glimpse of the wide range of residential provision for mentally handicapped children. Time and resources did not permit any systematic survey of this type of service, and 'special' schools coming under the auspices of education authorities have not been approached at all.

Nearly all of the 117 hospitals or units and 31 homes which reported having under-17-year-olds in residence on the census day provided details of overall numbers and which sex they were, and this data is presented in Table 8.2. There were 1,391 children and young people in all, over a thousand of them in hospitals. Over half of the juvenile hospital population was in mental handicap hospitals; nearly a quarter in adolescent units which were usually attached to psychiatric hospitals. This overall figure is already higher than that which the parallel survey identified in penal institutions in the four jurisdictions and if, as seems likely, the response rate to the survey of juveniles in hospitals has been no better than 50 per cent, the real figure could be around 3,000 (this estimate is confirmed by the Mental Health Act Commission, 1985, p. 12). We have no idea how many children are in 'special' schools and homes and hostels for the mentally handicapped. It is particularly noticeable that the number of girls relative to boys is much higher than in penal institutions of secure child-care accommodation. Details of the personal characteristics and backgrounds of the children will be discussed later in the chapter.

Interpreting custody

Only a small proportion of children — 11 per cent in hospitals — were reported by survey respondents as having been prevented from leaving in circumstances which are consistent with our definition of custody. On that basis, if it is accepted that there are

Table 8.2   *Under-17-year-olds in hospitals and other residential health establishments on the census date*

	Sex			
	Male	*Female*	*Not given*	*Total*
Establishment				
Mental handicap hospital	282	224	56	562 = 53%
Psychiatric hospital	38	18	1	57
DGH psychiatric ward	14	12	—	26
Adolescent unit	107	90	49	246 = 23%
Children's hospital/ unit (Long-stay or psychiatric)	102	54	14	170
Secure hospital/RSU (unspecified)	7	—	—	7
Total hospitals	550 = 51%	398 = 37%	120 = 11%	1,068 = 100%
Home/hostel for mentally handicapped	190	129	4	323
Overall total	740	527	124	1,391

around 3,000 children in mental hospitals and if these 50 per cent survey results reasonably represent the whole population, some 330 children would have been in hidden custody in mental hospitals on the census date. This is about equal to the numbers in officially approved secure accommodation. But how an adult understands the position of a child in a mental hospital is very much a matter of professional and value judgement.

There is a sense in which all children in mental hospitals are in custody because they are not allowed to discharge themselves without their parents' consent and nearly always it was their parents, or occasionally care authority, who originally requested admission. Formal detention under the Mental Health Act is scarcely an issue; only one young person was shown by the survey to be currently detained under a section. Replies from several health authorities, all denying the relevance of the survey, illustrate this point. For example, a district administrator in the South West of England claimed to be

> rather puzzled as to whom you wished to include in the survey as I am not clear what 'those who are prevented from leaving the hospital or ward' means. Obviously we have young people in our hospitals from time to time and in such circumstances we act in loco parentis and obviously this leads to some restraint on their leaving the hospital while they are receiving treatment. I am not aware of any young person, including the mental illness and mental handicap hospitals, who are [sic] legally restricted from leaving.

The consultant psychiatrist from a children's psychiatric hospital made similar points:

> We have 24 children in this hospital, some over the age of 17, but I am not sure whether they come under your category of 'security' and 'custody'. We have a chain link fence around the hospital and the children are unable to go outside the outer perimeter, therefore their freedom is curtailed. None of them have been referred by Law Courts, but all have behaviour problems.

He did not provide details on any of these children, nor did the consultant psychiatrist from an adolescent unit who wrote:

> Three males and two females were in the Unit. The building was locked at night as always. No steps were taken by staff to 'remove or significantly restrict a young person's freedom of choice to leave', but each had been told to stay by people in parental authority — parents or social worker. The building is locked for general security reasons.

Similarly the unit administrator from a large mental handicap hospital in the South East wrote: 'The resident children are not legally detained in any way and are free to leave at any time in the care of their parents.' And a consultant child psychiatrist from a children's hospital in the North West: 'None were expected to leave without their parents' permission as they were mostly under 14 years. None were detained in the way you presumably envisage.' There were 12 boys and 5 girls in that hospital on the census date. Unexplained references to what the respondent assumed the researcher meant, but had not actually said, were not uncommon in this survey of mental hospitals, and illustrate a general communication difficulty. The distance that was seen to exist between the professional ideology of child psychiatry and the juvenile justice orientation of the research meant that only limited progress could be made through the medium of a postal questionnaire.

Another area where confusion over interpretation had clearly led many respondents to deny the relevance of the survey to children in their hospitals, was the connotations attached to 'security' and 'custody'. Although the definition which was offered specified that we were concerned with deprivation of liberty 'for whatever reason and for however short a period of time', many health workers had attached their own meanings. 'Custody' was thought to involve incarceration as a punishment for offending; 'security' meant physical precautions against dangerous patients, of the kind who were thought to inhabit regional and interim secure units in the health service. Thus a district administrator in the North of England wrote: 'We have no children in [the district's] hospitals who are "prevented from leaving" for security or custody reasons. The [county] hospital is the only hospital locally which admits children and this is for the usual medical reasons.'

One consequence of a punitive interpretation of custody is the argument that no patients of whatever age can be regarded as being in custody because they are in hospital for medical care and treatment which are, by definition, benevolent. So even if they are actually under restraint, this is done for their own good and is therefore fundamentally different from restraint exercised in a non-medical location. So a Scottish chief administrative medical officer (a doctor) wrote:

> On the odd occasion a young mentally handicapped patient might become a little aggressive and might have to be given a little more nursing care to prevent injury to another youngster. It does not seem. . . . at all comparable with the kind of situations with which you are trying to compare hospital services and other institutional services. I feel therefore that there is little point in attempting to complete the questionnaire.

On a similar line of reasoning any patients — children or adults — who would prefer to leave, and thereby reject their treatment, cannot be regarded as responsible for their actions because they would be acting against their best interests. Trying to leave is seen as a symptom of mental disorder which must be contained or acted out. Thus a child and family psychiatrist from an English teaching hospital wrote:

> Most do not want to leave but "go through the motions". They are allowed to leave usually and sometimes *sent home* on a temporary basis! Sometimes we encourage leaving to allow therapy to take place.

A particular interpretation difficulty arose with responses from mental handicap hospitals. Some health workers maintained that because the nature of mental handicap meant that patients were unable to make rational decisions, preventing them from leaving the hospital was not a relevant consideration. One telephone caller elaborated this argument in relation to her hospital by explaining that government policies of discharging mentally handicapped children to 'care in the community' meant that only the most severely handicapped and disturbed were left in the hospital. They were physically disabled as well and incapable of leaving unaided. The district administrator responsible for a hospital in the South East of England wrote that he had not completed the questionnaire 'as the residents concerned were unable to exercise a choice to leave owing to their mental handicap.' The sister in charge of an Irish Republic residential home accommodating 25 boys and 18 girls wrote that to ask about residents being prevented from leaving was 'not a relevant question for severely mentally handicapped children and adolescents.' The consultant psychiatrist responsible for a top-floor children's psychiatric ward in a mental handicap hospital in the South of England wrote that none of the 14 patients was prevented from leaving on the census date because 'mental handicap patients are non-ambulant', which was presumably why the ward was located on the top floor as an alternative to more conventional forms of security. On the other hand, the chief administrative medical officer responsible for a Scottish hospital wrote that, 'the wards for the mentally handicapped children are from time to time locked, but this is simply to prevent the children running away and becoming lost in the grounds of the hospital.'

These fundamental differences in interpreting the boundaries of the survey of children in mental hospitals make it particularly difficult to give a reliable estimate of the overall numbers who are prevented from leaving, by multiplying up from the limited survey returns. While the returns seem to show that 11 per cent of the children in hospitals on the census day were in 'hidden custody' this must be an underestimation. All of the 11 per cent were in situations recognized as secure by the respondents who returned the questionnaires. They did not include any children in the circumstances which have just been described, where the respondents denied that security was being operated. Yet it is clear that many of these circumstances would have involved hidden custody by our definition. So the relucatance of many health workers to accept that they are depriving many children of their liberty has produced an underestimation of the incidence of hidden custody among children in mental hospitals.

Had we been ready to accept the categorical definition, that all children in mental hospitals are in hidden custody by reason of the constraints imposed on their age group, there would have been no point in undertaking the survey, as we had little prospect of obtaining an accurate figure for the total number of children involved. So we accepted a more pragmatic position, that there is a difference between generally preventing self-discharge by a whole

Table 8.3   Children who were prevented from leaving mental hospitals
and other residential health facilities

	Sex			
	Male	Female	Not given	Total
Number and type of establishments				
2 adult psychiatric hospitals	1	4	—	5] 22
7 adolescent units	6	4	—	10] = 15%
1 special hospital	7	—	—	7]
8 mental handicap hospitals	49	23	25	97] 120
4 mentally handicapped children's homes	16	7	—	23] = 85%
Total 22 establishments	79 = 56% (68%)	38 = 27% (32%)	25 = 17%	142 = 100%

age group of patients and actually restraining individuals whose behaviour may be putting themselves and other patients at risk. The consultant psychiatrist from a Midlands adolescent unit highlighted this difference:

> Sixteen years of age is age of consent to medical treatment so that all our patients under 16 are admitted for treatment at request of parent or legal guardian and only parent or legal guardian may discharge them. Our patients are not free to come and go as they please. They are expected to conform to unit programme etc. I assume that it is only if child is forcibly prevented from leaving that information is required.

Taking this more pragmatic interpretation of custody, and by using survey returns, we can reassess the proportion of juvenile patients who are prevented from leaving mental handicap hospitals — by far the largest group overall, as Table 8.3 shows. The problems of interpretation are demonstrated by two returns received from the same mental handicap hospital (dual returns arrived on a few occasions and have been disconnected in the tables). One return, from the hospital records department, said there were 10 patients aged under 17, none of whom was prevented from leaving. The second, completed by the social work team attached to the hospital in cooperation with the ward nursing staff, said there were only 6 patients and that 3 of these, 2 boys and a girl, aged 14, 13 and

11, were restrained on the census date and had been for a number of years. They were severely handicapped informal patients who had been admitted because their parents were unable to cope with them and no other placement could be found. The room where they were held had specially high door handles with dual controls, inaccessible to disabled children.

The detail given in this account by the social workers and nurses in contact with the patients was much more convincing than the bald figures from the hospital records department, and suggests that half of the juvenile patients in that mental handicap hospital were detained. But questions arise from the discrepancy in numbers: were there another 4 juvenile patients somewhere else in the hospital? Had they just been discharged? Or perhaps the formal hospital records did not show patients' ages accurately? As Table 8.2 shows, the children's sex was not given in 11% of cases. This may have been an insignificant slip, but reports from people working in mental handicap hospitals suggest that the unit administration often cannot give an accurate sex breakdown of the patient population, because this most basic personal detail has not been systematically recorded. In these circumstances it is not surprising that relatively little information was given on many of the survey forms which were returned on individual young people.

The child patients
One hundred and forty-two children were reported to have been prevented from leaving mental hospitals and related facilities on the census day (details are in Table 8.3). Fifteen per cent of these children had been diagnosed as mentally ill; 85 per cent as mentally handicapped. About a third of them were girls; two-thirds boys. The children prevented from leaving hospitals constituted 11 per cent of the juvenile hospital population which had been identified by the census, though this must be regarded as a minimum proportion, for the reasons which have just been discussed above.

Usable returns were received about 77 children, just over half of those who were reported to have been prevented from leaving. They came from 16 establishments in England, Northern Ireland and the Irish Republic. These 77 children are not necessarily representative of the 142 from among whom they are drawn, though the sex breakdown, for instance, is comparable. And it is statistically most improbable that they are representative of 1,500 or so children whom we can estimate were actually being held in psychiatric custody at the time. But looking at the circumstances of these 77 children gives us some understanding of how children end up being held in mental hospitals, and how they differ from children in the penal and secure child-care sectors. Those with mental illness and mental handicap diagnostic labels are best considered as two separate groups.

Mentally ill The 10 children receiving treatment for mental illness were mainly in adolescent units, and the information was provided by psychiatrists and social workers attached to the units. Half of the children were in a locked building or room. A 14-year-old boy described as 'very violent' was 'transferred from adolescent unit to our closed (intensive care) ward' the day after being admitted to the hospital at his parents' request. There were 19 other patients on the ward, all adults and, although the doors were permanently locked on this upper-floor ward and it was intended to be secure, it was not a designated interim secure unit. A 16-year-old boy, also admitted 'voluntarily' by his parents when he was 12, was being held on a semi-permanent basis in a locked time-out room in the child psychiatric unit of an adult hospital. It was said that he had 'attacked' other children and that his 'freedom will be restricted until child is discharged to appropriate adult psychiatric or mental handicap residential service'. Three 16-year-old girls, all of whom were or had recently been in care, were in a 'special care' adolescent unit on a ward where the 'doors remain locked at all times, however some residents can "earn" parole (unescorted) dependent on progress in behaviour modification programme.' The social worker explained that, 'doors are locked as some residents are subject to remand by courts or compulsory detention.' As this did not currently apply to any of the three girls, it seems that they were being locked up on account of restrictions imposed on other patients. This is a common situation in mental handicap hospitals, as we shall see later.

The only patient who was held formally under Section 3 of the Mental Health Act, a 16-year-old boy, was 'not locked in, but would be brought back if he left Unit on his own'. His freedom was controlled through 'specialling' by a nurse: 'Level of supervision required varies for this boy, from time to time.' Besides being sectioned, he was also currently under a care order and had been an in-patient for nine months. A 16-year-old girl was also subject to 'supervision being provided by a designated nurse monitoring patient's location at all times. Front hall receptionist alerted to special needs of supervision — to inform nursing officer if patient should leave.'

The sanctions which prevented two other children from leaving were less tangible. A 14-year-old girl in an adult psychiatric hospital because she was anorexic was 'confined to bed', presumably without her clothes and in a weak physical condition. A 15-year-old boy was in an adolescent unit where 'youngsters' movements are restricted to the unit and grounds as a routine at the time of first admission for a period usually of two weeks. They may go out with a member of staff if this is convenient or with family when they visit. This is a voluntary agreement.' The boy concerned was not a new patient but had been put back on restriction for breaking the house rules. This type of restriction is common in therapeutic communities for drug-dependents run on hierarchical lines following the American Synanon model. The adolescent unit involved had formerly been concerned mainly with drug-dependents and seemed to have retained the hierarchical model of working. No current drug-dependence units responded to the census survey.

The regimes described by respondents from adolescent units involved therapeutic community, behaviour modification and a mixture of the two: 'Residents subject to behaviour modification programme which is undertaken on a "contract" basis, i.e. with resident's agreement.' 'Modified therapeutic community. Family, dynamic and community therapies.' 'Therapeutic community type of communication system. Many therapies available, e.g. Analysis, Family Therapy, Behaviour Modification.' 'Adolescent Unit emphasis on milieu therapy and social skills training (not just domestic skills).' 'A therapeutic milieu within a child psychiatry unit that includes (1) group work, (2) individual psychotherapy.'

Although all the children but one were informal patients, the circumstances of their admission varied. Some consultants regarded the parents' wishes as all-important, but the respondent from a therapeutic community wrote that, 'youngsters will only be admitted if they agree themselves that they want to come to the unit.' One girl, who was in care under Section 1 of the Children and Young Persons Act 1969, had been admitted at her social worker's request but was 'not detained in unit by virtue of this.' Another 16-year-old girl had been under both a care order (1948 Children's Act) and Section 2 of the Mental Health Act when she was admitted. But by the time of the census, three months later, she was an informal patient and the care order had been revoked so, as the social worker pointed out, legally she could 'demand to leave. This person could terminate "contract" designed to modify anti-social behaviour.'

Six of these 10 children in mental illness hospitals were aged 16, and the others were 14 and 15. Two-thirds had been first referred to a psychiatrist when they were under 14, usually through the child guidance service. Only 4 of the children had never been under a care or supervision order. Respondents from other adolescent units who did not supply details of the children prevented from leaving also confirmed this, for example: 'We have several children under care orders and most have behavioural disorders and/or depression.'

In most cases it was unclear whether being in care was associated with offending, but if it was, this seems not to have been a major consideration. No information was supplied about the 7 boys aged under 17 who were on the adolescent ward of Moss Side Special Hospital on the census day, on the grounds of confidentiality. But personal details which were published in a parliamentary answer only six weeks later show that 4 of the 6 16-year-olds who were then in Moss Side and Rampton were not there as offenders (*Hansard*, 1984). None of the other secure hospitals in the four jurisidictions contained under-17-year-olds. The regional adolescent secure unit attached to Prestwich Hospital was not yet open at the time of the census survey.

All but one of the children were placed in hospitals within the boundaries of their home local authority, which would probably not have been the case had they been in residential child care. For half it was their first time away from their parents' home. The other half had already been in residential care. One girl had spent some time in secure accommodation in an assessment centre. No one had been in a penal institution. Four children out of the 10 had been to a special school for the educationally subnormal, suggesting that the division between mental illness and mental handicap may not, in these cases, be as fixed as the diagnostic labels suggest.

As in the other secure settings, respondents were asked why it had been decided to prevent each child from leaving. Seven reasons were given, up to three in the case of any one child. They are listed in descending order of frequency:

(1)   Aggressive or abusive behaviour.
(2 =)   Child's mental state.
(2 =)   Violence by child.
(4)   Absconding.
(5 =)   Promiscuity.
(5 =)   Substance abuse.
(5 =)   Breach of residential rules.

This range of reasons is similar to those given for placing children in secure child-care accommodation, as discussed in Chapter 7. But from the descriptions which were given of the circumstances in each setting it seems that the level of children's problems is generally more severe in secure accommodation than it is in psychiatric hospitals. A DHSS report recommended ten years ago that mental hospitals were not an appropriate place for children with particularly difficult and anti-social behaviour (DHSS, 1975). A recent study by the health advisory service, based on visits, suggests that the most disturbed children are to be found not in adolescent units but in residential child-care establishments (NHS, 1986). Our research confirms this.

The range of objectives in working with children in psychiatric custody similarly reflects those mentioned by workers in approved secure accommodation, but with different priorities. Nine objectives were suggested by respondents, up to five in the case of any one child. They are listed below in descending order of frequency:

(1)   Treatment.
(2)   Protect others.
(3=)   Control child's behaviour.
(3=)   For child's safety.
(5=)   Assessment.
(5=)   Insight, maturity, self-control.
(5=)   Improve relations with child's family.
(5=)   Hold or contain child.
(5=)   Prevent offending.

The possibility of harmful effects on the child was recognized in only three cases; a typical response to that question was 'not applicable'.

Facilitating treatment was the main objective in preventing the majority of the children from leaving: 'the opportunity to engage in therapeutic regime'; instilling 'a strong commitment to the unit's programme'. Where the objective with one boy was 'treatment of a severe mental illness', the psychiatrist expected that 'damage to person/property' might also be a consequence of confining him: 'Was paranoid about neighbours before admission and put brick through window of their house. It took nine male nurses culled from other wards in hospital to control him and implement transfer. Nurses on closed ward regard him as one of most disturbed admissions to ward.' The possibiliy of 'self damage and failure to change' was mentioned by another psychiatrist who did not send returns on individual patients.

Only the boys were thought to be violent. Another boy was kept in a secure single room so that there would be 'less danger of aggression towards others and of possible criminal involvement.' No harm was anticipated from this, although he had already been an in-patient for over 4 years. The objectives with the only boy who was under a Section were: 'Access to parents etc. can be controlled until he is more stable and can handle very difficult relationships. Eventual sorting out of relationships within his family. Prevention of violence, and of exploitation by others.' The psychiatrist also feared 'institutionalism in all its insidious forms — over-dependent on psychiatric institution.' A 15-year-old girl who had been admitted to a child psychiatric unit after an overdose was subject to:

> Specialling by a nurse as a part of a programme to help her stay in school for the required period. The reason is to show that we care enough about her and her problems to spend time helping her cope with difficult situations. End result — that she is important and worth more than she believes, and can't run away from problems that may be behind the school refusal. [But there is] a danger of too much emphasis on keeping her in school and forgetting the reasons behind her difficulties.

Criteria for discharge from security were specified in most cases, up to three being cited in relation to any one child:

(1) Complete, respond to treatment.
(2) Achieve self-control.
(3) Family accepts child.
(4=) Peer group accepts child.
(4=) New placement is arranged.

Again, these are similar to the criteria given for discharge from secure accommodation. Sometimes it was a matter of showing motivation: 'Consistent good behaviour and full use of the unit's programme'. In another case it would be a 'medical/nursing decision. Depends on response to medication, parents' views.' 'Clinical assessment of her ability to control impulse, the support of the group, the alleviation of mental disturbance. Period of restriction lasted two weeks — by then she was able and prepared to resume responsibility for her own movements.' For this patient and another no move was involved to end security; the restrictions were lifted. Others moved back to an open ward or on to another hospital. One went into residential care; two were expected to return home; another discharged herself from the hospital altogether when she was 17.

Mentally handicapped While significant similarities can be seen between the children in mental illness hospitals and units and those in secure child-care accommodation, the children in mental handicap hospitals and homes have, on the whole, the characteristics of a very different group. Of the 67 mentally handicapped children on whom individual returns were received, 47 were in hospitals and 20 were in residential homes run by three English social services departments. From the homes, responses were received from the residential workers, and in the hospitals the forms had been completed by psychiatrists (mainly), social workers and nurses.

All but one of the children were in locked buildings or wards. A nursing officer wrote about the 16-year-old girl who was controlled only by staff supervision, that she was 'not strictly speaking prevented from leaving as she shows no wish to leave.' But had she so wished she would not have been allowed to: 'The young lady is severely mentally handicapped and remains within staff supervision for her own safety as she has no ability to orientate herself outside of the ward area.'

The principal social worker from one mental handicap hospital reported an extreme custodial device which was said to be a thing of the past: 'This unit has a "time out box" that was set up two years ago for one resident. Due to better management techniques this facility is no longer needed and has been dismantled. A "seclusion" room exists on the site but this has never been used for disturbed children.' This device sounds like a large wicker cage which is still to be seen sometimes in the grounds of another mental handicap hospital which I know. However, the custodial measures employed in mental handicap hospitals are generally routine rather than unusual and individualized. For example the consultant psychiatrist from one hospital reported 25 child in-patients of whom 4 boys and 7 girls were prevented from leaving: 'The doors are kept locked. In common with the other residents they were able to move around the day room and in to the toilet areas. The people referred to are all resident in one of two wards for ambulant, disturbed, mentally handicapped young people.' In another recently built hospital, 'the villa on which the child is placed has the main door always locked. The windows are locked. Staff carry keys. There is no other way out of the villa. Some villas are locked all the time, others are locked when patients who may abscond are inside.' This arrangement meant that some children were sometimes locked up for reasons which had nothing to do with them personally. So the hospital social worker wrote about a 15-year-old boy who had been a patient for 10 years: 'The villa is locked to prevent another child from absconding — not this child!' The matron of a hospital and special school for autistic and emotionally disturbed children reported a similar situation which applied to 16 boys and 6 girls: 'Exit doors are locked. Children are locked in bedrooms at night. The level of security fits the needs of the most disturbed children — many of the children do not require this level of security.'

Similarly, in a short-stay local authority home for mentally handicapped children, the 'outside doors are locked' because that was the 'policy of the home', although the residents had varying degrees of handicap and difficult behaviour. One severely handicapped 11-year-old boy was 'allowed to move from room to room under watchful supervision due to epilepsy (frequent fits).' Another 16-year-old boy who was described as 'mentally incapable' was 'allowed to move around the unit without supervision. Also allowed to go outside and hang washing out without supervision.' An 8-year-old girl in respite care was 'prevented from leaving the establishment due to the fact that due to her profound mental handicap she could not leave the premises unattended, and staff cover was not available to facilitate her desire to leave the premises at that time.'

Two establishments, one a long-stay hospital and the other a mentally handicapped children's home, mentioned the use of inaccessible double door handles as a substitute for conventional locks on internal doors: 'Our doors are either often kept locked or have a double handle. Two single rooms with double handles. Most doors double handled except front door with key lock, back door bolt lock.' In the hospital, the 'door knobs [were] out of reach of children.' In both cases the children concerned suffered from varying degrees of physical disability which prevented them from manipulating the two door handles together: 'limited mobility'; 'unable to walk'; 'difficulty in walking and balance'; 'due to the child's physical and mental handicap has not the ability to abscond.'

Only half of these mentally handicapped children were in establishments which claimed to operate any particular regime. One hospital run by a religious order had 'behaviour modification programmes; high staff-child ratio.' Care in another hospital was described as 'basically custodial'. It seemed to depend on resources and staffing levels, as a hospital social worker explained: 'Custodial care on the villa, with low level of staff. High level of staff in the school where behaviour modification programmes are well operated.' In some establishments behaviour modification methods were used only with selected individuals, as with a 13-year-old boy in a hospital who had been 'assigned key worker and teacher operating behavioural programme designed to prevent vomiting.' All of the hospital patients and home residents had been admitted informally, nearly always at the request of their parents, though there was apparently no record of how 6 of the children came to be in a long-stay hospital. Seven of the hospital patients were or had been in local authority care, and this was usually connected with the circumstances of their admission. Other informal patients had been admitted because of withdrawal of care by their parents, which could otherwise have resulted in reception into local authority care. A 16-year-old girl with Down's syndrome had been abandoned in hospital by her mother two months after birth. A social services department had assumed parental rights and one of the hospital social workers was effectively responsible for her. A 14-year-old girl who was also under a full care order had been an: 'illegitimate child. Placed for adoption. Turned down when mental handicap diagnosed.' She had originally been fostered, then placed in two voluntary children's homes, then a mental handicap hospital before being admitted to the mentally handicapped children's homes where she was living on the census day.

An epileptic boy of 15 had been admitted to hospital when he was 5, 'informally at request of father, consequent upon suicide of mother.' A boy of 16 who was severely subnormal, deaf and blind with rubella syndrome caused by his mother catching German measles during pregnancy, had been an informal patient since he was 3: 'Admission requested when mother sent to prison. Has remained an in-patient ever since.' According to the hospital social worker, social services had never been involved in either case. Another 14-year-old boy with severe epilepsy had been admitted informally when he was 3 at the request of the social services department. Seven years later he was made the subject of a full care order, but the reasons for social services' involvement were not explained by the hospital social worker who filled in the form.

It seems likely that a common reason for informal admission to hospital of a mentally handicapped child would be the stress caused by the child's presence in a family. The family of an 11-year-old girl who had been admitted nine months previously were said to have been, 'unable to cope with conduct disorder in deaf, mentally handicapped child.' The mother of a 7-year-old girl, who was also recently admitted, was described as a 'deserted wife unable to control child's reactive behaviour disorder and hyperactivity.' Three patients from one hospital were simply described as 'informal resident — parents unable to cope.' For most of the children no details were given at all about the circumstances of their admission and it is at least possible that this was because the staff concerned did not know.

Boys among these mentally handicapped children outnumbered girls by about two to one, in both the hospitals and residential homes. This is still a much higher proportion of girls than were locked up in the penal and secure child-care sectors. The children also tended to be younger, again in both settings: two-thirds were aged under 14, and a quarter were less than 10 years old. Nearly three-quarters had been aged under 5 when they were first in contact with mental health services, much younger than the group of child patients who had been diagnosed as mentally ill. Only half were placed within their home local authority.

Fifteen per cent of the children in mental handicap hospitals were known to be, or to have been, in care, and 70 per cent of those in residential homes. However, this latter finding was a consequence of local authority policies rather than a reflection of the needs of the individual children concerned. Of the two authorities whose homes accommodated all but one of the 20 children in residential homes, one authority seems to have had a standard practice of taking an interim care order on every child admitted, even for respite care, while the other did not. None of the children in either setting was identified as an offender.

Four-fifths of the children had been living with their parents immediately before admission to the hospital or home. A fifth had been in residential care or another hospital. But it was their first time away from home for only about two-fifths of the children. Overall at least a quarter had been in residential care and a fifth had been in a hospital, at some time in the past. While living with their families nearly all had received non-residential services, particularly special education. Two-thirds of the children were admitted to their present placement when they were aged under 8, and at least three-quarters went direct into custody, the others spending time in an open ward first.

By far the most common reason given for placing a child in security was his or her mental state, but other reasons were also identified: violent or aggressive behaviour; absconding; self-injury or attack by other children; damage to property. The effect of children's mental condition was described. In the case of an 8-year-old girl: 'She is profoundly mentally handicapped and cannot "manage" herself unsupervised outside the establishment.' And about an 11-year-old boy who was said to be only mildly handicapped: 'In view of age, mental handicap, conduct disorder and communication difficulty he would be unable to take care of self.' This assessment does not in itself explain why it was thought that the boy had to be locked up, and in many other cases no convincing account was given. A hospital social worker wrote that a 13-year-old boy who showed 'hindered physical and mental development, constant vomiting. . . . is not prevented from leaving this establishment by any order, but remains here because no other, more appropriate home is available yet.' The social worker in one hospital wrote about 5 different children:

> The villa on which this child is placed is locked in order to prevent another child absconding. . . . Hospital practice results in this child being secured. No decision as such has been taken. . . . Main reason is that this villa is locked because of *another* patient. . . . . This villa has to be locked even though most of the patients do not need secure conditions — traditional hospital practice.

A majority of respondents — more than four-fifths — made some reply to the question about their objectives in working with the children who were prevented from leaving. The most frequent responses concerned the child's safety, acquisition of social and communication skills, and controlling or modifying the child's behaviour. Other objectives mentioned were: protecting others or relieving the family; holding or containing the child; facilitating treatment, assessment, maturity; preventing offending. It is not useful to attach any numbers to these objectives as in several cases standardized responses seem to have been given for 'batches' of mentally handicapped children as if they were homogeneous groups. There was very little evidence of this being done in any of the other surveys. For example, a psychiatrist wrote that his expectation in preventing 4 boys and 7 girls from leaving the hospital, was 'their own safety, [otherwise] that they will wander, get lost and be unable to take shelter.' The alternative was 'adequate supervision by another method', but he expected them to stay locked up in the hospital for 'probably a lifetime'.

A few respondents described positive goals for individual patients, for example: 'modification of behaviour to level where care at home possible'; and 'it is expected that her behaviour will improve to a level where she can be discharged home.' But more usually objectives were described in negative terms: 'she will come to no physical harm'; 'guard him from danger'; 'prevention of accident'; 'containment, prevention of aggression to self and others, protection of family'. Two respondents, one a hospital psychiatrist and the other an officer in charge of a residential home, sent separate letters with their forms explaining their point of view:

> I think it is important to point out to you that the young people in question on whom we have completed forms, effectively represent a multiply handicapped and damaged group. Most are children who would, developmentally, require the sort of supervision and care that would normally be reserved for toddlers and pre-school children. That is to say, for many of them there is the risk of self injurious behaviour by virtue of running away or attack from other and older young people who have poor self control and potential for aggressive outburst (consultant psychiatrist).

> A brief word of explanation about our unit. We are a ten bed hostel offering permanent and respite care for severely mentally and physically handicapped children and young people. Therefore, for their own safety we are unable to allow our residents out of the premises unaccompanied — that is, if they are able to anyway. All of them are taken out under supervision as often as we are able. Several are hyperactive, and again for their own safety we have to ensure that they do not leave unaccompanied. For this reason our doors are often kept locked. . . . It is only in this way do we in any way classify ourselves as a 'secure unit' and, indeed, think of the unit as being a home, which it is for several residents (officer in charge).

The possibility of harm resulting from confinement was mentioned in relation to only 9 children. Examples were a 14-year-old boy under a care order, where it was feared the consequences would continue to be 'accidental injury to himself and deliberate injury to other patients. Institutionalisation.' A social worker from the same hospital said that the effects of custody on a 16-year-old boy who had been an in-patient since he was 3 were 'institutionalisation. Reduction in curiosity and stimulation.' But by far the most common response to this question was 'not applicable', or as the social worker put it, from a hospital where 3 children were confined: 'None, due to mental handicap.' This suggests an attitude to mentally handicapped children as a homogeneous group who cannot be expected to show individual reactions to their social environment and who, by implication, therefore do not require any particular consideration.

Lengths of stay for children in mental handicap hospitals were extended. Two-thirds had already been in their current placement for more than 2 years. Only a few children who were in the residential homes for respite care had been there for a month or less. Respondents would not estimate when nearly three-quarters of the children were likely to leave, or expected them to stay in their present circumstances indefinitely. It was thought that more than a third of the children would spend the rest of their lives locked up in a mental handicap hospital. Alternative placements were being sought for children in some of the hospitals, but without clear promise of success. Comments about the children in respite care suggested that when their parents were no longer able to look after them these children could revert to the same position as their peers in long-term custody: 'Unlikely to improve, handicapping condition is such that this child is likely to always need close supervision.' 'Due to severity of his mental handicap, unlikely that he will be able to manage alone outside although he does have independence training.' 'Will always need special care as he is severely sub-normal, doubly incontinent, no speech, partially deaf.'

In a few cases change in the child was considered to be a possibility though probably not a likelihood: 'Change in his behaviour — less aggressive and end of absconding'. 'Dependent on the time span in which her ability may be improved to a level where she is capable of personally making a decision to act independently.'

> His behaviour 'improving', i.e. cessation of attacks on other people and damage to property. Commencement of speech (he does not speak as yet). I predict he will remain on a locked villa in this hospital until he dies, probably from epileptic attacks. That could be many years hence. N.B. This is a *social worker's personal opinion*, not a psychiatric assessment.

Answers to the question: 'What are the criteria for removing restrictions on this person's freedom of choice to leave?' were often unrelated to the needs of the particular child but rather reflected other people's needs or the availability of resources, for example: 'extra team members'; 'provision of alternative placement for him elsewhere than in hospital.' 'provision of alternative accommodation which is not locked and has more staff. There is a chance that he may be moved to a new small children's hostel during the next year. If he stays in this hospital, I fear he will remain on a locked villa either with children or adults.' 'I predict he will stay where he is for a further two years then he will be moved to an adult villa which will probably also be locked for the same reason — that of preventing other patients from absconding.' Another 15-year-old boy in the same position could expect to be given his freedom only if there was 'alternative provision for the other patient or improvement in behaviour by the other patient.' His needs and rights as an individual had become submerged.

Note

1. Concern over the issue of 'hidden custody' first emerged in the United States in the late 1970s where academic commentators demonstrated the phenomenon as an unintended consequence of government's initiative to reform juvenile justice practice (Lerman, 1980). In particular a Federal government initiative was intended to remove status offenders from the juvenile justice system and to release offenders from state detention centres and training schools by means of directly funding 'alternatives' under the Juvenile Justice and Delinquency Prevention Act of 1974. In practice, reductions in the numbers of juveniles so dealt with were offset by the development of new youth control systems using child welfare services, mental health resources and chemical control agents (Krisberg and Schwartz, 1983; Lerman, 1980). A particular feature of this development in the United States was that it took place predominantly in the private sector and was financed by the health insurance industry. Concern over developments in England and Wales have been expressed by Rutherford (1986), although he does not provide empirical data on the nature and extent of such control networks.

9 Comparisons

It was an original premise of the study group that differences in legislation and policy at a national level between the four jurisdictions of the British Isles would produce differences in the disposal of children within them. Conversely, it was assumed that the likelihood of children being put in custodial settings, and their experiences therein, would be crucially influenced by legislation and policy in the different jurisdictions. The census survey was intended to test these premises. They have been proved valid only to a certain extent.

The influence of formal national policies is most clear at a level of absolutes. First, special penal institutions for sentenced under-17-year-old boys exist only in England: junior detention centres. It is more than likely that the availability of these specialist institutions accounts for the relatively high proportion of children in penal institutions, compared to secure units, in England and the relatively high proportion of young boys (under 16) within the English penal population compared to the other jurisdictions (see Tables 5.1, p.109 and Table 6.1, p. 117). Where such a specialist facility exists, the executive authorities expect it to be used. Social workers alone should not be blamed for sometimes recommending custody in social enquiry reports (SERs). If the detention centre sentence did not exist for children, social workers could not be expected to recommend it. As it does exist, magistrates do expect that social workers will recommend custody for some children, if their SERs in general are to be taken seriously.

The second absolute is the Scottish virtual prohibition on penal custody sentence for under 16-year-olds, which alone accounts for the absence of 14- and 15-year-olds under sentence in Scottish penal institutions. This also illustrates the arbitrary nature of age thresholds to adulthood. Had the legal end of childhood in Scotland been at 17 instead to 16, as it is in England and Wales, Scotland could have appeared as a shining example of how to deal with juvenile offenders. But 'unruly' Scottish children can be remanded in custody, and are more likely in Scotland than in any other jurisdiction to be sent to an adult prison because no more appropriate institution exists locally. Overall, more children are officially locked up in Scotland and Northern Ireland than in England and Wales, in

Table 9.1   14-16-year-old males* in official custody (both sectors) related to total comparable populations in each jurisdiction

	Total pop. 14-16 males*	14-16 males* in custody	As % of total pop.
England & Wales	1,244,650	1,147 =	0.09%
Scotland	138,033	138 =	0.10%
Northern Ireland	45,187	43 =	0.10%
Republic of Ireland	103,273	47 =	0.05%
Within England & Wales			
North	80,839	145 =	0.18%
North-West	170,755	228 =	0.13%
Yorks. & Humberside	126,010	168 =	0.13%
East Midlands	97,975	101 =	0.10%
Wales	70,263	69 =	0.10%
West Midlands	135,965	129 =	0.09%
East Anglia	45,316	35 =	0.08%
South West	105,898	60 =	0.06%
South East	411,629	212 =	0.05%
All metropolitan districts	298,254	433 =	0.15%
All shire counties	791,703	617 =	0.08%
Greater London	154,693	88 =	0.06%

Note:

* 14-16-year-old males have been selected because they constitute 82 per cent of juveniles in official custody and thus form the most useful point of comparison with the census populations of the four jurisdictions. Numbers of girls and younger boys in custody were so small as to be statistically insignificant in relation to total population.

Sources:

Office of Population Censuses and Surveys (1983), *Census 1981, National Report Part 1,* HMSO

Department of Health and Social Services, Registrar General Northern Ireland (1983), *The Northern Ireland Census 1981, Summary Report,* HMSO.

General Statistics Office (1981), *Census of Population of Ireland Vol. 2,* Stationery Office, Dublin.

relation to the total population, with the Irish Republic clearly in fourth place. This is demonstrated in Table 9.1, using national census figures.

Beyond the level of absolutes, there are as many geographical differences within the jurisdicitions, particularly England and Wales, as there are between them. These differences, which were discussed in Chapter 6, probably arise from the sentencing practice of local courts, perhaps supported by SERs, and the historical legacy of the location of penal institutions. So a tendency is evident for children from economically depressed cities in the North of England to be sent to penal institutions in the relatively affluent South. Three times as many children who come from the North of England are locked up as from the South East and South West, in relation to total regional populations of the age group (see Table 9.1, also Table 7.5 (p.159) related to children in care). Equivalent movements from poor to rich areas are evident in the other jurisdictions. This major similarity between the jursidictions reflects shared inequalities in their social class structure.

The current debate on the geography of juvenile justice has focussed on 'going Scottish', whether other jurisdictions should adopt the Scottish policy of separating penal and child-care legislation and services and setting an age threshold banning children from penal custody sentences (e.g. ADSS, 1985). The English *Review of Child Care Law* has recommended only a minor adjustment, moving non-criminal child-care proceedings from the juvenile court to a domestic court. Post-Black proposals for change in Northern Ireland similarly seek to separate offenders from non-offenders, but will retain the existing training schools.

The 'going Scottish' debate rests on assumptions which equate punishment with penal institutions and care with whatever is done by local authorities. Decarceration is to be achieved by removing children from penal custody. The debate is thus based on comparisons between the two sectors: penal and child-care. But secure child-care accommodation must also be regarded as custodial. At a policy level, its regulation originates from a Criminal Justice Act, where its purposes are specified as being to stop children absconding or to remand in secure conditions. Workers in secure units regard them as custodial: as was shown in Chapter 7, their main objectives are to control children's behaviour and hold them when they want to run away. What we can gather from workers' comments and, for example from NAYPIC's (National Association of Young People in Care) evidence to the Short Committee (House of Commons, 1984), confirms that children also regard secure accommodation as custodial.

Children who are subject to secure accommodation orders (and the Irish equivalents) stay in custody longer than those serving penal sentences or on remand. One reason for this is that sentences are remittable while secure accommodation orders are renewable, which makes the two non-comparable on a formal basis. But comparison of the lengths of time already spent in custody by children on the census day (Tables 6.4 and 7.6; see pp. 132, 165) clearly shows the difference between the two sectors. Only 10 per cent of children in penal institutions had been there for more than four months, compared with 37 per cent of children in official secure accommodation. And among the latter group, the comparative figures for the four jurisdictions were: England and Wales 30 per cent, Scotland 46 per cent, Northern Ireland 52 per cent, Irish Republic 63 per cent.

The likely reason for these differences between the jurisdictions, with English children spending considerably shorter periods of time in security than the rest, is the concentration of types of secure unit. Nearly half the English children were in units attached to assessment centres (including multi-purpose centres) while the great majority of the children in the other jurisdictions were in establishments which are comparable to the English CHE: List D schools, training schools, reformatories (Table 7.2, p. 149). Ninety-three per cent of children in assessment (and multi-purpose) centres throughout the four jurisdictions had been there for less than three months, compared with only half the children in CHEs and equivalent. Some of the longest stays of all were in youth treatment centres, both of which are in England (Table 7.7, p. 166); without these, the average English length of stay would have been shorter. Three months is the maximum unremitted detention centre sentence which is given to under-16-year-olds in England. About half of the children in secure units in Scotland, where there is virtually no penal sentencing, had already been in custody for more than three months — and some of them had committed no offence at all.

An absolute preference for secure accommodation over penal institutions for juvenile offenders, as expressed recently by Bignell (1986) and Reynolds and Williamson (1985) for example, rests on value judgements about the innate superiority of care and what constitutes the 'best interests' of children. By what standards could the best interests of children be tested? Justice? Availability and effectiveness of treatment? Quality of life? On justice criteria, it must be recognized that there are serious inequalities in a system which produces custodial outcomes for offenders and non-offenders alike. Secure units contain both dangerous and violent offenders and those who have committed no offence at all, with no obvious differentiation in 'sentence'. In the secure child-care sector, length of stay seems unrelated to what a child has done, but rather follows from what s/he is perceived to be, that is behaviour. Meanwhile, the most overtly punitive disposal, in a penal institution, is reserved for mainly minor property offenders. Children in custody can see evidence of confused values at work when they compare each other's histories. Such inequalities must seriously undermine the deterrent and socially controlling capacities of policies for juvenile offenders.

While treatment, or helping, remains the paramount objective in child-care services and the survey has provided evidence that this is generally true within secure units, help in the form of probation officers is being deliberately withdrawn from penal institutions for juveniles, as a matter of government policy. The implications of this have been discussed in Chapter 6. However at least this means that child prisoners cannot be expected to be responsive to help which they are not receiving. Children in secure accommodation are expected to show motivation to change and respond to treatment before they will be let out. In mental hospitals those who might be thought most in need of treatment — severely mentally handicapped children with physical disabilities and disturbed behaviour — are least likely to receive help and personal attention. Mentally handicapped children still tend to be regarded as an undifferentiated and unchanging population.

Measuring children's best interests by their quality of life is perhaps the most difficult test of all, as it involves evaluating experiences. No researchers seem to have assessed the quality of life for children in penal institutions or secure accommodation, nor attempted to compare the two. The current juvenile justice debate has virtually ignored 'hidden custody', thereby excluding two major areas of children's experience. Comparisons of the relative value of the two officially custodial sectors are confused by the existence of a potentially large semi-secure child-care sector. This is 'hidden' only in the sense that widespread practices of local authorities, courts and children's panels are not explicitly recognized by central governments. Policy makers and researchers alike have been turning a blind eye to the implications of what is going on outside officially secure settings.

Mental hospitals probably contain the largest numbers of children in custody of all the sectors, and they are the least regulated. The tendency so far to omit them from the juvenile justice debate may be based partly on ignorance or unawareness of their significance. But it can equally be interpreted as blindness to the existence of children with mental disorders, particularly mental handicaps, and an implicit rejection of their right to consideration as citizens. Children in mental hospitals constitute a risk to themselves rather than to society, to which they are more of an embarrassment.

The census survey of children in custody actually found 1,902 who were recognized by respondents as being deprived of their liberty on 12 September 1984 in the British Isles. Adjustment to take account of misunderstandings and incomplete returns makes 3,600 a truer figure, plus an unknown number in semi-secure child-care accommodation. This may not seem a lot of children in custody compared with some countries (Tomasevski, 1986), but for a society which regards childhood as a time of special vulnerability it must represent a serious cause for concern.

Conclusion

**by Professor Norman Tutt, Chairman of the Study Group
on Children in Custody**

This study attempts to examine the four jurisdictions of England
and Wales, Scotland, Northern Ireland, and the Republic of Ireland,
each of which has both a different process and a different mechanism
of juvenile justice. By firstly examining the differences in the four
legislations and practices, and secondly examining the number and
types of children in custody, as the output of the four systems,
the study group hoped to identify which aspects of juvenile justice
systems generated increased numbers of children in custody. If this
could be achieved, and assuming that reductions in numbers in custody is an agreed objective, it should be possible to propose a system
of juvenile justice which would have the least detrimental impact
on the young people passing through it.

These were the aspirations with which the study group embarked
on its tasks. The first shock was to discover that the basic information
on numbers of children and young people deprived of their liberty is
not publicly available and in fact is not available at all. It seems extraordinary that given the high value put on freedom by the four jurisdictions, the safeguards which exist to protect that freedom by legal
means, and the high financial cost of both placing and retaining a
young person in custody, that basic data on numbers, institutions and
types of legal category are not systematically collected and published.

This failure occurs because of the very diffuse responsibility for
this relatively small number of children. The authorities involved in
the administration of custodial facilities for children are described in
the section on organising the survey (Chapter 5). In the four jurisdictions some 450 different and independent authorities were identified
as having some direct responsibility for the care of children in custody
or the administration of the institutions in which they were held.

Whilst acknowledging the difficulties involved in coordinating any
form of regular information return from such a diverse group of
authorities, and indeed having experienced the difficulties in collect-
ing the census data in this study, it is our belief that the deprivation
of liberty is such a major intervention on behalf of the state that
the state must be publicly accountable for its actions. To ensure
public accountability, regular, accurate information must be collected

and published enumerating the number of children, their sex, age, ethnic identity, and legal status, the institution in which they are held, and the length of time they are held in custody. This is the minimum information. We would like much more detail, which would allow some assessment to be made of the way in which the state is discharging its duty to its dependent but difficult citizens.

These figures published regularly over time would allow crucial decisions in this difficult policy area to be tackled. For example is the proportionate use of custody increasing? Are those held younger? Are girls and boys treated differently? Are ethnic minority groups receiving more or longer custodial sentences than their peers? Are all children held legally?

Inevitably at a time when public expenditure is limited, cost figures should also be published so that the public can determine whether the cost of custody is justified to protect the public or whether more may be achieved for both the child and public by more creative use of the same resource.

The issue of resources has been a key problem in interpretation of the census returns and their linkage with the system of juvenile justice in operation. The Republic of Ireland showed a very low use of secure facilities despite having a very high proportion of the population in the age group under consideration (Table 5.1, p. 109). It would be very tempting to assume that this low use was the result of systematic reform of the juvenile justice system. In fact it was almost the reverse. The Republic of Ireland had only limited legislation on child care since the 1908 Children's Act, and was mainly dependent upon the traditional 'training' school establishments set up under that legislation. Only recently had a new secure establishment been developed — Trinity House opened in 1983, some 20 years after the similar developments in England and Wales.

The experience of the Republic of Ireland clearly demonstrates that if special secure facilities are not developed, other ways of coping with difficult young people emerge. However it cannot determine whether those 'other ways' are more efficient, humane or effective, nor can it determine the converse, namely that if resources are available they will inevitably be used regardless of the appropriateness of the children (net widening). In fact this latter argument appeared to be defeated by the empirical evidence. As we show in Chapter 5, nearly a third of the secure units which were listed as being approved by the DHSS were closed at the time of the survey. Twelve units — 6 assessment centres and 6 community homes with education — had been closed after functioning for a time as secure units. The capital cost alone of this provision now not in use must be of the order of £10 million.

The evidence suggests that simple provision of secure units does not inevitably lead to their use, alternatively under-provision does not necessarily mean the development of more humane handling of young people. However it is difficult to draw firm conclusions given the lack of information, once again underscoring the need for government to collect adequate and appropriate information to plan resources effectively.

If the government administration of the four jurisdictions were to undertake this essential task of information-gathering it would force them to determine a clear definition of custody. The problems of definition, as experienced by the study group, are described in Chapter 1.

It seems scandalous that there is no clear legal definition of custody which can guide and protect practitioners, sentencers, and policy makers. More importantly the lack of definition endangers the liberty and rights of a number of children and young people each year. We believe that government has a clear responsibility to define the concepts of custody and ensure that it is agreed across the penal, educational, social and health services for children. The failure on the part of government to undertake this legal definition has led to the more 'punitive' treatment of children who, through disability, cannot be held personally accountable for their actions, than of those determined by a court of law as being guilty of a serious criminal offence. In Chapter 8 we discuss 'hidden custody', which can only arise because of the failure of government to define custody for practitioners. The current position is intolerable and requires immediate action. Consider for example the establishment mentioned in Chapter 8 in which 'two boys and a girl aged 14, 13 and 11 were restrained on the census date and had been for several years. They were severely handicapped informal patients who had been admitted because their parents were unable to cope with them and no other place could be found. The room where they were held had specially high door handles with dual controls, inaccessible to disabled children.'

These children were not deprived of their liberty because of staff 'malice' but because of staff ignorance, since the same hospital made a census return stating, that *no* children were deprived of their liberty. The ignorance of staff arises because no agreed definition of custody has been produced in legislation; consequently staff working in the same institution are able to interpret the deprivation of a child's liberty in very different ways. We believe this can no longer be allowed to continue and that the issue of children's rights generally, and the use of hidden custody specifically, is now part of the political agenda and will not readily disappear.

The concept of hidden custody has for the first time been tackled on an empirical basis in this study. We do not claim to have tackled the issue adequately, due to the methodological problems involved in asking people to record something which they should not legitimately be doing. However despite the inadequacies we have been able to move the study of hidden custody beyond the purely anecdotal level.

As Chapter 8 suggests, the use of hidden custody is most frequent within the mental handicap or mental health services. This is not surprising since, as we discuss in Chapter 4, the child-care and juvenile justice systems in the four jurisdictions have experienced considerable debate and reform in thinking, if not action, over the past decade because of the challenge of the so-called 'justice' ideology. As we argue,

> Clearly justice and welfare considerations may be seen as competing ideologies. In pure form they posit flatly non-complementary systems of delinquency control. At the level of debate they cause policy makers and practitioners alike to question taken-for-granted assumptions and resuscitate dormant issues of rights, due process and the nature and form of legal and welfare interventions.

However, as yet this debate has not radically challenged the operation of the mental health services. As we indicate in Chapter 2, young people under the age of 16 years are very much the 'property' of their parents who can accordingly 'volunteer' them for psychiatric treatment. The type of treatment, and its location in a custodial setting, is seen as very much an issue of medical discretion. The medical practitioner will advise the parent, who would have the right to refuse the treatment, but the 'rights' of the child in this process under mental health legislation are obscure. As Hoggett is quoted in Chapter 2:

> The principles leave a great deal of discretion in the hands of parents and doctors. There is every reason to believe that parents of handicapped or mentally disturbed children will find it hard to put their children's interests first all the time.

This legal observation is borne out in practice, as is shown by the responses to the survey:

> An epileptic boy of 15 had been admitted when he was 5 'informally at request of father, consequent upon suicide of mother'. A boy of 16. . . . had been an informal patient since he was 3. Admission requested when mother sent to prison. Has remained an in-patient ever since. (Chapter 8).

It would be a

> Medical/nursing decision. Depends on response to medication, parents' views. Clinical assessment of her ability to control impulse, the support of the group, the alleviation of mental disturbance. Period of restriction lasted two weeks — by then she was able and prepared to resume responsibility for her own movements. (Chapter 8)

We believe the extent of hidden custody operating in social and health services merits a thorough examination, and are supported in this by the recently published report of the Health Advisory Service. Moreover we believe the time has come for the issue of children's rights to be given serious consideration by the medical authorities. We hope the final outcome of the 'Gillick' case will lead the professional bodies of the Royal Colleges of Psychiatry, Nursing and others to determine to draw up a statement of children's rights in the psychiatric and mental handicap services.

Finally we would wish to comment on the position of staff and the practices they employ in their very difficult task of caring for some of the most difficult, neglected and rejected of our children. Whilst at times in this study we have been very critical of the operation of custodial facilities and the practices adopted by some staff we would not wish to condemn individuals personally for their use or abuse of custody. It is our belief that staff — whether social workers, courts, or practitioners in custodial institutions — all, at times, find themselves making or implementing decisions with which they personally are not content. It is evident that when staff are faced by a difficult young person and a shortage of resources whether real or perceived, they are likely to take expedient decisions or actions because they feel compelled 'to do something'.

The social worker admitting a mentally impaired child to an out-dated mental handicap hospital will put aside the likely long-term effect on the child because of the pressure of resolving the short-term problem of the parent who can no longer tolerate or cope with the pressure of caring for their child with little real help. The court faced by a 15-year-old charged with the latest in a series of persistent burglaries feels compelled to control the young person's behaviour, and if no other means is available custody is an all too attractive apparent solution. The residential social worker, with little experience or back-up from other staff, faced by a persistent absconder and pressure from the authorities to do something, will readily see locking up the young person as a quick and clean solution.

It is important that these practices, whilst understandable, are condemned, because ultimately it is the explicable and even rational decisions of individuals, often made in the child's best interests, that leads to the growth in the tide of custody for young people.

We would hope that each of the four jurisdictions would recognize the wide and increasing acceptance that custody for young people is detrimental and that the state has the responsibility to develop all other possible alternatives, so that eventually there would be no custodial provision for young people. We would hope such an abolition of custody would be undertaken sooner rather than later and would like to see each jurisdiction set clear and reducing annual targets for the numbers in custody and thereby move rapidly towards abolition.

In the meantime a number of young people will spend a substantial proportion of their young lives in highly restricted environments. The crucial element of childhood is that it is a period of rapid development, physical, intellectual and emotional. Much of this development depends upon adequate stimulation, and exposure to new experiences and relationships. It is for the limitations that custody imposes on the prospect of adequate development that its use for children must be condemned. Given that some children will continue to suffer these circumstances, most notably in mental handicap institutions, it is a responsibility upon the state to ensure that by its intervention into children's lives it has not further increased the deprivation of that individual. The only way the state can attempt to discharge this responsibility is to ensure that there are adequate numbers of staff and, as importantly, that they are adequately trained to redress some of the deficits inevitably arising from depriving children of their liberty.

We believe it is essential that training authorities in psychiatry, nursing, teaching and social work recognize the unique problems of staff and children in custody and offer adequate levels of training for this relatively small group of staff.

Ultimately the four jurisdictions of England and Wales, Scotland, Northern Ireland, and the Republic of Ireland must give serious consideration to the values and attitudes which underscore the legislation and social provision for young people. There is growing evidence that the British Isles is becoming more and more reactionary, compared with European governments, in its attitudes to youth policy issues, whether education, training, youth unemployment, drug abuse, housing or criminal policy. The time has come to stop the routine rhetorical condemnation of young people's behaviour which readily catches the media headlines. Instead politicians and those in the public service must ask themselves: is custody a response to youthful problems or have we, through recourse to custodial policies, created further and more serious problems for security and the young?

Appendix: Membership of the Study Group on Children in Custody

The Study Group on Children in Custody was funded by the Carnegie UK and Joseph Rowntree Memorial Trusts. Under the chairmanship of Professor Norman Tutt, the study group met ten times over a three-year period from June 1983 to June 1986. These included four wider meetings in Belfast, Birmingham, Dublin and Edinburgh, to which practitioners and other experts from the jurisdictions concerned were invited. Mrs G.M. Stewart was seconded from the University of Lancaster as secretary/research officer to the study group for eighteen months from October 1983.

Membership of the Study Group on Children in Custody was as follows:

Professor Norman Tutt (Chairman), *Professor of Applied Social Studies, University of Lancaster.*

Dr Susan Bailey, *Consultant Forensic Psychiatrist, Gardener Unit, Prestwich Hospital.*

Peter Bye, *Director of Social Services, Suffolk County Council.*

Miss Gillian Corsellis, *Independent Visitor; formerly DHSS Social Services Inspector.*

Peter Denley, *Assistant Chief Probation Officer, Probation Board for Northern Ireland.*

Alan Finlayson, *Reporter to Children's Panel, Lothian Regional Council.*

Henri Giller, *Managing Director, Social Information Systems; Fellow of University of Keele, formerly Lecturer in Law, University of Keele.*

Alex Hamilton, *Divisional Officer, Social Work Department, Grampian Regional Council.*

Dr Jean Harris, *Consultant Psychiatrist, Child and Family Psychiatric Service, North West Thames Regional Health Authority.*

Professor Frederick Martin, *Professor of Social Work, University of Glasgow.*

Professor Mary McAleese, *Reid Professor of Criminal Law, Criminology and Penology, School of Law, Trinity College, Dublin.*

Margot McAulay, *formerly Senior Research Officer, Adolescent Psychology and Research Unit for the Northern Ireland Training Schools.*

Séamus Ó Cinnéide, *Department of Social Studies, St Patrick's College, Maynooth; formerly member of the Task Force on Child Care Services.*

Max Paterson, *Consultant Psychologist; formerly Principal Psychologist, List D Schools.*

Ray Percival, *formerly Senior Advisor, Social Work Services Group, Scotland.*

James Wilkie, *Director, Glenthorne Youth Treatment Centre, Birmingham.*

Bibliography

Adler, M. and Asquith, S. (1981) 'Discretion and Power', in Adler, M. and Asquith, S. (eds), *Discretion and Welfare*, London: Heinemann.

Anderson, R. (1978) *Representation in the Juvenile Court*, London: Routledge and Kegan Paul.

Aries, P. (1962) *Centuries of Childhood*, Harmondsworth, Middlesex: Penguin.

Asquith, S. (1983) 'Justice, Retribution and Children', in Morris, A. and Giller, H. (eds), *Providing Criminal Justice for Children*, London: Edward Arnold.

ADSS (Association of Directors of Social Services) (1985), *Children Still in Trouble*, ADSS.

Balbernie, R. (1966), *Residential Work with Children*, London: Pergamon Press.

Bersoff, D. (1976) 'Representation of Children in Custody Decisions — all that Glitters is not Gault', *Journal of Family Law*, 15, pp. 27-49.

Bignell, G. (1986) 'Give care a chance', *Community Care*, 20 March, pp. 20-21.

Black Committee (1979) *Report of the Children and Young Persons Review Group*, Belfast: HMSO.

Blumenthal, G.J. (1985) *Development of Secure Units in Child Care*, Aldershot: Gower.

Bottomley, A.K. (1980) 'The "Justice Model" in America and Britain: Development and Analysis', in Bottoms, A.E. and Preston, R.H. (eds), *The Coming Penal Crisis*, Edinburgh: Scottish Academic Press.

Bowlby, J. (1953) *Child Care and the Growth of Love*, Harmondsworth, Middlesex: Penguin.

Brittan, L. (1985) *Attendance Centres: A Press Release*, London: Home Office.

Bunreacht na Heireann (1937) (Constitution of Ireland), Dublin: The Stationery Office.

Carlebach, J. (1970) *Caring for Children in Trouble*, London: Routledge and Kegan Paul.

Cawson, P. and Martell, M. (1979) *Children Referred to Secure Units,* Research Report, No. 5, London: DHSS Research Division.

CIPFA (Chartered Institute for Public Finance and Accountancy) (1986), *Personal Social Services Statistics 1984-85 Actuals,* London: CIPFA.

Children and Young Persons Review Group (1979) *Report,* Belfast: HMSO (Chairman: Sir Harold Black).

Childright (1983) *No Place for Children,* London: Children's Legal Centre, pp. 13-14.

Childright (various) The Journal of the Children's Legal Centre, London.

Chiswick, D. (Chairman) (1985), *Report of the Review of Suicide, Precautions at H.M. Detention Centre and H.M. Young Offenders' Institution, Glenochil,* Edinburgh: HMSO.

Cicourel, A. (1976) *The Social Organisation of Juvenile Justice,* London: Heinemann.

Clarke, S. and Koch, G. (1980) 'Juvenile Court: Therapy or Crime Control — Do Lawyers make a Difference?' *Law and Society Review,* 14, pp. 263-308.

Cohen, S. (1974) 'Criminology and the Sociology of Deviance in Britain', in Rock, P. and McIntosh, M. (eds), *Deviance and Social Control,* London: Tavistock.

Committee on Children and Young Persons (1960) *Report,* London: HMSO. (Cmnd. 1191) (Chairman: The Rt Hon. The Viscount Ingleby).

Criminal Procedure (Scotland) Act 1975.

Crowe, I. (1979) *The Detention Centre Experiment,* London: NACRO.

Denham, E.J.M. (1984) *The Use of Unruly Certificates,* Edinburgh: Scottish Office Central Research Unit.

DHSS (1971) *Care and Treatment in a Planned Environment,* London: HMSO.

DHSS (1975) *Better Services for the Mentally Ill,* London: HMSO. (Cmnd. 6233), para. 5.4.

DHSS (1980) *Observation and Assessment of Children — A Report of a Working Party,* London: DHSS.

DHSS (1981a) *Legal and Professional Aspects of the Use of Secure Accommodation for Children in Care,* (Report of a DHSS Internal Working Party) London: DHSS.

DHSS (1981b) *Offending by Young People: A Survey of Recent Trends,* London: DHSS.

DHSS (1983a) *The Mental Health Act (1983). Memorandum on Parts I to VI, VIII and X.*

DHSS (1983b) *Criminal Justice Act 1982 Section 25 — Restriction of Liberty — The Secure Accommodation Regulations 1983* (LAC(83)8), London: DHSS.

DHSS (1984) *Children in Care in England and Wales, March 1983*, London: DHSS.

DHSS (1985) *Review of Child Care Law*, London: HMSO.

Dingwall, R. *et al.* (1984) 'Childhood as a Social Problem: a Survey of the History of Legal Regulation', *Journal of Law and Society*, 11(2), pp. 207-33.

Ditchfield, J. (1976) *Police Cautioning in England and Wales*, Home Office Research Studies, No. 37, London: HMSO.

Donzelot, J. (1979) *The Policing of Families*, New York: Random House.

Duncan, W. (1984) 'Decision Making Relating to Children in the Republic of Ireland — Restraints on Introducing New Models', in Eekelaar, J. and Katz, S. (eds), *The Resolution of Family Conflict*, Toronto: Butterworth.

Durand, V. (1960) *Disturbances at the Carlton Approved School 29th and 30th August, 1959* (Cmnd. 137), London: HMSO.

Expenditure Committee of the House of Commons (1975) *Report on the Children and Young Persons Act 1969*, London: HMSO.

Family Law Reform Act (England and Wales) 1969.

Farrington, D. (1980) 'La dejudiciarisation des mineurs en Angleterre', *Deviance et Societé*, 4, pp. 257-77.

Farrington, D. and Bennett, T. (1981) 'Police Cautioning of Juveniles in London', *British Journal of Criminology*, 21 (2), pp. 123-35.

Foucault, M. (1977) *Discipline and Punishment — The Birth of the Prison*, London: Allen Lane.

Freeman, M.D.A. (1983) *The Rights and Wrongs of Children*, London: Francis Pinter.

Gelsthorpe, L. (1983) *Guidance on the Criminal Justice Act (1982)*, London: London Borough of Hounslow.

Giller, H. and Morris, A. (1981) *Care and Discretion: Social Workers' Decisions with Delinquents*, London: Burnett Books.

Giller, H. and Maidment, S. (1984) 'Legal Representation: Does More Mean Better?' in Eekelaar, J. and Katz, S. (eds), *The Resolution of Family Conflict*, Toronto: Butterworth.

Goldstein, J. Freud, A. and Solnit, A.J. (1979) *Beyond the Best Interests of the Child*, New York: Free Press.

Hansard, House of Commons Debates (1984): written answers 25 October 1984, Cols. 726-7.

Hansard, House of Commons Debates (1986): written answers 27 March and 3 April.

Hardiker, P. (1977) 'Social Work Ideologies in the Probation Service', *British Journal of Social Work*, 7 (2).

Henchy, Mr Justice, (Chairman) (1978) *Third Interim Report of the Inter-departmental Committee on Mentally Ill and Maladjusted Persons*, Dublin: Stationery Office.

HMSO *The Mental Health Act, (1959)*, London.

HMSO *The Mental Health (Scotland) Act, 1960, Patients Concerned in Criminal Proceedings* (Notes on Part V), Edinburgh.

HMSO (1962) *Mental Health (Scotland) Act 1960, Compulsory admission to hospital and guardianship* (Notes on Parts I and IV), Edinburgh.

HMSO *Mental Health Act (Northern Ireland) 1961*, Belfast.

HMSO *Social Work (Scotland) Act (1968)*, London.

HMSO *Health (Mental Services Act 1981)*, Dublin.

HMSO (1981) *Northern Ireland: Review Committee on Mental Health Legislation*, Belfast.

HMSO *The Mental Health Act, (1983)*, London.

HMSO *The Mental Health (Amendment) (Scotland) Act 1983*, London.

HMSO *The Mental Health (Scotland) Act, 1984*, London.

HMSO *Mental Treatment Acts*. Statutory provisions, regulations and explanatory notes, 1945-1961.

Hoggett, B. (1984) *Mental Health Law* (2nd edn) London: Sweet and Maxwell.

Hoghughi, M. (1978) *Troubled and Troublesome — Coping with Severely Disordered Children*, London: Burnett Books.

Home Office (1969) *Children and Young Persons Act 1969*, London: HMSO.

Home Office, DHSS, Department of Education and Science, and Welsh Office (1976), *Observations on the Eleventh Report of the Expenditure Committee* (Cmnd. 6494) London: HMSO.

Home Office (1977) *A Review of Criminal Justice Policy*, London: HMSO.

Home Office (1979) *Report of the Committee of Inquiry into the United Kingdom Prison Services* (Cmnd. 7673) London: HMSO.

Home Office (1980) *Young Offenders*, (Cmnd. 8045) London: HMSO.

Home Office (1983) *Criminal Justice Act 1982: Throughcare and Supervision of Young Offenders on Release from Custody* (Circular No. 58/1983), London: HMSO.

Home Office (1985) *Prison Statistics England and Wales, 1984* (Cmnd. 9622), London: HMSO.

Home Office (1986) 'The Ethnic Origins of Prisoners: the Prison Population on 30 June 1985 and Persons Received, July 1984 — March 1985', *Home Office Statistical Bulletin*, No. 17, HMSO.

House of Commons Social Services Commmittee (1984) *Children in Care*, 2nd Report, Session 1983-84, House of Commons Paper 360, London: HMSO.

Kelly, J.M. (1980) *The Irish Constitution, Irish Reports* (I.R.), Dublin: Jurist Publishing Co.

Kennedy Report (1980) Dublin: Stationery Office.

Kilbrandon, The Hon. Lord (1968) 'The Scottish Reforms', *British Journal of Criminology*, 8 (3), pp. 235-41.

Krisberg, B. and Schwartz, I. (1983) 'Rethinking Juvenile Justice', *Crime and Delinquency*, 24(4), pp. 333-64.

Lathaen, A. (1984) *Secure Accommodation in London: The Impact of the 1982 Criminal Justice Act*, London, London Boroughs Children's Regional Planning Committee.

Lerman, P. (1980) 'Trends and Issues in Deinstitutionalisation of Youths in Trouble', *Crime and Delinquency*, July, p. 282.

Lessels (1985) *Scots Law and the Mentally Disordered Child*, University of Aberdeen Publication.

Longford Report (1964) *Crime — A Challenge to us all*, London: Labour Party

Lunacy (Ireland) Acts 1821, 1837.

Criminal Lunatic Asylum Act 1845.

Lunatic Asylums (Ireland) Act 1875.

Trial of Lunatics Act 1883.

Criminal Lunatics Act 1884.

Martin, F., Fox, S.J., and Murray, K. (1981) *Children out of Court*, Glasgow: Scottish Academic Press.

Matza, D. (1964) *Delinquency and Drift*, New York: John Wiley and Sons.

Mental Health Act Commission (1985) *First Biennial Report of the Mental Health Act Commission 1983-85*, House of Commons Paper 586, Session 1984-85, London: HMSO.

Millham, S., Bullock, R. and Hosie, K. (1978), *Locking Up Children: Secure Units for Disturbed Children*, Farnborough: Saxon House.

Millham, S., Bullock, R. and Hosie, K. (1980) *Learning to Care* Farnborough: Gower Publishing.

Morris, A. and Giller, H. (1979) 'Juvenile Justice and Social Work in Great Britain', in Parker, H. (ed.), *Social Work and the Courts*, London: Edward Arnold.

Morris, A. and Giller, H. (1983) *Providing Criminal Justice for Children*, London: Edward Arnold.

Morris, A. Giller, H.J., Szwed, E. and Geach, H. (1980) *Justice for Children*, London: Macmillan.

Mungham, G. and Pearson, G. (1976) *Working Class Youth Culture*, London: Routledge Direct Editions.

NACRO (1984) *School Reports in the Juvenile Court*, London: NACRO.

NACRO (1985) *Young Offenders in Custody: Summary of the Home Office Report*, London: NACRO.

NAPO (1984) *The Future Provision for the Throughcare Needs of Prisoners*, Policy Document 1/84, NAPO.

NHS (National Health Service) Health Advisory Service (1986) *Bridges Over Troubled Waters: A Report from the N.H.S. Health Advisory Service on Services for Disturbed Adolescents*, NHSHAS, Sutton.

Parker, H. and Giller, H. (1981) 'More and Less the Same: British Delinquency Research since the Sixties', *British Journal of Criminology*, 21 (3), pp. 230-45.

Parker, H., Casburn, M., and Turnbull, D. (1981) *Receiving Juvenile Justice*, Oxford: Basil Blackwell.

Parliamentary All-Party Penal Affairs Group (1981) *The Prevention of Crime Among Young People*, Chichester: Barry Rose.

Petrie, C. (1980) *The Nowhere Boys*, Farnborough: Saxon House.

Pope, P.J. (1978) 'Children in Prisons and Remand Centres', *The Howard Journal of Penology and Crime Prevention*, 16 (3) pp. 134-43.

Priestley, P., Fears, D. and Fuller, R. (1977) *Justice for Juveniles*, London: Routledge and Kegan Paul.

Psychiatry, Royal College of (1983) *Mental Health Act 1983, Summary of the Main Provisions*, London: Royal College of Psychiatry.

Reid, I.D. (1982) 'The Development and Maintenance of a Behavioural Regime in a Secure Youth Treatment Centre', in Feldman, P. (ed.), *Developments in the Study of Criminal Behaviour*, Vol. I, London: John Wiley.

Reynolds, F. and Williamson H. (1985) 'Extending the Welfare Tariff for Juvenile Offenders', *Howard Journal*, 24 (1), pp. 29-39.

Richards, J. (1983) Personal communication, London: London Boroughs' Childrens Regional Planning Commitee.

Rushforth, M. (1978) *Committal to Care — A Case Study in Juvenile Justice,* London: HMSO.

Rutherford, A. (1986) *Growing Out of Crime,* Harmondsworth, Middlesex: Penguin, pp. 148-62.

Rutter, M. and Giller, H. (1983) *Juvenile Delinquency — Trends and Perspectives,* Harmondsworth, Middlesex: Penguin.

Schwartz, I., Jackson-Beeck, M. and Anderson, R. (1984) 'The "Hidden" System of Juvenile Control', *Crime and Delinquency,* vol. 30, 3, pp. 371-85.

Shatter, A.J. (1977) *Family Law in the Republic of Ireland,* Dublin: Wolfhound Press.

Smith, G. (1981) 'Discretionary Decision-making in Social Work', in Adler, M. and Asquith, S. (eds) *Discretion and Welfare,* London: Heinemann.

Social Services Committee (1984) *Children in Care,* House of Commons Paper 360, London: HMSO.

Stapleton, W. and Teitlebaum, L. (1972) *In Defense of Youth,* New York: Russell Sage.

Taskforce on Child Care Services (1975) *Interim report,* Dublin: Stationery Office.

Taskforce on Child Care Services (1980) *Final Report,* Dublin: Stationery Office.

Taylor, L., Lacey, R. and Bracken, D. (1980) *In Whose Best Interests?* London: MIND/Cobden Trust.

Thornton, D., Curran, L., Grayson, D. and Holloway, V. (1984) *Tougher Regimes in Detention Centres: Report of an Evaluation by the Young Offenders' Psychology Unit,* London: HMSO.

Thorpe, D., Smith, D., Green, D. and Paley, J. (1980) *Out of Care,* London: Allen and Unwin.

Tomasevski, K. (ed.) (1986) *Children in Adult Prisons: An International Perspective,* London: Frances Pinter.

Tutt, N. (1971) 'The Subnormal Offender', *British Journal of Mental Subnormality,* 17, pp. 42-7.

Tutt, N. (1981) 'New Hall — Old Way', *Community Care,* 10 September.

Tutt, N. (1984) 'Civil Liberties and Youth', in Wallington, P. (ed.), *Civil Liberties,* London: Martin Robertson.

Tutt, N. and Giller, H. (1983) *Social Inquiry Reports,* Lancaster: Information Systems.

US President's Commission on Law Enforcement and Administration of Justice (1967) *The Challenge of Crime in a Free Society,* Washington DC: Government Printing Office.

Walter, A. (1978) *Sent Away*, Farnborough: Saxon House.

West, D.J. (1973) *Who Becomes Delinquent?*, London: Heinemann.

Whitelaw, W. (1980) 'Address to the Conservative Party Conference', quoted in Young Offenders' Psychology Unit (1984) *Tougher Regimes in Detention Centres*, London: HMSO.

Wilkie, J. and Westwood, S. (1985), 'Co-education and the Treatment of Disturbed Adolescents with Special Reference to Glenthorne Y.T.C.', Glenthorne Publications No. 4, Birmingham.

Wringe, C.A. (1981) *Children's Rights — a philosophical study*, London: Routledge and Kegan Paul.

Index